KT-490-773

MOTHER INDIA

Katherine Mayo

Miss Mayo's grimly factual and harrowing picture of India in the twenties created an international sensation on its first publication in 1927, and it remains a book of more than passing interest. For this is India as it truly was—and as parts of it still are—in all its helplessness, hopelessness and horror. And this is the India all of us must know and understand if we are to have any chance at all of appreciating the magnitude of the many diverse and difficult problems which face that vast, teeming sub-continent today.

HUSBAND AND WIFE

Katherine Mayo

MOTHER INDIA

A HOWARD BAKER BOOK

Published by
Howard Baker Publishers Limited

in association with
REMPLOY LIMITED
Newcastle-under-Lyme

Katherine Mayo
MOTHER INDIA

Originally published in Great Britain by
Jonathan Cape, 1927

Eleventh impression, 1929

This edition, 1970

SBN 09 308630 X

This edition is published jointly by
Howard Baker Publishers Limited,
47 Museum Street, London, W.C.1
and Remploy Limited, Barracks Road,
Newcastle-under-Lyme, Staffs.

Printed in Great Britain by
J. W. Arrowsmith Limited, Bristol, BS3 2NT
and bound in Wales by
Remploy Limited, Ystradgynlais, Glamorgan

TO
THE PEOPLES OF INDIA
AND TO
THAT INDIAN FIELD-LABOURER
WHO, ONCE, BY AN ACT OF HUMANITY
SAVED MY LIFE

CONTENTS

CONTENTS

Part Five: Into the North

LIST OF ILLUSTRATIONS

FOREWORD

It would be a great pleasure to thank, by name, the many ersons, both Indian and English, who have so courteously acilitated my access to information, to records, and to those laces and things that I desired to see for myself. But the act that it was impossible to forecast the conclusions I hould reach, and that for these conclusions they are in no ay responsible, make it improper now to connect them herewith.

For this reason the manuscript of this book has not been ubmitted to any member of the Government of India, nor o any Briton or Indian connected with official life. It has, owever, been reviewed by certain public health authorities f international position who are familiar with the Indian ield.

I may, on the other hand, express my deep indebtedness o my friends, Miss M. Moyca Newell and Harry Hubert ield, the one for her constant and invaluable collaboration, he other for a helpfulness, both in India and here, beyond ither limit or thanks.

K. M.

EDFORD HILLS
NEW YORK

MOTHER INDIA

Part One: The Bus to Mandalay

CALCUTTA, second largest city in the British Empire, spread along the Ganges called Hooghly, at the top of the Bay of Bengal. Calcutta, big, Western, modern, with public buildings, monuments, parks, gardens, hospitals, museums, University, courts of law, hotels, offices, shops, all of which might belong to a prosperous American city; and all backed by an Indian town of temples, mosques, bazaars and intricate courtyards and alleys that has somehow created itself despite the rectangular lines shown on the map. In the courts and alleys and bazaars many little bookstalls, where narrow-chested, near-sighted, anæmic young Bengali students, in native dress, brood over piles of fly-blown Russian pamphlets.

Rich Calcutta, wide-open door to the traffic of the world and India, traffic of bullion, of jute, of cotton – of all that India and the world want out of each other's hands. Decorous, sophisticated Calcutta, where decorous and sophisticated people of all creeds, all colours and all costumes go to Government House garden parties, pleasantly to make their bows to Their Excellencies, and pleasantly to talk good English while they take their tea and ices and listen to the regimental band.

You cannot see the street from Government House Gardens, for the walls are high. But if you could, you would see it filled with traffic – motor traffic, mostly – limousines, touring cars, taxis and private machines. And rolling along among them now and again, a sort of Fifth Avenue bus, bearing the big-lettered label, 'Kali Ghat.'

This bus, if you happen to notice it, proceeds along the parkside past the Empire Theatre, the various clubs, St.

Paul's Cathedral, past the Bishop's House, the General Hospital, the London Missionary Society's Institution, and presently comes to a stop in a rather congested quarter, which is its destination as advertised.

'Kali Ghat' – 'place of Kali' – is the root-word of the name Calcutta. Kali is a Hindu goddess, wife of the great god Siva, whose attribute is destruction and whose thirst is for blood and death-sacrifice. Her spiritual domination of the world began about five thousand years ago, and should last nearly four hundred and thirty-two thousand years to come.

Kali has thousands of temples in India, great and small. This of Calcutta is the private property of a family of Brahmans who have owned it for some three centuries. A round hundred of these, 'all sons of one father,' share its possession to-day. And one of the hundred obligingly led me, with a Brahman friend, through the precincts. Let him be called Mr. Haldar, for that is the family's name.

But for his white petticoat-drawers and his white toga, the usual Bengali costume, Mr. Haldar might have been taken for a well-groomed northern Italian gentleman. His English was polished and his manner entirely agreeable.

Five hundred and ninety acres, tax free, constitute the temple holding, he said. Pilgrims from far and near, with whom the shrine is always crowded, make money offerings. There are also priestly fees to collect. And the innumerable booths that shoulder each other up and down the approaches, booths where sweetmeats, holy images, marigold flowers, amulets, and votive offerings are sold, bring in a sound income.

Rapidly cleaving a way through the coming and going mass of the devotees, Mr. Haldar leads us to the temple proper. A high platform, roofed and pillared, approached on three sides by tiers of steps of its own length and width. At one end, a deep, semi-enclosed shrine in which, dimly half-visible, looms the figure of the goddess. Black of face she is, with a monstrous lolling tongue, dripping blood. Of her four hands, one grasps a bleeding human head, one a knife, the third, outstretched, cradles blood, the fourth, raised in menace, is empty. In the shadows close about her feet stand the priests ministrant.

On the long platform before the deity, men and women prostrate themselves in vehement supplication. Among them stroll lounging boys, sucking lollypops fixed on sticks. Also, a white bull-calf wanders, while one reverend grey-beard in the midst of it all, squatting cross-legged on the pavement before a great book, lifts up a droning voice.

'He,' said Mr. Haldar, 'is reading to the worshippers from our Hindu mythology. The history of Kali.'

Of a sudden, a piercing outburst of shrill bleating. We turn the corner of the edifice to reach the open courtyard at the end opposite the shrine. Here stand two priests, one with a cutlass in his hand, the other holding a young goat. The goat shrieks, for in the air is that smell that all beasts fear. A crash of sound, as before the goddess drums thunder. The priest who holds the goat swings it up and drops it, stretched by the legs, its screaming head held fast in a cleft post. The second priest with a single blow of his cutlass decapitates the little creature. The blood gushes forth on the pavement, the drums and the gongs before the goddess burst out wildly. 'Kali! Kali! Kali!' shout all the priests and the suppliants together, some flinging themselves face downward on the temple floor.

Meantime, and instantly, a woman who waited behind the killers of the goat has rushed forward and fallen on all fours to lap up the blood with her tongue – 'in the hope of having a child.' And now a second woman, stooping, sops at the blood with a cloth, and thrusts the cloth into her bosom, while half a dozen sick, sore dogs, horribly misshapen by nameless diseases, stick their hungry muzzles into the lengthening pool of gore.

'In this manner we kill here from one hundred and fifty to two hundred kids each day,' says Mr. Haldar with some pride. 'The worshippers supply the kids.'

Now he leads us among the chapels of minor deities – that of the little red goddess of small-pox, side by side with her littler red twin who dispenses chicken-pox or not, according to humour; that of the five-headed black cobra who wears a tiny figure of a priest beneath his chin, to whom those make offerings who fear snakebite; that of the red monkey-god, to whom wrestlers do homage before the bout; that to which rich merchants and students of the university pray, before confronting examinations or risking new ventures in trade; that of 'the Universal God,' a mask, only, like an Alaskan totem. And then the ever-present phallic emblem of Siva, Kali's husband. Before them all, little offerings of marigold blossoms, or of red wads of something in baskets trimmed with shells, both of which may be had at the temple booths, at a price, together with sacred cakes made of the dung of the temple bulls.

Mr. Haldar leads us through a lane down which, neatly arranged in rows, sit scores of more or less naked holy men and mendicants, mostly fat and hairy and covered with ashes, begging. All are eager to be photographed. *Saddhus* – reverend ascetics – spring up and pose. One, a mad-man, flings himself at us, badly scaring a little girl who is being towed past by a young man whose wrist is tied to her tiny one by the two ends of a scarf. 'Husband and new wife,' says Mr. Haldar. 'They come to pray for a son.'

We proceed to the temple burning-ghat. A burning is in progress. In the midst of an open space an oblong pit, dug in the ground. This is now half-filled with sticks of wood. On the ground, close by, lies a rather beautiful young Indian woman, relaxed as though in a swoon. Her long black hair falls loose around her, a few flowers among its meshes. Her forehead, her hands and the soles of her feet are painted red, showing that she is blessed among women, in that she is saved from widowhood – her husband survives her. The relatives, two or three men and a ten-year-old boy, standing near, seem uninterested. Crouching at a distance, one old woman, keening. Five or six beggars like horse-flies nagging about.

Now they take up the body and lay it on the pile of wood in the pit. The woman's head turns and one arm drops, as though she moved in her sleep. She died only a few hours ago. They heap sticks of wood over her, tossing it on until it rises high. Then the little boy, her son, walks seven times around the pyre, carrying a torch. After that he throws the torch into the wood, flames and smoke rush up, and the ceremony is done.

'With a good fire everything burns but the navel,' explains Mr. Haldar. 'That is picked out of the ashes, by the temple attendants, and, with a gold coin provided by the dead person's family, is rolled in a ball of clay and flung into the Ganges. We shall now see the Ganges.'

Again he conducts us through the crowds to a point below the temple, where runs a muddy brook, shallow and filled with bathers. 'This,' says Mr. Haldar, 'is the most ancient remaining outlet of the Ganges. Therefore its virtues are accounted great. Hundreds of thousands of sick person come here annually to bathe and be cured of their sicknes just as you see those doing now. Also, such as would sup plicate the goddess for other reasons bathe here first, to b cleansed of their sins.'

As the bathers finished their ablutions, they drank of th water that lapped their knees. Then most of them devote a few moments to grubbing with their hands in the bottom bringing up handfuls of mud which they carefully sorte over in their palms. 'Those,' said Mr. Haldar, 'are lookin for the gold coins flung in from the burning ghat. The hope.'

Meantime, up and down the embankment, priests cam and went, each leading three or four kids, which they washe in the stream among the bathers and then dragged back screaming and struggling, toward the temple forecourt And men and women bearing water-jars, descending an ascending, filled their jars in the stream and disappeared b the same path.

'Each kid,' continued Mr. Haldar, 'must be purified i the holy stream before it is slain. As for the water-carriers they bring the water as an offering. It is poured over Kali' feet, and over the feet of the priests that stand before her.

As Mr. Haldar took leave of us, just at the rear of th outer temple wall, I noticed a drain-hole about the size of a man's hand, piercing the wall at the level of the ground By this hole, on a little flat stone, lay a few marigold flowers a few rose-petals, a few pennies. As I looked, suddenly ou of the hole gushed a flow of dirty water, and a woman, rushing up, thrust a cup under it and drank.

'That is our holy Ganges water, rendered more holy by having flowed over the feet of Kali and her priests. From th

Photo: H. H. Field.

IN KALI'S BURNING GHAT

›or of the shrine it is carried here by this ancient drain. is found most excellent against dysentery and enteric ver. The sick who have strength to move drink it here, 'st having bathed in the Ganges. To those too ill to come, eir friends may carry it.'

So we found our waiting motor and rolled away, past the eneral Hospital, the Bishop's House, the various Clubs, e Empire Theatre, straight into the heart of Calcutta in few minutes' time.

'Why did you go to Kali Ghat? That is not India. Only .e lowest and most ignorant of Indians are Kali wor-ıippers,' said an English Theosophist, sadly, next day.

I repeated the words to one of the most learned and dis-nguished of Bengali Brahmans. His comment was this:

'Your English friend is wrong. It is true that in the wer castes the percentage of worshippers of Kali is larger ıan the percentage of the worshippers of Vishnu, perhaps ːcause the latter demands some self-restraint, such as ›stinence from intoxicants. But hundreds of thousands ' Brahmans, everywhere, worship Kali, and the devotees Kali Ghat will include Hindus of all castes and conditions, nong whom are found some of the most highly educated ıd important personages of this town and of India.'

CHAPTER I

THE ARGUMENT

THE area we know as India is nearly half as large as t United States. Its population is three times greater th ours. Its import and export trade – as yet but the germ the possible – amounted, in the year 1924–5, to abo £500,000,000, or two and a half billion dollars.[1] A Bombay is but three weeks' journey from New York.

Under present conditions of human activity, where whether we will or no, the roads that join us to every part the world continually shorten and multiply, it would appe that some knowledge of main facts concerning so big a to-day so near a neighbour should be a part of our inte gence and our self-protection.

But what does the average American actually know abo India? That Mr. Gandhi lives there; also tigers. H further ideas, if such he has, resolve themselves into more less hazy notions more or less unconsciously absorbed fro professional propagandists out of one camp or another; fro religious or mystical sources; or from tales and travel-boo novels and verses, having India as their scene.

It was dissatisfaction with this status that sent me to Ind to see what a volunteer unsubsidized, uncommitted, a unattached, could observe of common things in daily hum life.

Leaving untouched the realms of religion, of politics, a of the arts, I would confine my inquiry to such workad

[1] *Review of the Trade of India in* 1924–5, Department of Commer Intelligence and Statistics, Calcutta, 1926, p. 51.

ound as public health and its contributing factors. I would to determine, for example, what situation would confront ublic health official charged with the duty of stopping an idemic of cholera or of plague; what elements would work and against a campaign against hookworm; or what ces would help or hinder a governmental effort to lower ant mortality, to better living conditions, or to raise ucational levels, supposing such work to be required.

None of these points could well be wrapped in 'eastern stery,' and all concern the whole family of nations in the ne way that the sanitary practices of John Smith of 23 ain Street concern Peter Jones at the other end of the ck.

Therefore, in early October, 1925, I went to London, led at India Office, and, a complete stranger, stated my n.

'What would you like us to do for you?' asked the gentle-n who received me.

'Nothing,' I answered, 'except to believe what I say. A eign stranger prying about India, not studying ancient hitecture, not seeking philosophers or poets, not even nting big game, and commissioned by no one, anywhere, y seem a queer figure. Especially if that stranger de-lops an acute tendency to ask questions. I should like it to accepted that I am neither an idle busybody nor a political ent, but merely an ordinary American citizen seeking test ts to lay before my own people.'

To such Indians as I met, whether then or later, I made same statement. In the period that followed, the intro-ctions that both gave me, coupled with the untiring urtesy and helpfulness alike of Indians and of British, icial or private, all over India, made possible a survey

more thorough than could have been accomplished in fi
times the time without such aid.

'But whatever you do, be careful not to generalize,' t
British urged. 'In this huge country little or nothing
everywhere true. Madras and Peshawar, Bombay a
Calcutta – attribute the things of one of these to any one
the others, and you are out of court.'

Those journeys I made, plus many another up and dov
and across the land. Everywhere I talked with heal
officers, both Indian and British, of all degrees, going o
with them into their respective fields, city or rural, to obser
their tasks and their ways of handling them. I visit
hospitals of many sorts and localities, talked at length wi
the doctors, and studied conditions and cases. I made lo
sorties in the open country from the North-West Frontier
Madras, sometimes accompanying a district commission
on his tours of chequered duty, sometimes 'sitting in'
village councils of peasants, or at Indian municipal boa
meetings, or at court sessions with their luminous parade
life. I went with English nurses into bazaars and cour
yards and inner chambers and over city roofs, visiting whe
need called. I saw, as well, the homes of the rich. I studie
the handling of confinements, the care of children and of t
sick, the care and protection of food, and the values place
upon cleanliness. I noted the personal habits of vario
castes and grades, in travel or at home, in daily life. I visite
agricultural stations and cattle-farms, and looked into t
general management of cattle and crops. I investigated t
animal sanctuaries provided by Indian piety. I saw t
schools, and discussed with teachers and pupils their ai
and experience. The sittings of the various legislatures, a
India and provincial, repaid attendance by the light the

hed upon the mind-quality of the elements represented. I ought and found private opportunity to question eminent ndians – princes, politicians, administrators, religious eaders; and the frankness of their talk, as to the mental and hysical status and conditions of the peoples of India, thrown ut upon the background of my personal observation, roved an asset of the first value.

And just this excellent Indian frankness finally led me to hink that, after all, there are perhaps certain points on vhich – south, north, east and west – you *can* generalize bout India. Still more: that you can generalize about the nly matters in which we of the busy West will, to a man, ee our own concern.

John Smith of 23 Main Street may care little enough bout the ancestry of Peter Jones, and still less about his eligion, his philosophy, or his views on art. But if Peter cul-ivates habits of living and ways of thinking that make him physical menace not only to himself and his family, but to ll the rest of the block, then practical John will want details.

'Why,' ask modern Indian thinkers, 'why, after all the ong years of British rule, are we still marked among the peoples of the world for our ignorance, our poverty, and our monstrous death rate? By what right are light and bread and life denied?'

'What this country suffers from is want of initiative, want of enterprise, and want of hard, sustained work,' mourns Sir Chimanlal Setalvad.[1] 'We rightly charge the English rulers for our helplessness and lack of initiative and originality,' says Mr. Gandhi.[2]

[1] *Legislative Assembly Debates*, 1925. Vol. VI, No. 6, p. 396.

[2] *Young India*, March 25, 1926, p. 112. This is Mr. Gandhi's weekly publication, from which much hereinafter will be quoted.

Other public men demand: 'Why are our enthusiasms so sterile? Why are our mutual pledges, our self-dedications to brotherhood and the cause of liberty so soon spent and forgotten? Why is our manhood itself so brief? Why do we tire so soon and die so young?' Only to answer themselves with the cry: 'Our spiritual part is wounded and bleeding. Our very souls are poisoned by the shadow of the arrogant stranger, blotting out our sun. Nothing can be done – nothing, anywhere, but to mount the political platform and faithfully denounce our tyrant until he takes his flight. When Britain has abdicated and gone, then, and not till then, free men breathing free air, may we turn our minds to the lesser needs of our dear Mother India.'

Now it is precisely at this point, and in a spirit of hearty sympathy with the suffering peoples, that I venture my main generality. It is this:

The British administration of India, be it good, bad, or indifferent, has nothing whatever to do with the conditions above indicated. Inertia, helplessness, lack of initiative and originality, lack of staying power and of sustained loyalties, sterility of enthusiasm, weakness of life-vigour itself – all are traits that truly characterize the Indian not only of to-day, but of long-past history. All, furthermore, will continue to characterize him, in increasing degree, until he admits their causes and with his own two hands uproots them. His soul and body are indeed chained in slavery. But he himself wields and hugs his chains and with violence defends them. No agency but a new spirit within his own breast can set him free. And his arraignments of outside elements, past, present, or to come, serve only to deceive his own mind and to put off the day of his deliverance.

Take a girl child twelve years old, a pitiful physical

pecimen in bone and blood, illiterate, ignorant, without any ort of training in habits of health. Force motherhood upon er at the earliest possible moment. Rear her weakling son n intensive vicious practices that drain his small vitality day y day. Give him no outlet in sports. Give him habits that nake him, by the time he is thirty years of age, a decrepit and uerulous old wreck – and will you ask what has sapped the nergy of his manhood?

Take a huge population, mainly rural, illiterate and loving ts illiteracy. Try to give it primary education without em-loying any of its women as teachers – because if you do mploy them you invite the ruin of each woman that you so xpose. Will you ask why that people's education proceeds lowly?

Take bodies and minds bred and built on the lines thus ndicated. Will you ask why the death rate is high and the eople poor?

Whether British or Russians or Japanese sit in the seat of he highest; whether the native princes divide the land, re-iving old days of princely dominance; or whether some utonomy more complete than that now existing be set up, he only power that can hasten the pace of Indian develop-nent toward freedom, beyond the pace it is travelling to-day, the power of the men of India, wasting no more time in lk, recriminations, and shiftings of blame, but facing and ttacking, with the best resolution they can muster, the task hat awaits them in their own bodies and souls.

This subject has not, I believe, been presented in com-non print. The Indian does not confront it in its entirety; e knows its component parts, but avoids the embarrass-nent of assembling them or of drawing their essential in-erences. The traveller in India misses it, having no occasion to delve below the picturesque surface into living things as they are. The British official will especially avoid it – will deprecate its handling by others. His own daily labours, since the Reforms of 1919, hinge upon persuasion rather than upon command; therefore his hopes of success, like his orders from above, impose the policy of the gentle word. Outside agencies working for the moral welfare of the Indian seem often to have adopted the method of encouraging their beneficiary to dwell on his own merits and to harp upon others short-comings, rather than to face his faults and conquer them. And so, in the midst of an agreement of silence or flattery, you find a sick man growing daily weaker, dying, body and brain, of a disease that only himself can cure, and with no one, anywhere, enough his friend to hold the mirror up and show him plainly what is killing him.

In shouldering this task myself, I am fully aware of the resentments I shall incur: of the accusations of muck-raking; of injustice; of material-mindedness; of lack of sympathy; of falsehood perhaps; perhaps of prurience. But the fact of having seen conditions and their bearings, and of being in a position to present them, would seem to deprive one of the right to indulge a personal reluctance to incur consequences.

Here, in the beginning of this book, therefore, stands the kernel of what seems to me the most important factor in the life and future of one-eighth of the human race. In the pages to come will be found an attempt to widen the picture, stretching into other fields and touching upon other aspects of Indian life. But in no field, in no aspect, can that life escape the influences of its inception.

CHAPTER II

'SLAVE MENTALITY'

'Let us not put off everything until Swaraj[1] is attained and thus put off Swaraj itself,' pleads Gandhi. 'Swaraj can be had only by brave and clean people.'[2]

But, in these days of the former leader's waned influence, it is not for such teachings that he gains ears. From every political platform stream flaming protests of devotion to the death to Mother India; but India's children fit no action to their words. Poor indeed she is, and sick – ignorant and helpless. But, instead of flinging their strength to her rescue, her ablest sons, as they themselves lament, spend their time in quarrels together or else lie idly weeping over their own futility.

Meantime the British Government, in administering the affairs of India, would seem to have reached a set rate of progress, which, if it be not seriously interrupted, might fairly be forecast decade by decade. So many schools constructed, so many hospitals; so many furlongs of highway laid, so many bridges built; so many hundred miles of irrigation canal dug; so many markets made available; so many thousand acres of waste land brought under homestead cultivation; so many wells sunk; so much rice and wheat and millet and cotton added to the country's food and trade resources.

This pace of advance, compared to the huge needs of the country, or compared to like movements in the United

[1] Self-government.

[2] *Young India*, Nov. 19, 1925, p. 399.

States or in Canada, is slow. To hasten it materially, one single element would suffice – the hearty, hard-working and intelligent devotion to the practical job itself, of the educated Indian. To-day, however, few signs appear, among Indian public men, of concern for the status of the masses, while they curse the one power which, however little to their liking, is doing practically all of whatever is done for the comfort of sad old Mother India.

The population of all India is reckoned, in round numbers, to be 319,000,000.[1] Setting aside Indian States ruled by Indian princes, that of British India is 247,000,000. Among these peoples live fewer than 200,000 Europeans, counting every man, woman and child in the land, from the Viceroy down to the haberdasher's baby. The British personnel of the Army, including all ranks, numbers fewer than 60,000 men. The British Civilian cadre, inclusive of the Civil Service, the medical men, the engineers, foresters, railway administrators, mint, assay, educational, agricultural and veterinary experts, etc., etc., totals 3,432 men. Of the Indian Police Service, the British membership approximates 4,000. This last figure excludes the subordinate and provincial services, in which the number of Europeans is, however, negligible.

Representing the British man-power in India to-day, you therefore have these figures:

Army	60,000
Civil Services	3,432
Police	4,000
	67,432

[1] *The Indian Year Book*, *Times* Press, Bombay, 1926, p. 13.

This is the entire local strength of the body to whose oppressive presence the Indian attributes what he himself describes as the 'slave mentality' of 247,000,000 human beings.

But one must not overlook the fact that, before Britain's day, India was ever either a chaos of small wars and brigandage, chief preying upon chief, and all upon the people; or else she was the flaccid subject of a foreign rule. If, once and again, a native king arose above the rest and spread his sway, the reign of his house was short, and never covered all of India. Again and again conquering forces came sweeping through the mountain passes down out of Central Asia. And the ancient Hindu stock, softly absorbing each recurrent blow, quivered – and lay still.

Many a reason is advanced to account for these things – reasons such as the devitalizing character of the Hindu religion, with its teachings of the nothingness of things as they seem; of the infinitude of lives – dreams all – to follow this present seeming. And this element, beyond doubt, plays its part. But we, as 'hard-headed Americans,' may, for a beginning, put such matters aside while we consider points on which we shall admit less room for debate and where we need no interpreter and no glossary.

The whole pyramid of the Hindu's woes, material and spiritual – poverty, sickness, ignorance, political minority, melancholy, ineffectiveness, not forgetting that subconscious conviction of inferiority which he for ever bares and advertises by his gnawing and imaginative alertness for social affronts – rests upon a rock-bottom physical base. This base is, simply, his manner of getting into the world and his sex-life thenceforward.

In the great orthodox Hindu majority, the girl looks for

motherhood nine months after reaching puberty[1] – or anywhere between the ages of fourteen and eight. The latter age is extreme, although in some sections not exceptional; the former is well above the average. Because of her years and upbringing and because countless generations behind her have been bred even as she, she is frail of body. She is also completely unlettered, her stock of knowledge comprising only the ritual of worship of the household idols, the rites of placation of the wrath of deities and evil spirits, and the detailed ceremony of the service of her husband, who is ritualistically her personal god.

As to the husband, he may be a child scarcely older than herself or he may be a widower of fifty, when first he requires of her his conjugal rites. In any case, whether from immaturity or from exhaustion, he has small vitality to transmit.

The little mother goes through a destructive pregnancy, ending in a confinement whose peculiar tortures will not be imagined unless in detail explained.

The infant that survives the birth-strain – a feeble creature at best, bankrupt in bone-stuff and vitality, often venereally poisoned, always predisposed to any malady that may be afloat – must look to his child-mother for care. Ignorant of the laws of hygiene, guided only by the most primitive superstitions, she has no helpers in her task other than the older women of the household, whose knowledge, despite their years, is little greater than hers. Because of her place in the social system, child-bearing and matters of procreation are the woman's one interest in life, her one subject of conversation, be her caste high or low. Therefore, the child growing up in the home learns, from earliest grasp of word and act, to dwell upon sex relations.

[1] Cf. *post*, p. 44.

Siva, one of the greatest of the Hindu deities, is represented, on highroad shrines, in the temples, on the little altar of the home, or in personal amulets, by the image of the male generative organ, in which shape he receives the daily sacrifices of the devout. The followers of Vishnu, multitudinous in the south, from their childhood wear painted upon their foreheads the sign of the function of generation.[1] And although it is accepted that the ancient inventors of these and kindred emblems intended them as aids to the climbing of spiritual heights, practice and extremely detailed narratives of the intimacies of the gods, preserved in the hymns of the fireside, give them literal meaning and suggestive power, as well as religious sanction in the common mind.[2]

'Fools,' says a modern teacher of the spiritual sense of the Phallic cult, 'do not understand, and they never will, for they look at it only from the physical side.'[3]

But, despite the scorn of the sage, practical observation in India forces one to the conclusion that a religion adapted to the wise alone leaves most of the sheep unshepherded.

And, even though the sex-symbols themselves were not present, there are the sculptures and paintings on temple walls and temple chariots, on palace doors and street-wall frescoes, realistically demonstrating every conceivable aspect and humour of sex contact; there are the eternal songs on the lips of the women of the household; there is, in brief, the

[1] Fanciful interpretations of this symbol are sometimes given.

[2] *Hindu Manners, Customs and Ceremonies*, Abbé J. A. Dubois, 1821. Edited and corrected by H. K. Beauchamp 1897 and 1925. Clarendon Press, Oxford, 1924, pp. 111–12, 628–31, etc.

[3] Swami Vivekananda, in *Bhakti Yoga*. For a brief and liberal discussion of the topic see Chapter XIII in *The Heart of Aryavarta*, by the Earl of Ronaldshay, Constable and Company, Ltd., London, 1925.

occupation and pre-occupation of the whole human worl within the child's vision, to predispose thought.

It is true that, to conform to the International Conventio for the Suppression of the Circulation of and Traffic i Obscene Publications, signed in Geneva on September 12 1923, the Indian Legislature duly amended the India Penal Code and Code of Criminal Procedure; and that thi amendment duly prescribes set penalties for 'whoever sell lets to hire, distributes, publicly exhibits . . . conveys . . or receives profit from any obscene object, book, representa tion or figure.' But its enactment, unqualified, althoug welcome to the Muhammadans, would have wrought havc with the religious belongings, the ancient traditions an customs and the priestly prerogatives dear to the Hind majority. Therefore the Indian Legislature, preponderantl Hindu, saddled the amendment with an exception, whic reads:[1]

'This section does not extend to any book, pamphlet writing, drawing or painting kept or used *bona fide* fo religious purposes or any representation sculptured, en graved, painted or otherwise represented on or in an temple, or on any car used for the conveyance of idols, o kept or used for any religious purpose.'

In many parts of the country, north and south, the littl boy, his mind so prepared, is likely, if physically attractive to be drafted for the satisfaction of grown men, or to b regularly attached to a temple, in the capacity of prostitute Neither parent as a rule sees any harm in this, but is, rather flattered that the son has been found pleasing.

This, also, is a matter neither of rank nor of specia

[1] *Indian Penal Code*, Act No. VIII of 1925, Section 292

gnorance. In fact, so far are they from seeing good and evil s we see good and evil, that the mother, high caste or low aste, will practise upon her children – the girl 'to make her leep well,' the boy 'to make him manly,' an abuse which he boy, at least, is apt to continue daily for the rest of is life.

This last point should be noticed. Highest medical uthority in widely scattered sections attests that practically very child brought under observation, for whatever reason, ears on its body the signs of this habit. Whatever opinion nay be held as to its physical effects during childhood, its ffect upon early thought-training cannot be overlooked. And, when constantly practised during mature life, its levastation of body and nerves will scarcely be questioned.

Ancient Hindu religious teachings are cited to prove that he marriage of the immature has not original Scriptural anction. Text is flung against text, in each recurrence of he argument. Pundits radically disagree. But against the og evoked in their dispute stand sharp and clear the facts of laily usage. Hindu custom demands that a man have a egitimate son at the earliest possible moment – a son to erform the proper religious ceremonies at and after the eath of the father and to crack the father's skull on the uneral pyre, according to his caste's ritual. For this reason s well as from inclination, the beginning of the average boy's exual commerce barely awaits his ability. Neither general abit nor public opinion confines that commerce to his wife r wives.

Mr. Gandhi has recorded that he lived with his wife, as uch, when he was thirteen years old, and adds that if he ad not, unlike his brother in similar case, left her presence or a certain period each day to go to school, he 'would either have fallen a prey to disease and premature death, or have le [thenceforth] a burdensome existence.'[1]

Forced up by Western influences, the subject of chil marriages has been much discussed of latter years and sentiment of uneasiness concerning it is perceptibly risin in the Indian mind. But as yet this finds small translatio into act, and the orthodox Hindu majority fights in strengt on the side of the ancient practice.

Little in the popular Hindu code suggests self-restrai in any direction, least of all in sex relations. 'My father,' sai a certain eminent Hindu barrister, one of the best men in h province, 'taught me wisely, in my boyhood, how to avoi infection.'

'Would it not have been better,' I asked, 'had he taugh you continence?'

'Ah – but we know that to be impossible.'

'No question of right or wrong can be involved in ar aspect of such matters,' a famous Hindu mystic, himself tl venerated teacher of multitudes, explained to me. 'I forg the act the moment I have finished it. I merely do it not be unkind to my wife, who is less illumined than I. To c it or not to do it, signifies nothing. Such things belong on to the world of illusion.'

After the rough outline just given, small surprise w meet the statement that from one end of the land to the oth the average male Hindu of thirty years, provided he ha means to command his pleasure, is an old man; and th from seven to eight out of every ten such males betwee the ages of twenty-five and thirty are impotent. The figures are not random, and are affected by little save th proviso above given; a cultivator of the soil, because of h

[1] *Young India*, Jan. 7, 1926

verty and his life of wholesome physical exertion during art of the year, is less liable than the man of means, or the y dweller. A side-light will be found by a glance down the vertisement space of Indian-owned newspapers. Magical ugs and mechanical contrivances, whether 'for princes and h men only,' or the humbler and not less familiar '32 llars of Strength to prop up your decaying body for One ipee[1] only,' crowd the columns and support the facts.

In the Punjab alone, between December 29, 1922, and cember 4, 1925, Government prosecuted vernacular pers eleven separate times for carrying ultra-indecent vertisements. In seven cases the publications were Hindu, ice Muhammadan, once Sikh. The fines imposed ranged m twenty-five to two hundred rupees, in one case plus iety days' rigorous imprisonment. And it should be duly ted that such prosecutions are never undertaken save iere the advertisement gives the grossest physical details in in and unmistakable language.

Following the eleventh prosecution, Government sent out iote to the Press informing the editors of this last con- tion with its relatively high fine, and advising them to utinize advertisements before publication. Upon this ggestion the editorial comment of the *Brahman Samachar*[2] iitted an informing ray:

'Government wants that such advertisements should not published and that the editors should go through them fore publishing them. It would have been better if the formation Bureau had published the obscene advertisement

[1] The market value of the rupee fluctuates with other international ex- nges. But for the purpose of this book, one rupee is taken to be worth 4*d.* sterling, 33 1/3 cents, three rupees one dollar, U.S. currency

[2] A Hindu paper of Lahore, issue of Feb. 16, 1926.

along with its report so that the subject matter and the mann of writing of the advertisement would have become know

Mr. Gandhi in his newspaper has, it is true, recorded disapproving cognizance. 'Drugs and mechanical contr ances,' he writes, 'may keep the body in a tolerable co dition, but they sap the mind.'[1]

But a far more characteristic general attitude was tl evidenced in the recent action of a Hindu of high positi whereby, before giving his daughter in marriage, he manded from his would-be son-in-law a British docto certificate attesting that he, the would-be son-in-law, v venereally infected. The explanation is simple: a barı wife casts embarrassment upon her parents; and barı marriages, although commonly laid to the wife, are often to the husband's inability. The father in this case v merely taking practical precaution. He did not want daughter, through fault not her own, to be either supplan or returned upon his hands. And no reproach whate attaches to the infected condition. No public opinion wo on the other side.

In case, however, of the continued failure of the wif any wife – to give him a child, the Hindu husband has a recourse; he may send his wife on a pilgrimage to a temp bearing gifts. And, it is affirmed, some castes habitu save time by doing this on the first night after the marria At the temple by day, the woman must beseech the god a son, and at night she must sleep within the sacred precin Morning come, she has a tale to tell the priest of what be her under the veil of darkness.

'Give praise, O daughter of honour!' he replies. 'It v the god!'

[1] *Young India*, Sept. 2, 1926, p. 309.

And so she returns to her home.

If a child comes, and it lives, a year later she revisits the nple, carrying, with other gifts, the hair from her child's ad.[1]

Visitors to the temples to-day sometimes notice a tree iose boughs are hung with hundreds of little packets und in dingy rags; around the roots of that tree lies a ick mat of short black locks of human hair. It is the votive e of the god. It declares his benefits. To maintain the nour of the shrine, the priests of this attribute are care-ly chosen from stout new brethren.

Every one, seemingly, understands all about it. The nost piety, nevertheless, truly imbues the suppliant's nd and contents the family.

As to the general subject, enough has now, perhaps, been d to explain and to substantiate the Hindu's bitter lament his own 'slave mentality.'

It may also suggest why he develops no real or lasting ders, and why such men as from time to time aspire to it rank are able only for a brief interval to hold the flitting nds of their followers.

The Indian perceives, to a certain degree, the condition; t he rarely goes all the way to the bottom thereof. Nor es he recognize its full significance and relate it to its con-quences. 'Why do our best men – those who should lead – die so young?' he repeats despondently, implying that only possible answer is: 'Karma – Kismet – an enigmatic e.' 'The average life of our inhabitants is 23 years,' says Hindu Doctor Hariprasad [2] – and lays the blame to bad nitation. Another characteristic Indian view is expressed

[1] Cf. *Hindu Manners, Customs and Ceremonies*, pp. 593–4.

[2] *Young India*, Nov. 5, 1925, p. 375.

by Manilal C. Parekh,[1] treating with dismay of the inroads tuberculosis – an infection that finds ideal encouragement the unresisting bodies and depleting habits of the people

'One need not think just now of the causes of this frightf increase. . . . The present writer wishes Swaraj to come India as early as possible in order that the people of the lar may be able to deal with this tremendously big problem.' . .

Thus they still contrive to shift the burden and avoid th fact.

Yet it was one of the most distinguished of Indian medic men, a Bombay Brahman, physician and pathologist, wh gave me the following appraisal:

'My people continually miss the association of the mental and material poverty with their physical extravaganc Yet our undeniable race deterioration, our natural lack power of concentration, of initiative and of continuity purpose cannot be dissociated from our expenditure of a vital energy on the single line of sexual indulgence.'

Once more, then, one is driven to the original conclusio Given men who enter the world physical bankrupts out bankrupt stock, rear them through childhood in influenc and practices that devour their vitality; launch them at th dawn of maturity on an unrestrained outpouring of the whole provision of creative energy in one single directio find them, at the age when the Anglo-Saxon is just comin into full glory of manhood, broken-nerved, low-spirite petulant ancients; and need you, while this remains un changed, seek for other reasons why they are poor and sic and dying and why their hands are too weak, too flutterin to seize or to hold the reins of Government?

[1] *Servants of India*, April 8, 1926, p. 124.

CHAPTER III

MARBLES AND TOPS

A STUDY of the attitude of the Government of India as to the subject of child-marriage shows that, while steadily exercising persuasive pressure toward progress and change, it has been dominated, always, by two general principles – the first, to avoid as far as possible interference in matters concerning the religion of the governed; the second, never to sanction a law that cannot be enforced. To run counter to the Indian's tenets as to religious duties, religious prohibitions, and god-given rights has ever meant the eclipse of Indian reason in madness, riot and blood. And to enforce a law whose keeping or breaking must be a matter of domestic secrecy, is, in such a country as India at least, impossible.

Indian and English authorities unite in the conviction that no law raising the marriage age of girls would be to-day effectively accepted by the Hindu peoples. The utmost to be hoped, in the present state of public mentality, is, so these experienced men hold, a raising of the age of consent within the marriage bonds. A step in this direction was accomplished in 1891, when Government, backed by certain members of the advanced section of the Indians, after a hot battle in which it was fiercely accused by eminent orthodox Hindus of assailing the most sacred foundations of the Hindu world, succeeded in raising that age from ten years to twelve. In latter-day Legislative Assemblies the struggle has been renewed, non-official Indian Assemblymen bringing forward Bills aiming at further advance only to see them, in one stage or another, defeated by the strong orthodox majority.

Upon such occasions, the attitude of the Viceregal Government has consistently been one of square approval of the main object in view, but of caution against the passage of laws so much in advance of public opinion that their existence can serve only to bring law itself into disrepute. This course is the more obligatory because of the tendency of the Indian public man to satisfy his sense of duty by the mere empty passing of a law, without thought or intention or accepted responsibility as to the carrying of his law into effect.

Not unnaturally, Government's course pleases no one. From the one side rise accusations of impious design against the sanctuaries of the faith; from the other come charges as bitter but of an opposite implication.

'What right have you to separate man and wife? cries an orthodox Brahman Assemblyman. 'You may lay your unholy hands on our ancient ideals and traditions, but we will not follow you.'[1] Yet, with equal vehemence a second member declares that 'every Englishman in the Government of India seems to be throwing obstacles in the way of other people going forward.'[2]

An examination of these debates gives a fair general view of the state of public opinion on the whole topic. Members seem well aware of conditions that obtain. The divergence comes in the weight they assign to those conditions.

Rai Bahadur Bakshi Sohan Lal, member from Jullundur, when introducing a non-official amendment to raise the age of consent within the marriage bond to fourteen years, argued:[3]

[1] *Legislative Assembly Debates*, 1925. Vol. V, Part III, p. 2890.
[2] *Ibid.* Vol. VI, p. 557.
[3] *Ibid.*, 1922. Vol. II, Part III, p. 2650.

'The very high rate of fatality amongst the high classes in is country of newly-born children and of young married ves is due to sexual intercourse and pregnancy of the girl fore she reaches the age of puberty or full development of r physical organs. The result of such consummation be-re bodily development not only weakens the health of the rl but often produces children who are weak and sickly, d in a large number of cases cannot resist any illness of an dinary type, or any inclemency of weather or climate. ius some of them die immediately after birth or during eir infancy. If they live at all, they are always in need of edical attendance, medical advice or medical treatment, to ger on their lives; or in other words they are born more to nister to the medical profession than themselves and their nilies or their country. Neither can they be good soldiers r good civilians, neither good outdoor workers nor good door workers; neither can they be fit to attack an enemy r defend themselves against attacks of an enemy, or against e raid of thieves or dacoits.[1] In a few words, his birth is ry often the cause of ruining the health, strength and pros-rity of his parents without resulting in a corresponding nefit to society. The husband, in the majority of cases, . has to arrange for his re-marriage several times during s life-time, on account of the successive deaths of his young ves or on account of his wife bearing children who are not ig-lived.'

Successive debates expose the facts that few or none of the dian parliamentarians dispute the theoretical wisdom of stponing motherhood until the maturity of the mother; t all agree that it is impossible to effect such a result with-

[1] Gang robbers.

out prohibiting the marriage of girls of immature age. Y this they say, with one accord, cannot be done – and fo three reasons:

First, because immutable custom forbids, premarita pubescence being generally considered, among Hindus, social if not a religious sin.[1]

Second, because the father dare not keep his daughter a home lest she be damaged before she is off his hands. An this especially in joint-family households, where several me and boys – brothers, cousins, uncles – live under the sam roof.

Third, because the parents dare not expose the girl, afte her dawning puberty, to the pressure of her own desire u satisfied.

With these intimate dangers in view a learned Brahma Assemblyman, Diwan Bahadur T. Rangachariar, Membe from Madras, spoke earnestly against the unofficial Bill 1925, raising the age of consent within the marriage bon to fourteen years. Any pretence at enforcing such a la would, it was generally conceded, demand the keeping of th wife away from her husband, retaining her in her own father *zenana*.[2] Said the Madrassi Assemblyman, warning, im ploring:[3]

'Remember the position of girls in our country betwee 12 and 14. Have we not got our daughters in our hous Have we not got our sisters in our house? Remember tha and remember your own neighbours. Remembering o

[1] See *Legislative Assembly Debates* of 1925, March 23 and 24 in Vol. Part III, and Sept. 1, in Vol. VI.

[2] Women's quarters.

[3] *Legislative Assembly Debates*, 1925. Vol. V, Part III, p. 2884.

habits, remembering our usages, remembering the precociousness of our youth, remembering the condition of the climate, remembering the conditions of the country, I ask you to give your weighty judgment to this matter.'

Another Brahman member vehemently protests: [1]

'The tradition of womanhood in this country is unapproached by the tradition of womanhood in any other country. Our ideal of womanhood is this: Our women regard their husbands – they have been taught from the moment they were suckling their mothers' milk to regard their husbands as their God on earth. . . . To the Brahman girl-wife the husband is a greater, truer, dearer benefactor than all the social reformers bundled together! . . . What right have you to interfere with this ancient, noble tradition of ours regarding the sanctity of wedlock? . . . What is the object of this legislation? Do you want to make the women of India strong and their children stalwart? But remember that in trying to do that, you may otherwise be doing a lot of evil, far worse than the evil you seek to remove. . . . By all means take care of [the girl's] body; but fail not to train her morals, to train her soul, so as to enable her to look upon her husband as her God, which indeed is the case in India, among Hindus at least. . . . Don't destroy, I beg of you – don't ruin our Hindu Homes.'

To reasoning of this sort another member – Mr. Shanmukhan Chetty, of Salem and Coimbatore – hotly retorts: [2]

'The fact that a so-called marriage rite precedes the commission of a crime does not and cannot justify that crime. I

[1] *Legislative Assembly Debates, ante*, p. 2890 *et seq.*
[2] *Ibid.* Vol. VI, p. 558.

have no doubt that if you were to ask a cannibal, he would plead his religion for the heinous act he does.'

And Dr. S. K. Datta, Indian Christian representative from Calcutta:[1]

'If ever there was "a man-made law," this compulsion of young girls to become mothers is one of them.'

The Bill raising the age of consent to fourteen was finally thrown out, buried under an avalanche of popular disapproval. In the next Assembly Sir Alexander Muddiman, leader of the Viceroy's Government, brought in an official Bill drafted with a view of breaking the *impasse* and securing that degree of advance that would be conceded by the conservative Indian element. This Bill, fixing the woman's age of consent within and without the marriage bond respectively at thirteen and fourteen years, was enacted into law as Act XXIX of 1925.

The discussion that it evoked on the floor of the Assembly gave still further light upon the attitude of Indians.

Some speakers pointed to the gradual growth of public opinion as expressed in caste, party and association councils as the best hope of the future. These deprecated legislation as both irritating and useless, calling attention to the fact that the orthodox community, comprising as it does the great majority of Hindus all over India, would regard legal abolition of child-marriage as, literally, a summons to a holy war.

Similarly, any active attempt to protect the child-wife during her infancy would, it was shown, be held as an attack upon the sacred marital relation, impossible to make effective and sure to let loose 'bloodshed and chaos.'

[1] *Legislative Assembly Debates*, 1925. Vol. V, Part III, p. 2839.

Rai Sahib M. Harbilas Sarda, of Ajmer-Merwara, maintained, it is true, that[1]

'where a social custom or a religious rite outrages our sense of humanity or inflicts injustice on a helpless class of people, the Legislature has a right to step in. Marrying a girl of three or four years and allowing sexual intercourse with a girl of nine or ten years outrages the sense of humanity anywhere.'

But Pundit Madan Mohan Malaviya, of Allahabad, thought differently, saying:[2]

'I have to face the stern realities of the situation, realities which include a general permission or rather a widespread practice of having marriages performed before twelve and consequently of the impossibility of preventing a married couple from meeting. . . . I submit that it is perhaps best that we should reconcile ourselves to leave the law as it is in the case of married people for the present, and to trust to the progress of education and to social reform to raise the age of consummation of marriage to the proper level. . . . I am sure, Sir, that a great deal of advance has been made in this matter. In many provinces among the higher classes the marriageable age has been rising. . . . It is the poorer classes who unfortunately are the greatest victims in this matter. Early marriages take place among the poorer classes in a larger measure than among the higher classes.'

And Mr. Amar Nath Dutt, of Burdwan, combated the action proposed, thus:[3]

[1] *Legislative Assembly Debates, ante.* Vol. VI, p. 561.
[2] *Ibid.*, pp. 573–4. [3] *Ibid.*, pp. 558–9.

'We have no right to thrust our advanced views upon our less advanced countrymen. . . . Our villages are torn with factions. If the age of consent is raised to 13, rightly or wrongly we will find that there will be inquisitions by the police at the instance of members of an opposite faction in the village and people will be put to disgrace and trouble. . . . I would ask [Government] . . . to withdraw the Bill at once. Coming as I do, Sir, from Bengal, I know what is the opinion of the majority of the people there.'

Mr. M. K. Acharya, of South Arcot, also strongly adverse to change, declared that [1]

'. . . what is sought to be done is to make that an offence which is not an offence now, to make that a crime which is not at present a crime, and which we are unable to regard as a crime, whatever may be the feelings of some few people to the contrary.'

To which the same speaker added, a few moments later: [2]

'There is very little opinion of any respectable body of men in India which wants this reform very urgently. It may come, and there is no harm in it, in its own course. Really this is . . . merely to give Honourable Members some legislative marbles and tops to play with during the time that we happen to be in Simla.' [3]

[1] *Legislative Assembly Debates*, Vol. VI, p. 551.

[2] *Ibid.*, p. 556.

[3] Simla is the summer seat of the Central Government.

CHAPTER IV

EARLY TO MARRY AND EARLY TO DIE

UPON the unfruitful circlings of the Hindus breaks, once and again, a voice from the hardy North. Rarely, for the subject carries small interest there; yet, when it comes, weighted with rough acumen.

Nawab Sir Sahibzada Abdul Qaiyum is, as his name suggests, a Muhammadan. Speaking as of the distant North-West Frontier Province, he said: [1]

'I should like to say only a few words on the practical side of it. In my part of the country, we do not have early marriages. So the Bill is not likely to affect us very much. . . . I should have thought . . . the proper remedy . . . fixing the age of marriage for a man at a certain point and for a woman at another point . . . [but] I do not think the country is prepared. . . . Well, just consider: Who is going to be the prosecutor, who is going to be the investigator, who are going to be the witnesses, and who is going to enforce the verdict? . . . Then there is another difficulty . . . that you allow a young couple to be married and to live together and give them the opportunity of sharpening their sexual appetite and then prevent them by law from having their natural intercourse simply because they have not reached a certain age. . . . Well, suppose this law is enacted, and the young couple are prevented from having intercourse, I should think that in the majority of cases you would thus be

[1] *Legislative Assembly Debates*, 1925. Vol. VI, pp. 571–2.

sending the young boy into the streets . . . but so long a you allow people to be married young, there is no sufficien reason why you should enact laws which may interfere wit their private life.'

The handling of child-wives, many finally affirm, must regardless of legal enactment, continue to be guided b natural instincts under the husbands' sacred rights.

Throughout the Hindu argument, however, the genera conviction appears that law-making for social advance, whil entirely hopeless of enforcement, exerts an educational in fluence upon the community and is therefore to be regarde with satisfaction as a completed piece of work. 'The peopl should be educated,' the Indian public man declares. 'The should follow the course that I hereby indicate.' Havin spoken, he washes his hands. His task is done.

The voice of Diwar. Bahadur T. Rangachariar, the Ma drassi Brahman Assemblyman before quoted, was one of th few raised in criticism of this characteristic view-point. Ad dressing a fellow Assemblyman, proponent of the reforn amendment, he says: [1]

'May I ask my Honourable friend how many platform he has addressed in this connection outside this hall? (A voice: "Never.") Has he ever summoned a meeting in hi own province and addressed the people on the value of thes reforms? Sir, it is easy to avail yourself of the position whic you occupy here appealing to an audience where all ar wedded to your views and to get them to aid in this legis lation. But . . . it is not so easy a task to go to the countr and convince your own countrymen and countrywomen.'

Thus throughout these councils, the weight of respon-

[1] *Legislative Assembly Debates*, 1925 Vol. V, Part III, p. 2847.

sibility tosses back and forth, a beggar for lodgment. 'It is only the Brahmans who marry their girls in infancy.' Or, equally, 'It is only the low castes that follow such practice'; and, 'In any case the evils of early marriages are much exaggerated, interference is unwise, and volunteer social and religious reform associations may be trusted to protect young wives.'

But, turning from the shifts and theories of politicians – from their vague affirmations of progress attained, to cold black and white – you are pulled up with a jerk. Says the latest Census of India:[1]

'It can be assumed for all practical purposes that every woman is in the married state at or immediately after puberty and that cohabitation, therefore, begins in every case with puberty.'

And the significance of the thing is further driven home by the estimate that in India each generation sees the death of 3,200,000 mothers in the agonies of childbirth[2] – a figure greater than that of the united death-roll of the British Empire, plus that of France, Belgium, Italy and the United States, in the World War; and that the average physical rating of the population is at the bottom of the international list.

To turn again to the Legislative Assembly: Once more, it is a man from the north who speaks – a grey-beard yeoman, tall, straight, lean and sinewy, hard as nails, a telling contrast to the Southerners around him who jeer as he talks – Sardar Bahadur Captain Hira Singh Brar, of the Punjab, old Sikh fighting man.[3]

[1] *Census of India*, 1921, Appendix VII.

[2] *Legislative Assembly Debates*, 1922. Vol. III, Part I, p. 882.

[3] *Ibid.*, 1925. Vol. V, Part III, pp. 2829–31.

'I think, Sir, the real solution for preventing infant mortality lies in smacking the parent who produces such children and more so, in slapping many of our friends who alway oppose the raising of the age to produce healthy children . . . Is it not a sin when they call a baby of 9 or 10 years o a boy of 10 years husband and wife? It is a shame. (Voices "No, no!") . . . a misfortune for this generation and fo the future generation. . . . Girls of 9 or 10, babies themselves who ought to be playing with their dolls rather tha becoming wives, are mothers of children. Boys who ough to be getting their lessons in school are rearing a larg family of half a dozen boys and girls. . . . I do not like t go into society. I feel ashamed, because there is no manhood, there is no womanhood. I should feel ashamed mysel to go into society with a little girl of 12 years as my wife . . . We all talk, talk and talk a hundred and one thing here, but what happens? All left in this House, all left o the platform and nothing carried to our homes, nothing happens. . . . Healthy children are the foundation of a strong nation. Every one knows that the parents canno produce healthy children. To be useful we must have long life which we cannot have if early marriage is not stopped "Early to marry and early to die," is the motto of Indians.

The frank give-and-takes of the Indian Legislature, between Indian and Indian, deal with facts. But it is instructive to observe the robes that those facts can wear when arrayed by a poet for foreign consideration. Rabindranath Tagore in a recent essay on 'The Indian Ideal of Marriage,' explains child-marriage as a flower of the sublimated spirit, a conquest over sexuality and materialism won by exalted intellect for the eugenic uplift of the race. His explanation, however gically implies the assumption, simply, that Indian women ust be securely bound and delivered before their woman- ›od is upon them, if they are to be kept in hand. His ›rds are:[1]

'The "desire" . . . against which India's solution of the arriage problem declared war, is one of Nature's most ›werful fighters; consequently, the question of how to over- ›me it was not an easy one. There is a particular age, said ıdia, at which this attraction between the sexes reaches its :ight; so if marriage is to be regulated according to the cial will [as distinguished from the choice of the individual ›ncerned], it must be finished with before such age. Hence e Indian custom of early marriage.'

In other words, a woman must be married before she ıows she is one.

Such matter as this, coming as it does from one of the ost widely known of modern Indian writers, may serve to ıggest that we of the 'material-minded West' shall be misled we too quickly accept the Oriental's phrases as making literal ctures of the daily human life of which he seems to speak.

All thus far written here concerns the fate of children ithin the marriage bond. The general subject of pros- .ution in India need not enter the field of this book; but rtain special aspects thereof may be cited because of the ›mpass bearings that they afford.

In some parts of the country, more particularly in the :esidency of Madras and in Orissa, a custom obtains ıong the Hindus whereby the parents, to persuade some vour from the gods, may vow their next born child, if it be

[1] *The Book of Marriage.* Keyserling, Jonathan Cape Ltd., London, 26.

a girl, to the gods. Or, a particularly lovely child, for o reason or another held superfluous in her natural surroun ings, is presented to the temple. The little creature, accor ingly, is delivered to the temple women, her predecesso along the route, for teaching in dancing and singing. Oft by the age of five, when she is considered most desirable, s becomes the priests' own prostitute.

If she survives to later years she serves as a dancer a singer before the shrine in the daily temple worship; and the houses around the temple she is held always ready, a price, for the use of men pilgrims during their devotio sojourns in the temple precincts. She now goes beautifu attired, often loaded with the jewels of the gods, and leads active life until her charms fade. Then, stamped with t mark of the god under whose ægis she has lived, she is turn out upon the public, with a small allowance and with t acknowledged right to a beggar's livelihood. Her paren who may be well-to-do persons of good rank and caste, ha lost no face at all by the manner of their disposal of h Their proceeding, it is held, was entirely reputable. And s and her like form a sort of caste of their own, are call *devadassis*, or 'prostitutes of the gods,' and are a recogniz essential of temple equipment.[1]

Now, if it were asked how a responsible Government p mits this custom to continue in the land, the answer is n far to seek. The custom, like its background of pub sentiment, is deep-rooted in the far past of an ultra-cons vative and passionately religiose people. Anyone curious to the fierceness with which it would be defended by t people, both openly and covertly, and in the name of religic

[1] Cf. *The Golden Bough*. J. G. Frazer. Macmillan & Co., London, 19 *Adonis, Attis, Osiris*, Vol. I, pp. 61–5.

ainst any frontal attack, will find answer in the extra-dinary work,[1] and in the too-reticent books[2] of Miss my Wilson-Carmichael.

A province could be roused to madness by the forcible .thdrawal of girl-children from the gods.

'You cannot hustle the East.' But the underground work-gs of western standards and western contacts, and the ady, quiet teachings of the British official through the ars have done more, perhaps, toward ultimate change than y coercion could have effected.

Thus, when one measure came before the Legislative ssembly to raise the age of consent outside the marriage nd it was vigorously resisted by that conspicuous member, e then Rao Bahadur T. Rangachariar. His argument was, at such a step would work great hardships to the temple ostitutes.

And why?

Because, as he explained, the daughters of the *devadassis* nnot be married to caste husbands; so,[3]

s these girls cannot find wedlock, the mothers arrange with certain class of Zemindars – big landlords – that they ould be taken into alliance with the Zemindar.'

And the sympathetic legislator goes on in warning that the girl's age is raised, no *zemindar* will desire her, with e result that a good bargain is lost and the child is planted her poor mother's hands.

But the interesting point in the debate is not the eminent rahman's voicing of the mass-sentiment of his people, but e opposition that his words call forth from the seats around

[1] In Dohnavur, Tinnevelly District, South India.

[2] *Lotus Buds, Things As They Are*, etc. Morgan & Scott, London.

[3] *Legislative Assembly Debates*, 1923. Vol. III, Part IV, pp. 2807–8.

him, which are almost at one in their disapproval of an argu ment that, a generation earlier, would have met anoth reception.

Then followed the member from Orissa, Mr. Misra, wit his views on '*devadassis* or ordinary *dassis* or prostitutes':

'They have existed from time immemorial. . . . They ar regarded as a necessity even for marriage and other partie and for singing songs in invocation of God. . . . Much ha been said about girls being disposed of to Zemindars an Rajas.[2] . . . Zemindars never get any girls from procurer What happens is this. When Zemindars or Rajas marry their wives or Ranis bring with them some girls as mai servants. . . . Such a thing as procuring of girls does no exist, and no gentleman, whether he be a Zemindar or a Raj or an ordinary man, would ever adopt such a nefariou means to procure girls. . . . Why should we think so muc about these people [minor girls] who are able to take car of themselves?'

Mr. Misra's speech, although it dealt with simple facts evoked another manifestation of western influence, in that i definitely jarred upon many of his co-legislators. Howeve true, they did not want it spread in the record. Cries o 'Withdraw!' repeatedly interrupted him, and the words o other speakers gave ample proof of stirrings, intellectually at least, of a new perception in the land.

To translate intellectual perception into concrete ac requires yet another subversive mental process, in a peopl whose religion teaches that freedom from all action is th crown of perfect attainment.

[1] *Legislative Assembly Debates*, 1923. Vol. III, Part IV, pp. 2826–7.

[2] A Hindu title, inferior to Maharaja.

CHAPTER V

SPADES ARE SPADES

To visualize the effects of child-marriage as outlined by the legislators just quoted, one of the most direct means that the foreigner in India can take is to visit women's hospitals. This I have done from the Punjab to Bombay, from Madras to the United Provinces. This a man can scarcely do, for the reason that, doctor or not, he will rarely be admitted to the sight of a woman patient.

In one of the cities of the north-east is a little *purdah*[1] hospital of great popularity among Indian women. The timid creatures who crowd it are often making thereby their first excursion outside the walls of their own homes, nor would they have ventured now save for the pain that drove them. Muhammadans always, Hindus often, arrive in *purdah* conveyances – hidden in curtained carriages, or in little close-draped boxes barely high enough to hold their crouching bodies, swinging on a pole between bearers like bales of goods. Government clerks' wives they are, wives of officials or of professional men, rich women sometimes, sometimes poor, women of high caste, women of low caste – too desperate, all, for the help they are dying for, to set up against themselves their cherished bars of religious hatreds and caste repulsions.

The hospital consists of a series of little one-story bungalows, partly in wards, partly in single rooms. At the start, years ago, it was slow business getting the women to come; the first season producing a total of nine midwifery cases.

[1] The seclusion of women as in a harem.

But now every bed is full, even the verandas are crowded with cots, and women by scores, for whom there is no space, are pleading for admission.

Walking down the aisles you see, against the white plane of the pillows, dark faces of the non-Aryan stock, lighter faces of Brahmans, fine-cut faces of the northern Persian-Muhammadan strain, coarse faces of the south, all alike looking out from behind a common veil of helplessness and pain. Most of the work, here, is gynæcological. Most of the women are very young. Almost all are venereally affected.

Some come because they are childless, begging for either medicine or an operation to give them the one thing that buys an Indian wife a place in the sun. 'Among such,' says the British surgeon-superintendent, 'we continually find that the patient has had one child, often dead, and that then she has been infected with gonorrhœa which has utterly destroyed the pelvic organs. The number of young girls that come here, so destroyed in their first years of married life, is appalling. Ninety per cent. of the pelvic inflammation is of gonorrhœal origin.

'Here,' she continues, as we stop at the bedside of a young girl who looks up at us with the eyes of a hungry animal, 'here is a new patient. She has had several children, all still-born. This time, because her husband will no longer keep her unless she bears him a living child, she has come to us for confinement. As usual, it is a venereal case. But I hope we can help her.'

'And what about this one?' I ask, pausing by another cot in inward revolt against the death-stricken look on the young face before us.

'That,' answers the doctor, 'is the wife of a Hindu official.

e brought her to us three days ago, in the very onset of her cond confinement, because, by the first, she had failed to ve him a living child. Also she is suffering from heart-sease, asthma and a broken leg! I had to set her leg and nfine her at practically one and the same time. It was a rceps case. Dead twins. She, too, is an internal wreck, om infection, and can never give birth again. But that she es not yet know; I think it would kill her if she heard it ow.

'Her age? Thirteen and a few months.'

'Now what can be wrong here?' I inquire, catching the nile of a wan-faced child whose bird's-claw hands are asped around a paper toy.

'Ah!' says the doctor, 'this one was a pupil in a Govern-ent primary school, a merry wee thing, and so bright that e had just won a prize for scholarship. During the holiday e months ago her brother sent her home to the man to hom they had married her. That man is fifty years old. om their point of view he is a Hindu gentleman beyond proach. From our point of view he is a beast. . . . What ppened, this mite was too terrified to tell. For weeks she ew worse and worse. At last she went completely off her ad. Then her sister, an old patient of ours, stole her away d dragged her here.

'I have never seen a creature so fouled. Her internal ounds were alive with maggots. For days after she got re, she lay speechless on her bed. Not a sound did she ter – only stared, with half blank, half terror-stricken eyes. hen one day it chanced that a child with a fractured arm as brought in and put in a bed near hers. And I, going rough the ward, began playing with that child. This little e, watching, evidently began to think that here, perhaps, we were not all cruel monsters. Next day as I passed, sh smiled. The day after that she put her arms around my neck in a sort of maudlin fashion. That was the turning point i her mind. Now her mental balance is mending, though he body is still sick. Her memory, fortunately, has not re covered the immediate past. She lies there with her toy wondering at them, feebly playing with them, or with her bi eyes following our movements about the room. She pitifully content.

'Meantime her husband is suing her to recover his marit rights and force her back into his possession. She is not ye thirteen years old.'

Such instances of mental derangement are commo enough. Where should child-fabric, even though its in heritance had been the best instead of the weakest, fin strength to withstand the strain? The case last cited was c well-to-do, educated, city-dwelling stock. But it differed i no essential from that of a younger child whom I saw in village some three hundred miles distant. Married as a baby sent to her husband at ten, the shock of incessant use was to much for her brain. It went. After that, beat her as h would, all that she could do was to crouch in the corner little twisted heap, panting. Not worth the keep. And so a last, in despair and rage over his bad bargain, he slung he small body over his shoulder, carried her out to the edge c the jungle, cast her in among the scrub thicket, and left he there to die.

This she must have done, but that an Indian witness t the deed carried the tale to an English lady who herself wer out into the jungle, found the child, and brought her in Her mind, they said, was slow in emerging from its stupor But under the influence of peace and gentleness and th handling proper to a child, she began at last to blossom into normal intelligence. When I first saw her, a year and four months after her abandonment, she was racing about a pleasant old garden, romping with other happy little children, and contentedly hugging a doll. Her English protectors will keep her as long as they can. After that, what?

Except well to the north, the general condition thus indicated is found in most sections of India. Bombay Presidency has an outstanding number of educated and progressive women, but the status of the vast majority in that province, as in the rest, would more fairly be inferred from the other extreme – from, for example, the wife whom I saw, mother at nine and a half, by Cæsarean operation, of a boy weighing one and three-quarter pounds.

Strike off across the peninsula, a thousand miles east of Bombay, and you have the same story. 'What can be hoped from these infant wives?' says the superintendent of a hospital here – a most competent and devoted British woman doctor. 'Their whole small stock of vitality is exhausted in the first pregnancy. Thence they go on, repeating the strain with no chance whatever of building up strength to give to the children that come so fast. A five-pound baby is large. In the neighbourhood of four is the usual weight. Many are born dead; and all, because of their low vitality, are predisposed to any and every infection that may come along. My patients, here, are largely the wives of University students. Practically every one is venereally infected. When I first came out to India, I tried going to the parents of each such case to tell them of their daughter's state, in the hope that they would act in her behalf. But when I found that they had known the husband's diseased condition before giving their daughter in marriage, and could still see neither shame nor harm therein, I gave up the attempt. They do not look on it as an inconvenience, nor will they give weight to the fact that they are passing on a vile thing to the children.

'Now my question is, whether, in view of the chronic inadequacy of our hospital funds, I am right in giving the cure to these patients. It costs about twenty rupees (£1 7*s*. 6*d*.), and the woman is reinfected the day she returns to her own home. I could do so many other things with those precious twenty rupees! And yet –'

Again, in the great Madras Presidency, east or west, the tale is no better. 'For the vast majority of women here,' says a widely experienced surgeon, 'marriage is a physical tragedy. The girl may bring to birth one or two sound children, but is by that time herself ruined and crippled, either from infection or cruel handling. In the thousands of gynæcological cases that I have treated and am still treating, I have never found one woman who had not some form of venereal disease.'

In other provinces of India, other medical men and women, European and western-educated Indian alike, gave me ample corroborative statements as to the effects of child motherhood. On the mother's part, increased predisposition to tuberculosis; displacement of organs; softening of immature bones, due to weight on spine and pelvis, presently causing disastrous obstructions to birth; hysteria and pathological mental derangements; stunting of mental and physical growth.

'A very small percentage of Indian women seem to me to be well and strong,' adds a woman physician of wide present-day Indian experience. 'This state I believe to be accounted for by a morbid and unawakened mentality, by venereal infection, and by sexual exhaustion. They commonly experience marital use two and three times a day.'

Thirty-six years ago, when the Age of Consent Bill was being argued in the Indian Legislature, all the women doctors then working in India united to lay before the Viceroy a memorial and petition for the relief of those to whose help their own lives were dedicated. Affirming that they instanced only ordinary cases – cases taken from the common personal practice of one or another of their own number – they give as follows the conditions in which certain patients first came into their hands: [1]

'A. – Aged 9. Day after marriage. Left femur dislocated, pelvis crushed out of shape. Flesh hanging in shreds.

'B. – Aged 10. Unable to stand, bleeding profusely, flesh much lacerated.

'C. – Aged 9. So completely ravished as to be almost beyond surgical repair. Her husband had two other living wives and spoke very fine English.

'I. – Aged about 7. Living with husband. Died in great agony after three days.

'M. – Aged about 10. Crawled to hospital on her hands and knees. Has never been able to stand erect since her marriage.'

The original list is longer than here given. It will be found in the appendix of this book.[2]

This was in 1891. In 1922, the subject being again before the Indian Legislature, this same petition of the women surgeons was once more brought forward as equally applic-

[1] *Legislative Assembly Debates*, 1922. Vol. III, Part I, pp. 881–3, and Appendix, p. 919.

[2] See Appendix I.

able after the lapse of years. No one disputed, no one can yet dispute, its continued force. The Englishman who now introduced it into the debate could not bring himself to read its text aloud. But, referring to the Bill raising the Age of Consent then under discussion, he concluded his speech thus:

'A number of persons . . . have said that this Bill is likely to give rise to agitation. No one dislikes agitation more than I do. I am sick of agitation. But when, Sir, it is a case of the lives of women and children, I can only say, in the words of the Duke of Wellington: "Agitate and be damned!"'

In a recent issue of his weekly paper, *Young India*,[1] Mr. Gandhi printed an article over his own name entitled 'Curse of Child Marriage.' Said Mr. Gandhi:

'It is sapping the vitality of thousands of our promising boys and girls on whom the future of our society entirely rests.

'It is bringing into existence every year thousands of weaklings – both boys and girls – who are born of immature parenthood.

'It is a very fruitful source of appalling child-mortality and still-births that now prevail in our society.

'It is a very important cause of the gradual and steady decline of Hindu society in point of (1) numbers, (2) physical strength and courage, and (3) morality.'

Not less interesting than the article itself is the reply that it quickly elicits from an Indian correspondent whom Mr. Gandhi himself vouches for as 'a man occupying a high position in society.' This correspondent writes:[2]

[1] *Young India*, August 26, 1926, p. 302. [2] *Ibid.*, Sept. 9, 1926, p. 318.

'I am very much pained to read your article on "Curse of :hild Marriage." . . .

'I fail to understand why you could not take a charitable iew of those whose opinion differs from you. . . . I think : improper to say that those who insist on child marriage are steeped in vice." . . .

'The practice of early marriage is not confined to any rovince or class of society, but is practically a universal ustom in India. . . .

'The chief objection to early marriage is that it weakens he health of the girl and her children. But this objection is ot very convincing for the following reasons. The age of narriage is now rising among the Hindus, but the race is ecoming weaker. Fifty or a hundred years ago the men and vomen were generally stronger, healthier and more long-ived than now. But early marriage was then more in vogue. . . From these facts it appears probable that early marriage loes not cause as much physical deterioration as some people elieve. . . .'

The type of logic employed in the paragraph last quoted s so essentially Indian that its character should not be passed y without particular note. The writer sees no connection etween the practice of the grandparents and the condition f the grandchildren, even though he sets both down in lack and white on the paper before him.

A voice in the wilderness, Mr. Gandhi continues the ttack, printing still further correspondence drawn forth by is original article. He gives the letter of a Bengali Hindu ady, who writes :[1]

'I don't know how to thank you for your speaking on

[1] *Young India*, Oct. 7, 1926, p. 349.

behalf of the poor girl-wives of our Hindu society. . . . Ot women always bear their burden of sorrow, in silence, wit meekness. They have no power left in them to fight again any evil whatever.'

To this Mr. Gandhi rejoins by adducing from his ow knowledge instances in support, such as that of a sixty-yea old educationalist, who, without loss of public respect, h taken home a wife of nine years. But he ends on a rare ne note, arraigning India's western-taught women who spen their energies in politics, publicity-seeking and empty ta to the utter neglect of the crucial work for India that on they can do.[1]

'May women always throw the blame on men and salv their consciences? . . . They may fight, if they like, fc votes for women. It costs neither time nor trouble. It pr vides them with innocent recreation. But where are the bra women who work among the girl-wives and girl-widows, an who would take no rest and leave none for men, till gir marriage became an impossibility?'

It has been the habit, in approaching these matters, t draw a veil before their nakedness and pass quickly b Searching missionaries' reports for light out of their lon experience, one finds neat rows of dots, marking the sile tombs of the indecorous. For the missionary is thinkin first, of the dovecotes at home whence his money comes, an on whose sitting-room tables his report will be laid; anc second, of the super-sensitive Indians on whose sufferance h depends for whatever measure of success he may attai Again, laymen who know the facts have written aroun

[1] *Young India*, Oct. 7, 1926.

ather than about them, swathing the spot in euphemisms, artly to avoid the Indian's resentment at being held up to disapproval whose grounds he can neither feel nor under-tand, partly out of respect to the occidental reader's taste.

Yet, to suppress or to veil the bare truth is, in cases such s this, to belie it. For few western readers, without plain elling, spade by spade, will imagine the conditions that xist.

Given, then, a constructive desire really to understand ndia's problems, it is merely what Mr. Gandhi calls 'self-leception, the worst of sins,' to beg off from facing the facts n these fundamental aspects of Indian life. And if anyone s inclined to bolt the task, let him stop to consider whether ie has a right so to humour himself, a right to find it too hard ven to speak or to hear of things that millions of little hildren, and of women scarcely more than children, are this ery day enduring in their tormented flesh.

Part Two: The Grand Trunk Road

THE Grand Trunk Road, at the Khyber. Black, barren, jagged hills scowl into the chasm that cleaves them. Tribesmen's villages on either side – each house in itself a fortalice, its high fighting towers surrounded by high, blind walls loop-holed for rifles.

'What is your calling?' you ask the master. 'What but the calling of my people?' says he. 'We are raiders.'

They may not shoot across the road, it being the highway of the King-Emperor. But on either side to it they shoot as they please, the country being their country. Their whole life is war, clan on clan, house on house, man on man, yet, for utter joy, Muslim on Hindu. Hills are bare, food is scarce, and the delight of life is stalking human prey, excelling its cunning.

Two miles of camels, majestic, tail to nose, nose to tail, bearing salt, cotton and sugar from India to Asia, swinging gloriously past two miles of camels, nose to tail, tail to nose, bearing the wares of Asia into India. Armed escorts of Afridi soldiers. Armed posts. Frequent roadside emplacements for three or four sharp-shooters with rifles. Barbed wire entanglements. Tribesmen afoot, hawk-nosed, hawk-eyed, carrying two rifles apiece, taking the lay of the land on the off-chance. Tramp – tramp – a marching detachment of the 2nd Battalion Royal Fusiliers – open-faced, bright-skinned English lads, smart and keen – an incredible sight in that setting. Yet because of them and them only may the Hindu to-day venture the Khyber. Until the Pax Britannica reached so far, few Hindus came through alive, unless mounted and clad as women.

The Grand Trunk Road rolls south and south – a broad,

smooth river of peace whose waves are unthinking humanity Monkeys of many sorts play along its sides. Peacocks Deer. Herds of camels shepherded by little naked boys entirely competent. Dust of traffic. White bullocks almond-eyed, string upon string of sky-blue beads twisted around their necks and horns, pulling wains heaped high with cotton for Japan. Villages – villages – villages – true homes of India, scattered, miles apart, across the open country. Each just a handful of mud-walled huts clustered beside the hole they took the mud from, now half full of stagnant water in which they wash and bathe and quench their thirst. In villages such as these live nine-tenths of all the peoples of India. Hindu or Muhammadan alike – hard working cultivators of the soil, simple, illiterate, peaceful kindly, save when men steal amongst them carrying fire

Sunset. The ghost of a ghost – a thin long veil of blue floating twice a man's height above the earth. Softly it widens, deepens, till all the air is blue and the tall tree trunks and the stars themselves show blue behind it. Now comes its breath – a biting tang of smoke – the smoke of all the hearth-fires in all the villages. And this is the hour, this the incense, this the invocation of Mother India, walking among the tree-trunks in the twilight, veiled in the smoke of the hearth-fires of her children, her hands outstretched in entreaty, blue stars shining in her hair.

For the rest, the Grand Trunk is just *Kim*. Read it again for all of it is true. Zam Zammah still stands in Lahore Mahbub Ali died three years ago, but his two boys are in England at school. And the Old Lady still travels in her bullock-cart, scolding shrilly through her curtains into the clouds of dust.

CHAPTER VI

THE EARTHLY GOD

. BEAUTIFUL Rolls-Royce of His Highness's sending was hirling us along the road from the Guest House to the ılace. My escort, one of the chief officials of the Prince's ɔusehold, a high-caste orthodox Brahman scholar easily at ɔme in his European dress, had already shown readiness to ɔnverse and to explain.

'Let us suppose,' I now asked him, 'that you have an fant daughter. At what age will you marry her?'

'At five – at seven – but I must surely marry her,' he plied in his excellent English, 'before she completes her nth year.'

'And if you do not, what is the penalty, and upon whom ɔes it fall?'

'It falls upon me; I am outcasted by my caste. None of ıem will eat with me or give me water to drink or admit ıe to any ceremony. None will give me his daughter to ıarry my son, so that I can have no son's son of right birth. shall have, in fact, no further social existence. No fellow ıste-man will even lend his shoulder to carry my body to ıe burning-ghat. And my penance in the next life will be eavier still than this.'

'Then as to the child herself, what would befall her?'

'The child? Ah, yes. According to our law I must turn er out of my house and send her into the forest alone. There must leave her with empty hands. Thenceforth I may not otice her in any way. Nor may any Hindu give her food r help from the wild beasts, on penalty of sharing the curse.'

'And would you really do that thing?'

'No; for the reason that occasion would not arise. I cou[l] not conceivably commit the sin whose consequence it is.'

It was noticeable that in this picture the speaker saw [n] suffering figure save his own.

A girl child, in the Hindu scheme, is usually a heavy an[d] unwelcome cash liability. Her birth elicits the formal co[n]dolences of family friends. But not always would one find [s]ingenuous a witness as that prosperous old Hindu landown[er] who said to me: 'I have had twelve children. Ten girl[s] which, naturally, did not live. Who, indeed, could ha[ve] borne that burden! The two boys, of course, I preserved[.']

Yet Sir Michael O'Dwyer records a similar instance [of] open speech from his own days of service as Settleme[nt] Commissioner in Bharatpur:[1]

'The sister of the Maharaja was to be married to a gre[at] Punjab Sirdar. The family pressed [the Maharaja being [a] minor] for the lavish expenditure usual on those occasions [–] £30,000 to £40,000 – and the local members of the Sta[te] Council supported their view. The Political Agent – th[e] State being then under British supervision – and I strong[ly] protested against such extravagance in a year of seve[re] scarcity and distress. Finally, the matter was discussed i[n] full Council. I asked the oldest member of the Council t[o] quote precedents – how much had been sanctioned o[n] similar marriages of the daughter or sister of a Maharaja i[n] the past. He shook his head and said there was no preceden[t]. I said, "How can that be? – the State has been in existenc[e] over two hundred years, and there have been eleven suc[-]

[1] *India As I Knew It*, Sir Michael O'Dwyer. Constable & Co., Lt[d.] London, 1925, p. 102.

ssions without adoption, from father to son; do you mean tell me that there were never any daughters?" The old an hesitated a little, and then said, "Sahib, you know our ıstoms, surely you know the reason. There were daughters ›rn, but till this generation they were not allowed to grow ›." And it was so.'

But it is fair to remember that infanticide has been ›mmon not with primitive races only but with Greece, with ome, with nearly all peoples known to history save those ho have been affected by Christian or Muhammadan ılture. Forbidden in India by Imperial law, the ancient actice, so easily followed in secret, seems still to persist in any parts of the country.[1]

Statistical proof in such matters is practically unattainable, will be realized later in this chapter. But the statement of e Superintendent of the United Provinces Census[2] re- ırding girl children of older growth is cautious enough to oid all pitfalls:

'I very much doubt whether there is any active dislike of rl babies. . . . But if there is no active dislike, there is ıquestionably passive neglect. "The parents look after the ›n, and God looks after the daughter." The daughter is ss warmly clad, she receives less attention when ill, and less ıd worse food when well. This is not due to cruelty, or en to indifference; it is due simply to the fact that the son preferred to the daughter and all the care, attention and ıinties are lavished on him, whilst the daughter must be ›ntent with the remnants of all three. . . . The result is

[1] See *Census of India*, Vol. I, Part I, 1921, Appendix VI. See also *The ınjab Peasant in Prosperity and Debt*, M. L. Darling, Oxford, 1925, › 58–9.

[2] *Census of India*, 1911. Vol. XV, p. 190.

that [the female] death-rate between 1 and 5 is almost i variably somewhat higher than the male death-rate.'

This attitude toward the unwanted was illustrated in a incident that I myself chanced upon in a hospital in Benga The patient, a girl of five or six years, had fallen down a we and sustained a bad cut across her head. The mother, wi the bleeding and unconscious child in her arms, had rushe to the hospital for help. In a day or two tetanus develope Now the child lay at death's door, in agony terrible to se The crisis was on, and the mother, crouching beside her, figure of grief and fear, muttered prayers to the gods whi the English doctor worked. Suddenly, there at the bedsid stood a man – a Bengali *babu* – some sort of small official clerk.

'Miss Sahib,' he said, addressing the doctor, 'I have con for my wife.'

'Your wife!' exclaimed the doctor sternly. 'Look at you wife. Look at your child. What do you mean!'

'I mean,' he went on, 'that I have come to fetch my wi home, at once, for my proper marital use.'

'But your child will die if her mother leaves her now. Yo cannot separate them – see!' and the child, who had som how understood the threat even through her mortal pai clung to her mother, wailing.

The woman threw herself prostrate upon the floo clutched his knees, imploring, kissed his feet, and with h two hands, Indian fashion, took the dust from his feet an put it upon her head. 'My lord, my lord,' she wept, 'b merciful!'

'Come away,' said he. 'I have need of you, I say. Yo have left me long enough.'

'My lord – the child – the little child – my Master!'

He gave the suppliant figure a thrust with his foot. 'I ave spoken' – and with never another word or look, turning n the threshold, he walked away into the world of sun.

The woman rose. The child screamed.

'Will you obey?' exclaimed the doctor, incredulous for all er years of seeing.

'I dare not disobey,' sobbed the woman – and, pulling her eil across her stricken face, she ran after her man – crouch-ıg, like a small, weak animal.

The girl, going to her husband by her ninth or twelfth ear, or earlier, has little time and less chance to learn from ooks. But two things she surely will have learned – her duty ›ward her husband and her duty toward those gods and evils that concern her. Her duty toward her husband, as of ld laid down in the *Padmapurana*,[1] is thus translated:[2]

'There is no other god on earth for a woman than her hus-and. The most excellent of all the good works that she can o is to seek to please him by manifesting perfect obedience › him. Therein should lie her sole rule of life.

'Be her husband deformed, aged, infirm, offensive in his ıanners; let him also be choleric, debauched, immoral, a runkard, a gambler; let him frequent places of ill-repute, ve in open sin with other women, have no affection what-ver for his home; let him rave like a lunatic; let him live ʼithout honour; let him be blind, deaf, dumb or crippled, in word, let his defects be what they may, let his wickedness e what it may, a wife should always look upon him as her od, should lavish on him all her attention and care, paying

[1] The *Puranas*, ancient religious poems, are the Bible of the Hindu peoples.

[2] *Hindu Manners, Customs, and Ceremonies*, pp. 344–9.

no heed whatsoever to his character and giving him no caus
whatsoever for displeasure. . . .

'A wife must eat only after her husband has had his fill If the latter fasts, she shall fast, too, if he touch not food she also shall not touch it; if he be in affliction, she shall b so, too; if he be cheerful, she shall share his joy. . . . Sh must, on the death of her husband, allow herself to be burn alive on the same funeral pyre; then everybody will prais her virtue. . . .

'If he sing she must be in ecstasy; if he dance she mus look at him with delight; if he speak of learned things sh must listen to him with admiration. In his presence, indeed she ought always to be cheerful, and never show signs o sadness or discontent.

'Let her carefully avoid creating domestic squabbles o the subject of her parents, or on account of another woma whom her husband may wish to keep, or on account of an unpleasant remark which may have been addressed to her To leave the house for reasons such as these would expos her to public ridicule, and would give cause for much evi speaking.

'If her husband flies into a passion, threatens her, abuse her grossly, even beats her unjustly, she shall answer hin meekly, shall lay hold of his hands, kiss them, and beg hi pardon, instead of uttering loud cries and running awa from the house. . . .

'Let all her words and actions give public proof that sh looks upon her husband as her god. Honoured by every body, she shall thus enjoy the reputation of a faithful an virtuous spouse.'

The Abbé Dubois found this ancient law still the code o

ineteenth-century Hinduism, and weighed its aspect with hilosophic care. His comment ran:[1]

'A real union with sincere and mutual affection, or even eace, is very rare in Hindu households. The moral gulf hich exists in this country between the sexes is so great that the eyes of a native the woman is simply a passive object ho must be abjectly submissive to her husband's will and ncy. She is never looked upon as a companion who can are her husband's thoughts and be the first object of his re and affection. The Hindu wife finds in her husband ly a proud and overbearing master who regards her as a rtunate woman to be allowed the honour of sharing his bed d board.'

In the handling of this point by the modern, Rabindranath agore, appears another useful hint as to the caution we ight well observe in accepting, at their face value to us, the pressions of Hindu speakers and writers. Says Tagore,[2] esenting the Hindu theory:

'For the purpose of marriage, spontaneous love is unre-able; its proper cultivation should yield the best results . . and this cultivation should begin before marriage. herefore from their earliest years, the husband as an idea held up before our girls, in verse and story, through remonial and worship. When at length they get this usband, he is to them not a person but a principle, like yalty, patriotism, or such other abstractions. . . .'

As to the theory of the matter, let that be what it may. s to the actual practice of the times, material will be re-alled from the previous pages of this book bearing upon the

[1] *Hindu Manners, Customs and Ceremonies*, p. 231.

[2] *The Book of Marriage*, Keyserling, pp. 112-13.

likeness of the Hindu husband, as such, to 'loyalty, 'patriotism,' or any impersonal abstraction.

Mr. Gandhi tirelessly denounces the dominance of the ol teaching. 'By sheer force of a vicious custom,' he repeat 'even the most ignorant and worthless men have been enjoy ing a superiority over women which they do not deserve an ought not to have.'[1]

But a creed through tens of centuries bred into weak ignorant, and fanatical peoples is not to be uprooted in on or two hundred years; neither can it be shaken by the wrat of a single prophet, however reverenced. The general bod of the ancient law relating to the status and conduct c women yet reigns practically supreme among the grea Hindu majority.

In the Puranic code great stress is laid upon the duty c the wife to her mother-in-law. Upon this foundation rest a tremendous factor in every woman's life. A Hind marriage does not betoken the setting up of a new home stead; the little bride, on the contrary, is simply added t the household of the groom's parents, as that househol already exists. There she becomes at once the acknowledge servant of the mother-in-law, at whose beck and call she live The father-in-law, the sister-in-law, demand what they lik of her, and, bred as she is, it lies not in her to rebel. The ver idea that she possibly could rebel or acquire any degree c freedom has neither root nor ground in her mind. She exist to serve. The mother-in-law is often hard, ruling withou mercy or affection; and if by chance the child is slow to bea children, or if her children be daughters, then, too fre quently, the elder woman's tongue is a flail, her hand heav in blows, her revengeful spirit set on clouding her victim'

[1] Quoted in *The Indian Social Reformer*, Oct. 29, 1922, p. 135.

ıfe with threats of the new wife who, according to the Hindu ode, may supplant and enslave her.

Not infrequently, in pursuing my inquiry in the rural listricts, I came upon the record of suicides of women be-ween the ages of fourteen and nineteen. The commonest ause assigned by the Indian police recorder was 'colic ains, and a quarrel with the mother-in-law.'

As to the direct relation of wife to husband, as understood n high-class Hindu families to-day, it has thus been de-cribed by that most eminent of Indian ladies, whose know-edge of her sisters of all ranks and creeds is wide, deep, and ind, Miss Cornelia Sorabji: [1]

'Chief priestess of her husband, whom to serve is her re-igion and her delight . . . moving on a plane far below him or all purposes religious, mental and social; gentle and doring, but incapable of participation in the larger interests f his life. . . . To please his mother, whose chief hand-naiden she is, and to bring him a son, these are her two mbitions. . . . The whole idea of marriage in the East re-olves simply on the conception of life; a community of nterests, companionship, these never enter into the general alculation. She waits upon her husband when he feeds, ilent in his presence, with downcast eyes. To look him in he face were bold indeed.'

Then says Miss Sorabji, continuing her picture: [2]

'When she is the mother of a son, greater respect is hers rom the other women in the *zenana* . . . she has been suc-essful, has justified her existence. The self-respect it gives

[1] *Between the Twilights*, Cornelia Sorabji. Harper and Brothers, ondon, 1908, pp. 125–32.

[2] *Ibid.*, pp. 45–6.

the woman herself is most marked. She is still a faithf slave to her husband, but she is an entity, a person, in so fa as that is possible in a Hindu *zenana*; she can lift her hea above the women who taunted her, her heart above the fea of a rival.'

This general characterization of the wife in the *zenana* c educated, well-to-do, and prominent Hindus finds its faith ful echo in one of many similar incidents that came to m notice in humbler fields. For the orthodox Hindu woman whoever she be, will obey the law of her ancestors and he gods with a pride and integrity unaffected by her socia condition.

The woman, in this case, was the wife of a small land owner in a district not far from Delhi. The man, unusuall enlightened, sent her to hospital for her first confinemen But he sent her too late, and, after a severe ordeal, the chil was born dead.

Again, the following year, the same story was repeatec The patient was brought late, and even the necessar Cæsarean operation did not save the child. Still a third tim the *zemindar* appeared, bringing the wife; but now, taugh by experience, he had moved in time. As the woman cam out of the ether, the young English nurse bent over her, al aglow with the news.

'Little mother, happy little mother, don't you want to se your baby – don't you want to see your boy?'

The head on the pillow turned away. Faintly, slowly th words came back out of the pit of hopeless night:

'Who wants to see – a dead baby! I have seen – to many – too many – dead – dead –' The voice trailed int silence. The heavy eyelids closed.

Then Sister picked up the baby. Baby squealed.

On that instant the thing was already done – so quickly lone that none could measure the time of its doing. The ifeless figure on the bed tautened. The great black eyes lashed wide. The thin arms lifted in a gesture of demand. For the first time in all her life, perhaps, this girl was think-ng in the imperative.

'Give me my son!' She spoke as an empress might speak. Send at once to my village and inform the father of my son hat I desire his presence.' Utterly changed. Endued with lignity – with self-respect – with importance.

The father came. All the relatives came, heaping like flies nto the little family quarters attached, in Indian women's ospitals, to each private room. Ten days they sat there – over a dozen of them, in a space some fifteen by twenty feet quare. And on the tenth, in a triumphant procession, they ore home to their village mother and son.

Rich or poor, high caste or low caste, the mother of a son vill idolize the child. She has little knowledge to give him, ave knowledge of strange taboos and fears and charms and eremonies to propitiate a universe of powers unseen. She vould never discipline him, even though she knew the mean-ng of the word. She would never teach him to restrain passion or impulse or appetite. She has not the vaguest con-eption how to feed him or develop him. Her idea of a ufficient meal is to tie a string around his little brown body nd stuff him till the string bursts. And so through all his hildhood he grows as grew his father before him, back into he mists of time.

Yet, when the boy himself assumes married life, he will onour his mother above his wife, and show her often a real ffection and deference. Then it is that the woman comes into her own, ruling indoors with an iron hand, stoutl maintaining the ancient tradition, and, forgetful of he former misery, visiting upon the slender shoulders of he little daughters-in-law all the burdens and the wrath that fe upon her own young back. But one higher step is perhap reserved for her. With each grandson laid in her arms she i again exalted. The family line is secure. Her husband' soul is protected. Proud is she among women. Blessed b the gods!

CHAPTER VII

WAGES OF SIN

THE reverse of the picture shows the Hindu widow – the ccursed. That so hideous a fate as widowhood should befall woman can be but for one cause – the enormity of her sins n a former incarnation. From the moment of her husband's ecease till the last hour of her own life, she must expiate hose sins in shame and suffering and self-immolation, hained in every thought to the service of his soul. Be she child of three, who knows nothing of the marriage that ound her, or be she a wife in fact, having lived with her usband, her case is the same. By his death she is revealed s a creature of innate guilt and evil portent, herself coninced, when she is old enough to think at all, of the justice f her fate. Miss Sorabji thus treats the subject:[1]

'The orthodox Hindu widow suffers her lot with the erce enjoyment of martyrdom . . . but nothing can mininize the evils of that lot. . . . That she accepts the fact nakes it no less of a hardship. For some sin committed in a revious birth, the gods have deprived her of a husband. Vhat is left to her now but to work out his "salvation" and y her prayers and penances to win him a better place in his ext genesis? . . . For the mother-in-law, what also is left ut the obligation to curse? . . . But for this luckless one, er son might still be in the land of the living. . . . There is o determined animosity in the attitude. The person cursing s as much an instrument of Fate as the person cursed. . . .

[1] *Between the Twilights*, pp. 144–6.

[But] it is all very well to assert no personal animosity tc ward her whom you hold it a privilege to curse and to burde with every unpleasant duty imaginable. Your practice is ap to mislead.'

The widow becomes the menial of every other person i the house of her late husband. All the hardest and uglie tasks are hers, no comforts, no ease. She may take but on meal a day and that of the meanest. She must perform stric fasts. Her hair must be shaven off. She must take care t absent herself from any scene of ceremony or rejoicing, fror a marriage, from a religious celebration, from the sight of a expectant mother or of any person whom the curse of he glance might harm. Those who speak to her may speak i terms of contempt and reproach; and she herself is th priestess of her own misery, for its due continuance is he one remaining merit.

The old French traveller, Bernier, states that the pains c widowhood were imposed 'as an easy mode of keeping wive in subjection, of securing their attention in times of sicknes and of deterring them from administering poison to thei husbands.' [1]

But once, however, did I hear this idea from a Hindu' lips. 'We husbands so often make our wives unhappy,' sai this frank witness, 'that we might well fear they woul poison us. Therefore did our wise ancestors make th penalty of widowhood so frightful – in order that the woma may not be tempted.'

In the female wards of prisons in many parts of India have seen women under sentence for the murder of thei

[1] *Travels in the Mogul Empire, A.D. 1656–1668*, François Bernie Oxford University Press, 1916, pp. 310–11.

usbands. These are perhaps rare mentalities, perhaps ysteria cases. More characteristic are the still-recurring ıstances of practical *suttee*, where the newly-widowed wife eliberately pours oil over her garments, sets them afire and urns to death, in a connived-at secrecy. She has seen the ıte of other widows. She is about to become a drudge, a lave, starved, tyrannized over, abused – and this is the acred way out – 'following the divine law.' Committing a ious and meritorious act, in spite of all foreign-made ıterdicts, she escapes a present hell and may hope for appier birth in her next incarnation.

Although demanded in the scripture already quoted, the ractice of burning the widow upon the husband's funeral yre is to-day unlawful. But it must be noted that this hange represents an exceptional episode; it represents not a atural advance of public opinion, but one of the rare incurions of the British strong hand into the field of native eligions. *Suttee* was forbidden by British Governors [1] some wenty-nine years before the actual taking over by the rown of direct government. That advanced Indian, Raja am Mohan Roy, supported the Act. But other influential engali gentlemen, vigorously opposing, did not hesitate to ush their fight for the preservation of the practice even to he court of last resort – the Privy Council in London.

Is it conceivable that, given opportunity, the submerged oot of the matter might come again to life and light? In Ar. Gandhi's weekly [2] of November 11, 1926, a Hindu riter declares the impossibility of a widow's re-marriage o-day, without the death-bed permission of the deceased usband. No devout husband will give such permission, the

[1] Regulation XVII of 1829.

[2] *Young India.*

correspondent affirms, and adds: 'He will rather fain agre to his wife's becoming *sati* [suttee] if she can.'

An inmate of her husband's home at the time of his deat the widow, although she has no legal claim for protectio may be retained there on the terms above described, or sh may be turned adrift. Then she must live by charity – or b prostitution, into which she not seldom falls. And he dingy, ragged figure, her bristly, shaven head, even thoug its stubble be white over the haggard face of unhappy ag is often to be seen in temple crowds or in the streets pilgrimage cities, where sometimes niggard piety doles he a handful of rice.

As to re-marriage, that, in orthodox Hinduism, is im possible. Marriage is not a personal affair, but an etern sacrament. And it must never be forgotten that the gre majority of the Hindus are orthodox to the bone. Whethe the widow be an infant and a stranger to the man whos death, she is told, was caused by her sins, or whether she b twenty and of his bed and board, orthodoxy forbids her re marriage. Of recent years, however, the gradual if un recognized influence of western teaching has aroused certain response. In different sections of India sever associations have sprung up, having the re-marriage of virgi widows as one of their chief purported objects. The move ment, however, is almost wholly restricted to the mos advanced element of Hindu society, and its influence is, yet, too fractional appreciably to affect statistics.

The observations on this point made by the Abbé Dubo a century since still, in general, hold good. He saw that th marriage of a small child to a man of sixty and the forbiddin of her re-marriage after his death must often throw the chil as a widow, into a dissolute life. Yet widow re-marriage wa ınknown. Even were it permitted, says the Abbé, 'the trange preference which Brahmans have for children of ·ery tender years would make such a permission almost ıominal in the case of their widows.' [1]

And one cannot forget, in estimating the effect of the ·oung widow on the social structure of which she is a part, hat, in her infancy, she lived in the same atmosphere of exual stimulus that surrounded the boy child, her brother. f a girl child so reared in thought and so sharpened in desire e barred from lawful satisfaction of desire, it is strange if the lesire prove stronger with her than the social law? Her amily, the family of the dead husband, will, for their credit's ake, restrain her if they can. And often, perhaps most ften, she needs no restraint save her own spirit of sacrifice. But the opposite example is frequently commented upon by ndian speakers. Lala Lajpat Rai, Swarajist politician, aments: [2]

'The condition of child-widows is indescribable. God nay bless those who are opposed to their re-marriage, but heir superstition introduces so many abuses and brings ıbout so much moral and physical misery as to cripple ociety as a whole and handicap it in the struggle for life.'

Mr. Gandhi acquiescently cites another Indian writer on child marriage and enforced child widowhood, thus: 'It is bringing into existence thousands of girl-widows every year who in their turn are a source of corruption and dangerous infection to society.' [3]

[1] *Hindu Manners, Customs and Ceremonies*, p. 212.

[2] Presidential Speech delivered before the Hindu Mahasabha Conference, in Bombay, December, 1925.

[3] *Young India*, Aug. 26, 1926, p. 302.

Talk there is, resolutions passed, in caste and association conventions, as to changing these things of oppression and of scornings. But a virgin widow's re-marriage is still a headline event, even to the reform newspapers, while the re-marriage of a Hindu widowed wife is still held to be inconceivable.

And here, curiously enough, the very influence that, on the one hand most strongly operates to rescue the woman, on the other more widely enslaves her. While British practice and western education tend, at the top of the ladder, to breed discontent with ancient darkness, British public works, British sanitation and agricultural development, steadily raising the economic condition of the lower classes, as steadily breed aspirants to greater social prestige. Thus the census of 1921 finds restriction in widow re-marriage definitely increasing in those low ranks of the social scale that, by their own code, have no such inhibition. Hindu caste rank is entirely independent of worldly wealth; but the first move of the man of little place, suddenly awakening to a new prosperity, security and peace, is to mimic the manners of those to whom he has looked up. He becomes a social climber, not less in India than in the United States, and assumes the shackles of the elect.

Mr. Mukerjea of Baroda, an Indian official observer, thus writes of attempts to break down the custom of obligatory widowhood: [1]

'All such efforts will be powerless as long as authoritative Hindu opinion continues to regard the prohibition of widow re-marriage as a badge of respectability. Amongst the lower Hindu castes, the socially affluent sections are discounten-

[1] *Census of India*, 1921. Vol. I, Chapter VII, paragraph 134.

ncing the practice of widow re-marriage as actively as any rahman.'

It was a distinguished Bengali, the Pundit Iswar Chunder 'idyasagar, who, among Indians, started the movement for e-marriage of virgin widows and supported Government in he enactment of a law legalizing such re-marriages. But over im and the fruit of his work another eminent Indian thus ments:[1]

'I well remember the stir and agitation which the movement produced and how orthodox Hindus were up in arms gainst it. . . . The champion of the Hindu widows died a isappointed man, like so many of those who were in advance f their age, leaving his message unfulfilled. . . . The proress which the movement has made since his death in 1891 as been slow. A new generation has sprung up, but he has ound no successor. The mantle of Elijah has not fallen upon Elisha. The lot of the Hindu widow to-day remains very nuch the same that it was fifty years ago. There are few to ipe her tears and to remove the enforced widowhood that s her lot. The group of sentimental sympathizers have erhaps increased – shouting at public meetings on the 'idyasagar anniversary day, but leaving unredeemed the nessage of the great champion of the Hindu widow.'

Mr. Gandhi, always true to his light, himself has said:[2]

'To force widowhood upon little girls is a brutal crime for which we Hindus are daily paying dearly. . . . There is no warrant in any *shastra*[3] for such widowhood. Voluntary

[1] *A Nation in the Making.* Sir Surendranath Banerjea. Oxford University ress, 1925, pp. 8–9.

[2] *Young India*, August 5, 1926, p. 276.

[3] Hindu book of sacred institutes.

widowhood consciously adopted by a woman who has fel the affection of a partner adds grace and dignity to lif sanctifies the home and uplifts religion itself. Widowhoo imposed by religion or custom is an unbearable yoke an defiles the home by secret vice and degrades religion. An does not the Hindu widowhood stink in one's nostrils whe one thinks of old and diseased men over fifty taking or rathe purchasing girl wives, sometimes one on top of another?'

But this, again, is a personal opinion, rather than a publi force. 'We want no more of Gandhi's doctrines,' one con spicuous Indian politician told me; 'Gandhi is a delude man.'

That distinguished Indian, Sir Ganga Ram, C.I.E. C.V.O., with some help from Government has built an endowed a fine home and school for Hindu widows in th city of Lahore. This establishment, in 1926, had over fort inmates. In Bombay Presidency are five Government-aide institutes for widows and deserted wives, run by philan thropic Indian gentlemen. Other such institutions ma exist; but, if they do, their existence has escaped the officia recorders. I myself saw, in the pilgrim city of Nawadwip in Bengal, a refuge for widows maintained by local subscrip tion and pilgrims' gifts. It was fourteen years old and ha eight inmates – the extent, it appeared, of its intention an capacity.

The number of widows in India is, according to the lates published official computation, 26,834,838.[1]

[1] *Statistical Abstract for British India*, 1914–15 to 1923–24. Govern ment of India Publication, 1925, p. 20.

CHAPTER VIII

MOTHER INDIA

Row upon row of girl children – little tots all, four, five, six, ven seven years old, sitting cross-legged on the floor, facing he brazen goddess. Before each one, laid straight and tidy, ertain treasures – a flower, a bead or two, a piece of fruit – precious things brought from their homes as sacrificial offer-ngs. For this is a sort of day-school of piety. These babies re learning texts – 'mantrims' to use in worship – learning he rites that belong to the various ceremonies incumbent upon Hindu women. And that is all they are learning; that s all they need to know. Now in unison they pray.

'What are they praying for?' one asks the teacher, a grave-aced Hindu lady.

'What should a woman-child pray for? A husband, if she s not married; or, if she is, then for a better husband at her next re-birth.'

Women pray first as to husbands; then, to bear sons. Men must have sons to serve their souls.

Already we have seen some evidence of the general atti-ude of the Hindu toward this, the greatest of all his con-cerns, in its pre-natal aspect. But another cardinal point that, n any practical survey of Indian competency, can be neither contested nor suppressed, is the manner in which the Hindu of all classes permits his much-coveted son to be ushered nto the light of day.

We have spoken of women's hospitals in various parts of India. These are doing excellent work, mostly gynæco-logical. But they are few, relatively to the work to be done, nor could the vast majority of Indian women, in their present state of development, be induced to use a hospital, were it at their very door.

What the typical Indian woman wants in her hour of trial is the thing to which she is historically used – the midwife – the *dhai*. And the *dhai* is a creature that must indeed be seen to be credited.

According to the Hindu code, a woman in childbirth and in convalescence therefrom is ceremonially unclean, contaminating all that she touches. Therefore only those become *dhais* who are themselves of the unclean, 'untouchable' class, the class whose filthy habits will be adduced by the orthodox Hindu as his good and sufficient reason for barring them from contact with himself. Again, according to the Hindu code, a woman in childbirth, like the newborn child itself, is peculiarly susceptible to the 'evil eye.' Therefore no woman whose child has died, no one who has had an abortion, may, in many parts of India, serve as *dhai*, because of the malice or jealousy that may secretly inspire her. Neither may any widow so serve, being herself a thing of evil omen. Not all of these disqualifications obtain everywhere. But each holds in large sections.

Further, no sort of training is held necessary for the work. As a calling, it descends in families. At the death of a *dhai*, her daughter or daughter-in-law may adopt it, beginning at once to practice even though she has never seen a confinement in all her life.[1] But other women, outside the line of descent, may also take on the work and, if they are properly beyond the lines of the taboos, will find ready employment without any sort of preparation and for the mere asking.

[1] Cf. Edris Griffin, Health Visitor, Delhi, in *National Health*, Oct., 1925, p. 125.

Therefore, in total, you have the half-blind, the aged, the ·ippled, the palsied and the diseased, drawn from the ırtiest poor, as sole ministrants to the women of India in ıe most delicate, the most dangerous and the most im-ortant hour of their existence.

The expectant mother makes no preparations for the aby's coming – such as the getting ready of little garments. 'his would be taking dangerously for granted the favour of ıe gods. But she may and does toss into a shed or into a nall dark chamber whatever soiled and disreputable rags, ıcapable of further use, fall from the hands of the house-old during the year.

And it is into this evil-smelling rubbish-hole that the oung wife creeps when her hour is come upon her. 'Un-ean' she is, in her pain – unclean whatever she touches, nd fit thereafter only to be destroyed. In the name of ırift, therefore, give her about her only the unclean and the 'orthless, whether human or inanimate. If there be a roken-legged, ragged string-cot, let her have that to lie pon; it can be saved in that same black chamber for the next need it. Otherwise, make her a little support of cow-dung r of stones, on the bare earthen floor. And let no one waste ffort in sweeping or dusting or washing the place till this ccasion be over.[1]

When the pains begin, send for the *dhai*. If the *dhai*, ·hen the call reaches her, chances to be wearing decent lothes, she will stop, whatever the haste, to change ıto the rags she keeps for the purpose, infected and re-ıfected from the succession of diseased cases that have ome into her practice. And so, at her dirtiest, a bearer

[1] *National Health*, 1925, p. 70. See also Maggie Ghose, 'Puerperal ever,' in *Victoria Memorial Scholarship Fund Report*, Calcutta (1918), p. 153.

of multiple contagions, she shuts herself in with he victim.

If there be an air-hole in the room, she stops it up wit straw and refuse; fresh air is bad in confinements – it give fever. If there be rags sufficient to make curtains, she cobbl them together, strings them across a corner and puts th patient within, against the wall, still farther to keep away th air. Then, to make darkness darker, she lights the tinie glim – a bit of cord in a bit of oil, or a little kerosene lam without a chimney, smoking villainously. Next, she makes small charcoal fire in a pan beneath the bed or close by th patient's side, whence it joins its poisonous breath to th serried stenches.

The first *dhai* that I saw in action tossed upon this coa pot, as I entered the room, a handful of some special vil smelling stuff to ward off the evil eye – my evil eye. Th smoke of it rose thick – also a tongue of flame. By that ligh one saw her Witch-of-Endor face through its vermi infested elf-locks, her hanging rags, her dirty claws, as sh peered with festered and almost sightless eyes out over th stink-cloud she had raised. But it was not she who ran t quench the flame that caught in the bed and went writhin up the body of her unconscious patient. She was too blind too dull of sense to see or to feel it.

If the delivery is at all delayed, the *dhai* is expected t explore for the reason of the delay. She thrusts her long unwashed hand, loaded with dirty rings and bracelets an encrusted with untold living contaminations, into th patient's body, pulling and twisting at what she finds there. If the delivery is long delayed and difficult, a second or

[1] *V.M.S.F. Report*, 'Improvement of the Conditions of Child-Birth in India pp. 70 *et seq.*

hird *dhai* may be called in, if the husband of the patient vill sanction the expense, and the child may be dragged orth in detached sections – a leg or an arm torn off at a ime.[1]

Again to quote from a medical woman:[2]

'One often sees in cases of contracted pelvis due to osteo-nalacia, if there seems no chance of the head passing down that the *dhai*] attempts to draw on the limbs, and, if ossible, breaks them off. She prefers to extract the child y *main force*, and the patient in such cases is badly torn, often nto her bladder, with the resulting large vesico-vaginal istulæ so common in Indian women, and which cause them o much misery.'

Such labour may last three, four, five, even six days. During all this period the woman is given no nourishment vhatever – such is the code – and the *dhai* resorts to all her raditions. She kneads the patient with her fists; stands her gainst the wall and butts her with her head; props her up-ight on the bare ground, seizes her hands and shoves against ier thighs with gruesome bare feet,[3] until, so the doctors tate, the patient's flesh is often torn to ribbons by the *dhai's* ong, ragged toe-nails. Or, she lays the woman flat and walks ip and down her body, like one treading grapes. Also, she nakes balls of strange substances, such as hollyhock roots, or dirty string, or rags full of quince-seeds; or earth, or earth mixed with cloves, butter and marigold flowers; or nuts, or spices – any irritant – and thrusts them into the

[1] Dr. Marion A. Wylie, M.A., M.B., Ch.B., *V.M.S.F. Report*, p. 85, nd *Ibid.*, Appendix V, p. 69.

[2] *Ibid.*, p. 71.

[3] *Ibid.*, p. 99, Dr. K. O. Vaughan.

uterus, to hasten the event. In some parts of the country goats' hair, scorpions' stings, monkey-skulls, and snake skins are considered valuable applications.[1]

These insertions and the wounds they occasion commonly result in partial or complete permanent closing of the passage.

If the afterbirth be over five minutes in appearing, again the filthy, ringed and bracelet-loaded hand and wrist are thrust in, and the placenta is ripped loose and dragged away.

No clean clothes are provided for use in the confinement and no hot water. Fresh cow-dung or goats' droppings, or hot ashes, however, often serve as heating agents when the patient's body begins to turn cold.[3]

In Benares, sacred among cities, citadel of orthodox Hinduism, the sweepers, all of whom are 'Untouchables,' are divided into seven grades. From the first come the *dhais*; from the last and lowest come the 'cord-cutters.' To cut the umbilical cord is considered a task so degrading that in the Holy City even a sweep will not undertake it, unless she be at the bottom of her kind. Therefore the unspeakable *dhai* brings with her a still more unspeakable servant to wreak her quality upon the mother and the child in birth.

Sometimes it is a split bamboo that they use; sometimes a bit of an old tin can, or a rusty nail, or a potsherd or a fragment of broken glass. Sometimes, having no tool of their own and having found nothing sharp-edged lying about, they go out to the neighbours to borrow. I shall not soon forget the cry: 'Hi, there, inside! Bring me back that knife! I hadn't finished paring my vegetables for dinner.'

[1] *V.M.S.F. Report*, pp. 151–2, Mrs. Chowdhri, sub-assistant surgeon.

[2] *Ibid.*, p. 86, Dr. M. A. Wylie.

[3] *Ibid.*, p. 152, Miss Vidyabai M. Ram.

The end of the cut cord, at best, is left undressed, to take are of itself. In more careful and less happy cases, it is reated with a handful of earth, or with charcoal, or with everal other substances, including cow-dung. Needless to dd, a heavy percentage of such children as survive the train of birth, die of lock-jaw [1] or of erysipelas.

As the child is taken from the mother, it is commonly laid pon the bare floor, uncovered and unattended, until the *hai* is ready to take it up. If it be a girl child, many simple ules have been handed down through the ages for disconinuing the unwelcome life then and there.

In the matter of feeding, practice varies. In the Central rovinces, the first feedings are likely to be of crude sugar nixed with the child's own urine.[2] In Delhi, it may get ugar and spices, or wine, or honey. Or, it may be fed for he first three days on something called *gutli*, a combination f spices in which have been stewed old rust-encrusted lucky oins and charms written out on scraps of paper. These hings, differing somewhat in different regions, castes and ommunities, differ more in detail than in the quality of ntelligence displayed.

As to the mother, she, as already has been said, is usually ept without any food or drink for from four to seven days rom the outset of her confinement; or, if she be fed, she is iven only a few dry nuts and dates. The purpose here eems sometimes to be one of thrift – to save the family

[1] 'Ordinarily half the children born in Bengal die before reaching the age f eight years, and only one-quarter of the population reaches the age of forty ears. . . . As to the causes influencing infant mortality, 50 per cent. of the eaths are due to debility at birth and 11·4 per cent. to tetanus.' – *54th Annual eport of the Director of Public Health of Bengal*, pp. 8–10.

[2] *V.M.S.F. Report*, p. 86, Dr. M. A. Wylie.

utensils from pollution. But in any case it enjoys the prestig of an ancient tenet to which the economical spirit of th household lends a spontaneous support.[1]

In some religions or communities the baby is not put t the breast till after the third day[2] – a custom productive c dire results. But in others the mother is expected to feed nc only the newly born, but her elder children as well, if sh have them. A child three years old will not seldom be ser in to be fed at the mother's breast during the throes of difficult labour. 'It cried – it was hungry. It wouldn't hav other food,' the women outside will explain.

As a result, first, of their feeble and diseased ancestry second, of their poor diet; and, third, of their own infar marriage and premature sexual use and infection, a heav percentage of the women of India are either too small-bonec or too internally misshapen and diseased to give norm birth to a child, but require surgical aid. It may safely b said that all these cases die by slow torture, unless the receive the care of a British or American woman doctor, c of an Indian woman, British-trained.[3] Such care, eve though it be at hand, is often denied the sufferer, either b

[1] Edris Griffin, in *National Health*, Oct., 1925, p. 124.

[2] *V.M.S.F. Report*, p. 86.

[3] For the male medical student in India, instruction in gynæcology an midwifery is extremely difficult to get, for the reason that Indian women ca rarely be persuaded to come to hospitals open to medical men. With th exception of certain extremely limited opportunities, therefore, the India student must get his gynæcology from books. Even though he learns it abroa he has little or no opportunity to practise it. Sometimes, it is true, the wester diplomæd Indian doctor will conduct a labour case by sitting on the far sic of a heavy curtain calling out advice based on the statements shouted acro by the *dhai* who is handling the patient. But this scarcely constitut 'practice' as the word is generally meant.

e husband or by the elder women of the family, in their :votion to the ancient cults.

Or, even in cases where a delivery is normal, the results, om an Indian point of view, are often more tragic than :ath. An able woman surgeon, Dr. K. O. Vaughan, of the enana Hospital at Srinagar, thus expresses it:[1]

'Many women who are childless and permanently disabled e so from the maltreatment received during parturition; any men are without male issue because the child has been lled by ignorance when born, or their wives so mangled by ie midwives they are incapable of further childbearing. . . .

'I [illustrate] my remarks with a few cases typical of e sort of thing every medical woman practising in this untry encounters.

'A summons comes, and we are told a woman is in labour. n arrival at the house we are taken into a small, dark and irty room, often with no window. If there is one it is opped up. Puerperal fever is supposed to be caused by esh air. The remaining air is vitiated by the presence of a iarcoal fire burning in a pan, and on a *charpoy* [cot] or on ie floor is the woman. With her are one or two dirty old omen, their clothes filthy, their hands begrimed with dirt, ieir heads alive with vermin. They explain that they are iidwives, that the patient has been in labour three days, and iey cannot get the child out. They are rubbing their hands n the floor previous to making another effort. On inspecon we find the vulva swollen and torn. They tell us, yes, is a bad case and they have had to use both feet and hands their effort to deliver her. . . . Chloroform is given and ie child extracted with forceps. We are sure to find holly-

[1] *V.M.S.F. Report*, pp. 98–9.

hock roots which have been pushed inside the mother, som times string and a dirty rag containing quince-seeds in t uterus itself. . . .

'Do not think it is the poor only who suffer like this. can show you the homes of many Indian men with Unive sity degrees whose wives are confined on filthy rags a attended by these Bazaar *dhais* because it is the custom, a the course for the B.A. degree does not include a lit common sense.'

Doctor Vaughan then proceeds to quote further illustr tions from her own practice, of which the following is specimen:[1]

'A wealthy Hindu, a graduate of an Indian Universi and a lecturer himself, a man who is highly educated, ca us to his house, as his wife has been delivered of a child a had fever. . . . We find that [the *dhai*] had no disinfectan as they would have cost her about Rs. 3 [4*s*. 2*d*., $1 Ame can], and the fee she will get on the case is only R. 1 and few dirty clothes. The patient is lying on a heap of cast-c and dirty clothes, an old waistcoat, an English railway ru a piece of waterproof packing from a parcel, half a staine and dirty shirt of her husband's. There are no sheets clean rags of any kind. As her husband tells me: "We sha give her clean things on the fifth day, but not now; that our custom."

'That woman, in spite of all we could do, died of sept cæmia contracted either from the dirty clothing which saved from one confinement in the family to another [u washed], or from the *dhai*, who did her best in the absenc of either hot water, soap, nail-brush or disinfectants.'

[1] *V.M.S.F. Report*, pp. 99–100.

Evidence is in hand of educated, travelled and well-born ıdians, themselves holders of European university degrees, ho permit their wives to undergo this same inheritance of ırkness. The case may be cited of an Indian medical man, ılding an English University's Ph.D. and M.D. degrees, ›nsidered to be exceptionally able and brilliant and now tually in charge of a Government centre for the training *dhais* in modern midwifery. His own young wife being cently confined, he yielded to the pressure of the elder omen of his family and called in an old-school *dhai*, dirty ıd ignorant as the rest, to attend her. The wife died of ıerperal fever; the child died in the birth. 'When we have e spectacle of even educated Indians with English degrees lowing their wives and children to be killed off like flies by norant midwives,' says Doctor Vaughan again, 'we can intly imagine the sufferings of their humbler sisters.'

But the question of station or of worldly goods has small ırt in the matter. To this the admirable sisterhood of nglish and American women doctors unites to testify.

Dr. Marion A. Wylie's words are:[1]

'These conditions are by no means confined to the poorest r most ignorant classes. I have attended the families of ajahs where many of these practices were carried out, and ıet with strenuous opposition when I introduced ventilation nd aseptic measures.'

Sweeper-girl or Brahman, outcaste or queen, there is ssentially little to choose between their lots, in that fierce ıoment for which alone they were born. An Indian hristian lady of distinguished position and attainment, hose character has opened to her many doors that remain

[1] *V.M.S.F. Report*, p. 86.

to others fast closed, gives the following story of her visit mercy to a child-princess.

The little thing, wife of a ruling prince and just past h tenth year, was already in labour when her visitor entered t room. The *dhais* were busy over her, but the case was o viously serious, and priestly assistance had been called. Ou side the door sat its exponent – an old man, reading alo from the scriptures and from time to time chanting words direction deciphered from his book.

'Hark, within, there!' he suddenly shouted. 'Now it time to make a fire upon this woman's body. Make and lig a fire upon her body, quick!'

Instantly the *dhais* set about to obey.

'And what will the fire do to our little princess?' quiet asked the visitor, too practised to express alarm.

'Oh,' replied the women, listlessly, 'if it be her fate to li she will live, and there will, of course, be a great scar brand upon her. Or, if it be her fate to die, then she will die' – ar on they went with their fire-building.

Out to the ministrant squatting at the door flew the quic witted visitor. 'Holy One,' she asked, 'are you not afraid the divine jealousies? You are about to make the Fir sacrifice – but this is a queen, not a common mortal. W not Mother Ganges see and be jealous that no honour is pa to her?'

The old man looked up, perplexed. 'It is true,' he sai 'it is true the gods are ever jealous and easily provok to anger – but the Book here surely says –' And h troubled eyes turned to the ancient writ outspread upon h knees.

'Have you Ganges water here in the house?' interrupte the other.

'Surely. Dare the house live without it!' answered the old e.

'Then here is what I am given to say: Let water of Holy anges be put upon bright fire and made thrice hot. Let it en be poured into a marvel-sack that the gods, by my hand, all provide. And let that sack be laid upon the Maharani's dy. So in a united offering – fire and water together – all the gods be propitiated and their wrath escaped.'

'This is wisdom. So be it!' cried the old man. Then ick ran the visitor to fetch her Bond Street hot-water bag.

Superstition, among the Indian peoples, knows few undary lines of condition or class. Women in general are one to believe that disease is an evidence of the approach a god. Medicine and surgery, driving that god away, fend him, and it is ill business to offend the Great Ones; tter, therefore, charms and propitiations, with an eye to e long run.

And besides the gods, there are the demons and evil irits, already as many as the sands of the sea, to whose umber more must not be added.

Among the worst of demons are the spirits of women who ed in childbirth before the child was born. These walk ith their feet turned backward, haunting lonely roads and e family hearth, and are malicious beyond the rest.

Therefore, when a woman is seen to be about to breathe er last, her child yet undelivered – she may have lain for ys in labour for a birth against which her starveling bones e locked – the *dhai*, as in duty bound, sets to work upon recautions for the protection of the family.

First she brings pepper and rubs it into the dying eyes, at the soul may be blinded and unable to find its way out. hen she takes two long iron nails, and, stretching out her victim's unresisting arms – for the poor creature knows ar accepts her fate – drives a spike straight through each pal fast into the floor. This is done to pinion the soul to tl ground, to delay its passing or that it may not rise ar wander, vexing the living. And so the woman dies, piteous calling to the gods for pardon for those black sins of a form life for which she now is suffering.

This statement, horrible as it is, rests upon the testimor of many and unimpeachable medical witnesses in wide separated parts of India. All the main statements in th chapter rest upon such testimony and upon my own obse vation.

It would be unjust to assume, however, that the *dhai*, f all her monstrous deeds, is a blameworthy creature. Eve move that she makes is a part of the ancient and accepte ritual of her calling. Did she omit or change any part of i nothing would be gained; simply the elder women of tl households she serves would revile her for incapacity an call in another more faithful to the creed.

Her services include attendance at the time of confin ment and for ten days, more or less, thereafter, the approx mate interval during which no member of the family wi approach the patient because of her uncleanness. Durin this time the *dhai* does all that is done for the sick woma and the infant. At its end she is expected to clean the defile room and coat with cow-dung its floor and walls.

She receives her pay in accordance with the sex of the chil that was born. These sums vary. A rich man may give he for the entire period of service as much as Rs. 15 (abou £1 1*s.*) if the child be a son. From the well-to-do the mor usual fee is about R. 1 (1*s.* 4*d.*) for a son and eight anna (8*d.*) for a daughter. The poor pay the *dhai* for her for ht's work the equivalent of four or five cents for a son and o to three cents for a daughter. Herself the poorest of the or, she has no means of her own wherewith to buy as ich as a cake of soap or a bit of clean cotton. None are ywhere provided for her. And so, the slaughter goes on.[1]

Various funds subscribed by British charity sustain ternal and child-welfare work in many parts of India, and erywhere their labours include the attempt to teach the *ais*. But the task is extremely difficult. Invariably the *ais* protest that they have nothing to learn, in which their ents agree with them. One medical woman said in showg me her *dhai* class, an appalling array of decrepit old ones:

'We pay these women, out of a fund from England, for ning to class. We also pay some of them not to practise, mall sum, but just enough to live on. They are too old, stupid and too generally miserable to be capable of learng. Yet, when we beg them not to take cases because of the rm they do, they say: "How else can we live? This is our ly means to earn food." Which is true.'

A characteristic incident, freshly happened when it came my knowledge, concerned a Public Health instructor tioned by one of the funds above mentioned, in the north. visualize the scene, one must think of the instructor as at she is – a conspicuously comely and spirited young ly of the type that under all circumstances looks *chic* and ll-groomed. She had been training a class of *dhais* in hore, and had invited her 'graduates' when handling a ficult case to call her in for advice.

At three o'clock one cold winter's morning of 1926, a aduate summoned her. The summons led to the house of

[1] *V.M.S.F. Report*, p. 89.

an outcaste, a little mud hut with an interior perhaps eig by twelve feet square. In the room were ten people, thr generations of the family, all save the patient fast aslee Also, a sheep, two goats, some chickens and a cow, becau the owner did not trust his neighbours. No light but a gli in an earthen pot. No heat but that from the bodies of m and beast. No aperture but the door, which was closed.

In a small alcove at the back of the room four cot be planted one upon another, all occupied by members of t family. In the cot third from the ground lay a woman advanced labour.

'*Dhai* went outside,' observed Grandmother, stirri sleepily, and turned her face to the wall.

Not a moment to be lost. No time to hunt up the *dh* By good luck, the cow lay snug against the cot-pile. So o trig little English lady climbs up on the back of the plac and unobjecting cow, and from that vantage point succe fully brings into the world a pair of tiny Hindus – a girl a a boy.

Just as the thing is over, back comes the *dhai*, in a rag She had been out in the yard, quarrelling with the husba about the size of the coin that he should lay in her pal on which to cut the cord – without which coin already in h possession no canny *dhai* will operate.

And this is merely an ordinary experience.

Our Indian conduct of midwifery undoubtedly should otherwise than it is,' said a group of Indian gentlemen d cussing the whole problem as it existed in their own superi circle, 'but is it possible that enough English ladies will found to come out and do the work?'

A fractional percentage of the young wives are now fou ready to accept modern medical help. But it is from t der women of the household that resistance both deter-ined and effective comes.

Says Dr. Agnes C. Scott, M.B., B.S., of the Punjab, one the most distinguished of the many British medical women -day giving their lives to India:[1]

'An educated man may desire a better-trained woman to tend on his wife, but he is helpless against the stone wall of norance and prejudice built and kept up by the older omen of the *zenana* who are the real rulers of the house.'

Dr. K. O. Vaughan says upon this point:[2]

'The women are their own greatest enemies, and if any-ne can devise a system of education and enlightenment for andmother, great-grandmother and great-great-grand-other which will persuade them not to employ the ignorant, rty Bazaar *dhai*, they will deserve well of the Indian nation. my opinion that is an impossible task.'

And another woman surgeon adds:[3]

'Usually a mother-in-law or some ancient dame superin-nds the confinement, who is herself used to the old tradi-ons and insists on their observance. . . . It has been the immemorial custom that the management of a confinement the province of the leading woman of the house, and the en are powerless to interfere.'

Thus arises a curious picture – the picture of the man who s since time immemorial enslaved his wife, and whose most

[1] *V.M.S.F. Report*, p. 91. Cf. Sir Patrick Hehir, *The Medical Profession India*. Henry Frowde and Hodder & Stoughton, London, 1923, pp. 5–31.

[2] *V.M.S.F. Report*, p. 101.

[3] *Ibid.*, p. 71.

vital need in all life, present and to come, is the getting a son; and of this man, by means none other than the wi of his willing slave, balked in his heart's desire! He h thought it good that she be kept ignorant; that she for ev suppress her natural spirit and inclinations, walking cer monially, in stiff harness, before him, her 'earthly god She has so walked, obedient from infancy to death, throug untold centuries of merciless discipline, while he, fro infancy to death, through untold centuries, has given hin self no discipline at all. And now their harvests ripen i kind: hers a death-grip on the rock of the old law, makin her dead-weight negative to any change, however mercifu his, a weakness of will and purpose, a fatigue of nerve an spirit, that deliver him in his own house, beaten, into th hands of his slave.

Of Indian babies born alive about 2,000,000 die eac year. 'Available statistics show,' says the latest Census India, 'that over 40 per cent. of the deaths of infants occu in the first week after birth, and over 60 per cent. in the fir month.'[1]

The number of still-births is heavy. Syphilis and go orrhœa are among its main causes, to which must be adde the sheer inability of the child to bear the strain of comin into the world.

Vital statistics are weak in India, for they must large depend upon illiterate villagers as collectors. If a baby die the mother's wail trails down the darkness of a night or tw But if the village be near a river, the little body may just b tossed into the stream, without waste of a rag for a shrou Kites and the turtles finish its brief history. And it is mo than probable that no one in the village will think it wort

[1] *Census of India*, 1921. Vol. I, Part I, p. 132.

ile to report either the birth or the death. Statistics as to ›ies must therefore be taken as at best approximate.

It is probable, however, in view of existing conditions, .t the actual figures of infant mortality, were it possible to ow them, would surprise the western mind rather by their allness than by their height. 'I used to think,' said one the American medical women, 'that a baby was a delicate ature. But experience here is forcing me to believe it the ıghest fabric ever made, since it ever survives.'

CHAPTER IX

BEHIND THE VEIL

THE chapters preceding have chiefly dealt with the Hind who forms, roughly, three-quarters of the population India. The remaining quarter, the Muhammadans, diff considerably as between the northern element, whose blo contains a substantial strain of the old conquering Persi and Afghan stock, and the southern contingent, who a for the larger part, descendants of Hindu converts retainin in greater or less degree, many of the qualities of Hin character.

In some respects, Muhammadan women enjoy gre advantages over their Hindu sisters. Conspicuous amo such advantages is their freedom from infant marriage a from enforced widowhood, with the train of miseries evok by each. Their consequent better inheritance, supported a diet greatly superior to that of the Hindu, brings them the threshold of a maturity sturdier than that of the Hin type. Upon crossing that threshold the advantage Muhammadan women of the better class is, however, forfe For they pass into practical life-imprisonment within t four walls of the home.

Purdah, as this system of women's seclusion is calle having been introduced by the Muslim conquerors and them observed, soon came to be regarded by higher ca Hindus as a hall-mark of social prestige. These, there o adopted it as a matter of mode. And to-day, as a consequen of the growing prosperity of the country, this mediæ custom, like the interdiction of re-marriage of virgin wido nong the Hindus, seems to be actually on the increase. or every woman at the top of the scale whom western ıfluence sets free, several humbler but prospering sisters, ocially ambitious, deliberately assume the bonds.

That view of women which makes them the proper loot war was probably the origin of the custom of *purdah.* Vhen a man has his women shut up within his own four alls, he can guard the door. Taking Indian evidence on ie question, it appears that in some degree the same neces- ty exists to-day. In a part of India where *purdah* but little otains, I observed the united request of several Hindu dies of high position that the Amusement Club for English ıd Indian ladies to which they belong reduce the minimum ge required for membership to twelve, or, better, to eleven ears. This, they frankly said, was because they were afraid leave their daughters of that age at home, even for one ternoon, without a mother's eye and accessible to the men the family.

Far down the social scale the same anxiety is found. The Iindu peasant villager's wife will not leave her girl child at ome alone for the space of an hour, being practically sure ıat, if she does so, the child will be ruined. I dare not ffirm that this condition everywhere obtains. But I can ffirm that it was brought to my attention by Indians and y Occidentals, as regulating daily life in widely separated ections of the country.

No typical Muhammadan will trust another man in his *enana*, simply because he knows that such liberty would be egarded as opportunity. If there be a handful of Hindus f another persuasion, it is almost or quite invariably be- ause they are reflecting some part of the western attitude oward women; and this they do without abatement of their distrust of their fellow-men. Intercourse between men ar women which is both free and innocent is a thing well-nig incredible to the Indian mind.

In many parts of India the precincts of the *zenana*, amor better-class Hindus, are therefore closed and the wom cloistered within. And the cloistered Muhammadan wome if they emerge from their seclusion, do so under concealir veils, or in concealing vehicles. The Rolls-Royce of a Hinc reigning prince's wife may sometimes possess dark windo glasses, through which the lady looks out at ease, herself u seen. But the wife of a prosperous Muhammadan cook, she go out on an errand, will cover herself from the crown the head downward in a thick cotton shroud, through who scant three inches of mesh-covered eye-space she peers hal blinded.

I happened to be present at a '*purdah* party' – a party f veiled ladies attended by ladies only – in a private hou in Delhi when tragedy hovered nigh. The Indian ladi had all arrived, stepping heavily swathed from their clos curtained motor-cars. Their hostess, wife of a high Englis official, herself had met them on her threshold; for, out deference to the custom of the *purdah*, all the men-servan had been banished from the house, leaving Lady – alone conduct her guests to the drawing-room. There they ha laid aside their swathings. And now, in all the grace of the native costumes, they were sitting about the room, gent conversing with the English ladies invited to meet ther The senior Indian lady easily dominated her party. She wa far advanced in years, they said, and she wore long, light blu velvet trousers, tight from the knee down, golden slipper a smart little jacket of silk brocade, and a beautifully em broidered Kashmir shawl draped over her head.

We went in to tea. And again Lady –, single-handed, cept for the help of the English ladies, moved back and rth, from pantry to tea-table, serving her Indian guests.

Suddenly from the veranda without, arose a sound of cursion – a rushing – men's voices, women's voices, loud, uder, coming close. The hostess with a face of dismay ıshed for the door. Within the room panic prevailed. heir great white mantles being out of reach, the Indian dies ran into the corners, turning their backs, while the nglish, understanding their plight, stood before them to reen them as best might be.

Meantime, out on the veranda, more fracas had arisen – en a sudden silence and a whir of retreating wheels. ady – returned, panting, all apologies and relief.

'I am *too* sorry! But it is all over now. Do forgive it! othing shall frighten you again,' she said to the trembling dian ladies; and, to the rest of us: 'It was the young Roose- lts come to call. They didn't know!'

It was in the talk immediately following that one of the ungest of the Indian ladies exclaimed:

'You find it difficult to like our *purdah*. But we have ıown nothing else. We lead a quiet, peaceful, protected e within our own homes. And, with men as they are, we ould be miserable, terrified, outside.'

But one of the ladies of middle age expressed another ind: 'I have been with my husband to England,' she said, eaking quietly to escape the others' ears. 'While we were ere he let me leave off *purdah*, for women are respected in ngland. So I went about freely, in streets and shops and lleries and gardens and to the houses of friends, quite mfortable always. No one frightened or disturbed me and ıad much interesting talk with gentlemen as well as ladies.

Oh, it was wonderful – a paradise! But here – here there nothing. I must stay within the *zenana*, keeping stri *purdah*, as becomes our rank, seeing no one but the wom and my husband. We see nothing. We know nothing. V have nothing to say to each other. We quarrel. It is *du* But they,' nodding surreptitiously toward the oldest woma 'will have it so. It is only because of our hostess that su as she would come here to-day. More they would nev consent to. And they know how to make life horrible for in each household, if we offer to relax an atom of the *purd* law.'

Then, looking from face to face, one saw the illustratio of the talk – the pretty, blank features of the novices; t unutterable listlessness and fatigue of those of the speake age; the sharp-eyed, iron-lipped authority of the old.

The report of the Calcutta University Commission says

'All orthodox Bengali women of the higher classe whether Hindu or Muslim, pass at an early age behind t *purdah*, and spend the rest of their lives in the comple seclusion of their homes, and under the control of the elde woman of the household. This seclusion is more stri among the Musalmans than among the Hindus. . . . A fe westernized women have emancipated themselves, . [but] they are regarded by most of their countrywomen denationalized.'

Bombay, however, practises but little *purdah*, largely, doubt, because of the advanced status and liberalizing i fluence of the Parsi ladies; and in the Province of Madr it is as a rule peculiar only to the Muhammadans and t wealthy Hindus. From two Hindu gentlemen, both train

[1] Vol. II, Part I, pp. 4–5.

England to a scientific profession, I heard that they themselves had insisted that their wives quit *purdah*, and that they were bringing up their little daughters in a European school. But their wives, they added, unhappy in what seemed to them too great exposure, would be only too glad to resume their former sheltered state. And, viewing things as they are, one can scarcely escape the conclusion that much is to be said on that side. One frequently hears, in India and out of it, of the beauty of the sayings of the Hindu masters on the exalted position of women. One finds often quoted such passages as the precept of Manu:

> 'Where a woman is not honoured
> Vain is sacrificial rite.'

But, as Mr. Gandhi tersely sums it up: 'What is the teaching worth, if their practice denies it?' [1]

One consequence of *purdah* seclusion is its incubation of tuberculosis. Dr. Arthur Lankester [2] has shown that among the *purdah*-keeping classes the mortality of women from tuberculosis is terribly high. It is also shown that, among persons living in the same locality and of the same habits and means, the men of the *purdah*-keeping classes display a higher incidence of death from tuberculosis than do those whose women are less shut in.

The Health Officer for Calcutta declares in his report for 1917:

'In spite of the improvement in the general death-rate of the city, the death-rate amongst females is still more than 40 per cent. higher than amongst males. . . . Until it is real-

[1] Statement to the author, Sabarmati, Ahmedabad, March 17, 1926.

[2] *Tuberculosis in India*, Arthur Lankester, M.D. Butterworth & Co., London, 1920, p. 140.

ized that the strict observance of the *purdah* system in a larg city, except in the case of the very wealthy who can affor spacious homes standing in their own grounds, necessari involves the premature death of a large number of wome this standing reproach to the city will never be removed.'

Dr. Andrew Balfour, Director of the London School Hygiene and Tropical Medicine, in pointing out how pe fectly the habits of the Indian peoples favour the spread the disease, speaks of 'the system by which big families li together; the *purdah* custom relegating women to the da and dingy parts of the house; the early marriages, sappir the vitality of thousands of the young; the pernicious hab of indiscriminate spitting.'[1] These, added to dirt, bad san tation, confinement, lack of air and exercise, make a perfe breeding-place for the White Death. Between nine hundre thousand and one million persons, it is estimated, d annually of tuberculosis in India.[2]

It has been further estimated that forty million India women, Muhammadan and Hindu, are to-day in *purdah* In the opinion, however, of those experienced officers who I could consult, this estimate, if it is intended to represe the number of women kept so strictly cloistered that the never leave their apartments nor see any male save husbar and son, is probably three times too high. Those who nev see the outer world, from their marriage day till the day their death, number by careful estimate of minimum an maximum between 11,250,000 and 17,290,000 persons.

[1] *Health Problems of the Empire*. Dr. Andrew Balfour and Dr. H. Scott. Collins, London, 1924, p. 286.

[2] *Ibid.*, p. 285.

[3] *India and Missions*, The Bishop of Dornakal.

As to the mental effect of the *purdah* system upon those ho live under it, one may leave its characterization to ıdian authorities.

Says Dr. N. N. Parakh, the Indian physician:[1]

'Ignorance and the *purdah* system have brought the omen of India to the level of animals. They are unable to ok after themselves, nor have they any will of their own. 'hey are slaves to their masculine owners.'[2]

Said that outstanding Swarajist leader, Lala Lajpat Rai, his Presidential address to the Hindu Mahasabha Con- rence held in Bombay in December, 1925:

'The great feature of present-day Hindu life is passivity. Let it be so" sums up all their psychology, individual and ɔcial. They have got into the habit of taking things lying ɔwn. They have imbibed this tendency and this psychology ıd this habit from their mothers. It seems as if it was in ıeir blood. . . . Our women labour under many handicaps. : is not only ignorance and superstition that corrode their ıtelligence, but even physically they are a poor race. . . . Vomen get very little open air and almost no exercise. How n earth is the race, then, to improve and become efficient? . large number of our women develop consumption and die an early age. Such of them as are mothers, infect their ıildren also. Segregation of cases affected by tuberculosis almost impossible. . . . There is nothing so hateful as a ıarrelsome, unnecessarily assertive, impudent, ill-mannered oman, but even if that were the only road which the Hindu oman must traverse in order to be an efficient, courageous,

[1] *Legislative Assembly Debates*, Vol. III, Part I, p. 881.

[2] Cf., however, *ante*, pp. 77, 80, 109, 116, *et al.*

independent and physically fit mother, I would prefer it the existing state of things.'

At this point, the practical experience of a school-mistres the English principal of a Calcutta girls' college, may l cited. Dated eight years later than the Report of the Ca cutta Health Officer already quoted, it concerns tl daughters of the most progressive and liberal of Bengal families.[1]

'They dislike exercise and take it only under compulsio They will not go into the fresh air if they can avoid doir so. The average student is very weak. She needs good foo exercise, and often remedial gymnastics. The chest is co tracted, and the spine often curved. She has no desire f games. . . . We want the authority . . . to compel the st dent to take those remedies which will help her to grow in a woman.'

But the introduction of physical training as a help to tl bankrupt physiques of Hindu girls is thus far only a drea of the occidental intruder. Old orthodoxy will not have it s

'The Hindu father is prone to complain that he does n want his daughter turned into a *nautch* girl. She has to l married into one of a limited number of families; and the is always a chance of one of the old ladies exclaiming, "Th girl has been taught to kick her legs about in public. Sure such a shameless one is not to be brought into our house!" '

[1] Sister Mary Victoria, Principal of the Diocesan College for Girls, *Fi Quinquennial Review of the Progress of Education in Bengal*, paragrap 521–4.

[2] The Inspectress for Eastern Bengal, *Calcutta University Commissi Report*, Vol. II, Part I, p. 23.

'It is, indeed, only among the orthodox,' says the authority quoting this testimony, 'that this kind of objection is taken. But the orthodox are the majority.'[1]

Under the heading, 'Thou Shalt Do NO Murder,' the Oxford Mission of Calcutta printed, in its weekly journal of February 20, 1926, an editorial beginning as follows:

'A few years ago we published an article with the above heading in which was vividly described by a woman writer the appalling destruction of life and health which was going on in Bengal behind the *purdah* and in *zenanas* amongst the women herded there. We thought that the revelations then made, based on the health officer's reports, would bring to us a stream of indignant letters demanding instant reform. The effect amongst menfolk was entirely *nil*. Apparently not a spark of interest was roused. An article condemning the silly credulity of the use of charms and talismans at once evokes criticism, and the absurdities of superstition are vigorously defended even by men who are graduates. But not a voice was raised in horror at the fact that for every male who dies of tuberculosis in Calcutta five females die.'

Yet among young western-educated men a certain abstract uneasiness begins to appear concerning things as they are. After they have driven the Occident out of India, many of them say, they must surely take up this matter of women. Not often, however, does one find impatience such as that of Abani Mohan Das Gupta, of Calcutta, expressed in the journal just quoted.

'I shudder to think about the condition of our mothers and sisters in the "harem." . . . From early morn till late at

[1] The Inspectress for Eastern Bengal, *ante*, p. 24.

night they are working out the same routine throughout the whole of their lives without a murmur, as if they are patience incarnate. There are many instances where a woman has entered the house of her husband at the time of the marriage and did not leave it until death had carried her away. They are always in harness as if they have no will or woe but only to suffer – suffer without any protest. . . . I appeal to young Indians to unfurl their flag for the freedom of women. Allow them their right. . . . Am I crying in the wilderness?'

Bengal is the seat of bitterest political unrest – the producer of India's main crop of anarchists, bomb-throwers and assassins. Bengal is also among the most sexually exaggerated regions of India; and medical and police authorities in any country observe the link between that quality and 'queer' criminal minds – the exhaustion of normal avenues of excitement creating a thirst and a search in the abnormal for gratification. But Bengal is also the stronghold of strict *purdah*, and one cannot but speculate as to how many explosions of eccentric crime in which the young politicals of Bengal have indulged, were given the detonating touch by the unspeakable flatness of their *purdah*-deadened home lives, made the more irksome by their own half-digested dose of foreign doctrines.

CHAPTER X

WOMAN THE SPINSTER

ESS than 2 per cent. of the women of British India are erate in the sense of being able to write a letter of a few mple phrases, and read its answer, in any one language or alect. To be exact, such literates numbered, in 1921, ghteen to the thousand.[1] But in the year 1911 they ımbered only ten to the thousand. And, in order to timate the significance of that increase, two points should e considered: first, that a century ago literate women, save r a few rare stars, were practically unknown in India; and, cond, that the great body of the peoples, always heavily pposed to female education, still so opposes it, and on ligio-social grounds.

Writing in the beginning of the nineteenth century, the bbé Dubois said:[2]

'The social condition of the wives of the Brahmins differs ry little from that of the women of other castes. . . . They e considered incapable of developing any of those higher ental qualities which would make them more worthy of nsideration and also more capable of playing a useful part life. . . . As a natural consequence of these views, female lucation is altogether neglected. A young girl's mind reains totally uncultivated, though many of them have good bilities. . . . It would be thought a disgrace to a respectable oman to learn to read; and even if she had learnt she would e ashamed to own it.'

[1] *India in* 1924–25. L. F. Rushbrook Williams, C.B.E., p. 276.

[2] *Hindu Manners, Customs and Ceremonies*, pp. 336–7.

This was written of the Hindu. But Islam in India ha also disapproved of the education of women, which, there fore, has been held by the vast majority of both creeds to b unnecessary, unorthodox, and dangerous.

In the year 1917, the Governor-General of India i Council appointed a commission to inquire and recommen as to the status of the University of Calcutta and of tributar educational conditions in Bengal. This commission com prised eminent British educators from the faculties of th Universities of Leeds, Glasgow, Manchester, and London allied with eminent Indian professionals. Bengal, the field c inquiry, has long stood distinguished among all othe provinces of British India for its thirst for learning. Th testimonies accumulated by the Commission during it three years' work may consequently be taken as not unkindl reflecting the wider Indian horizon.

With regard to the education of women, it is therefore c interest to find Mr. Brajalal Chakravarti, Secretary of th Hindu Academy at Daulatpur, affirming:[1]

'It is strictly enjoined in the religious books of the Hindu that females should not be allowed to come under any influ ence outside that of the family. For this reason, no system c school and college education can be made to suit their re quirements. . . . Women get sufficient moral and practica training in the household and that is far more important tha the type of education schools can give.'

Another of the Commission's witnesses, Mr. Harida Goswamy, Head Master of the High School at Asanso amplified the thought, saying:[2]

[1] *Calcutta University Commission Report*, Vol. XII, p. 414.
[2] *Ibid.*, p. 426.

'It is not wise to implant in [girls] by means of education astes which they would not have an opportunity to gratify in heir after life, and thus sow the seeds of future discontent nd discord.'

And Mr. Rabindra Mohan Dutta,[1] member of the faculty f the University itself, even while deploring that 'darkness f ignorance and superstition' which, he asserts, puts the omen of India 'in continual conflict and disagreement with heir educated husbands, brothers or sons,' would yet follow he orthodox multitude, genuinely fearful of importing into he Indian home, from the distaff side,

the spirit of revolutionary and rationalistic iconoclasm condemning all our ancient institutions that are the outcome of long past and are part of our flesh and blood as it were.'

When, however, the topic of women's education comes p for discussion in Indian political bodies, speakers arise on he side of change. In the Delhi Legislative Assembly, Dr. Hari Singh Gour[2] denounces the sequestration and suppression of women. And Munshi Iswar Saran,[3] member for he cities of the United Provinces, points out, in a spirit of idicule, that it is

. . . the sin of this *Kali Yuga* [Age of Destruction] that oungsters receive education and then decline to be ordered about by their elders. . . . Such is our foolhardiness that we have started giving education to our girls. . . . If this is going on, I ask whether you believe that you will be able to dictate to your daughters?'

[1] *Calcutta University Commission Report*, Vol. XII, p. 422.
[2] *Legislative Assembly Debates*, 1921. Vol. I, Part I, p. 363.
[3] *Ibid.*, 1922. Vol. II, Part II, p. 1631.

I recall the heat with which a wealthy young Hindu of m acquaintance, but just returned from an English university asserted that he would never, never take an Indian bride because he would not tie himself to 'a wife of the tent century.' And among western-educated Indians in th higher walks of life, the desire for similarly educated wive sometimes rises even to a willingness to accept such bride with dowries smaller than would otherwise be exacted.

But this factor, though recognizable, is as yet small Bombay, perhaps, gives its women more latitude than doe any other province. Yet its Education Report asserts:[1]

'Educated men desire educated wives for their sons anc presumably educate their daughters with the same object in view, but they generally withdraw them from school on any manifestation of a desire to . . . push education to any length which might interfere with or delay marriage.'

The Report of the Central Provinces affirms:[2]

'Even those parents who are not averse to their daughters being literate consider that the primary course is sufficient and that after its completion girls are too old to be away fron their homes.'

And Assam adds:[3]

'[Parents] send their girls to school in order to enabl themselves to marry them better and occasionally on easier terms. But as soon as a suitable bridegroom is available the girl is at once placed in the seclusion of the *purdah*.'

Certainly the great weight of sentiment remains intact in its loyalty to ancient conditions. To disturb them were to

[1] Quoted in *Progress of Education in India*, 1917–22, Eighth Quinquennial Review, pp. 129–30. [2] *Ibid.* [3] *Ibid.*

k the mould of manhood. The metaphor of Dr. Brajendnath Seal, M.A., PH.D., Professor of Mental and Moral ience in Calcutta University, implies the dreaded risk: lan,' writes this Hindu philosopher, 'is a home-brew in the t of woman the brewster, or, as the Indian would put it, a me-spun in the loom of woman the spinster.' [1]

On such general grounds, says the Calcutta University ommission,[2] is the feeling against women's education 'very mmonly supported by the men, even by those who have ssed through the whole course of western education.' If e child be sent to school at all, it is more often to put her in afe place out of the family's way, rather than to give her struction for which is felt so faint a need and so great a strust.

To use the words of Mr. B. Mukherjee, M.A., F.R. ON. SOC.: [3]

'The strict social system which makes the marriage of a l religiously compulsory at the age of twelve or so also ts an end to all hope of continuing the education of the dinary Hindu girl beyond the [marriageable] age.'

It is estimated that over 73 per cent. of the total number girls at school are withdrawn before they achieve literacy, d in the year 1922, in the great Bengal Presidency, out of ery hundred girls under instruction but one was studying ove the primary stage.[4]

Such small advance as has been achieved, in the desper-

[1] *Calcutta University Commission Report*, Vol. XII, p. 62.

[2] *Ibid.*, Vol. II, Part I, p. 5.

[3] *Ibid.*, Vol. XII, p. 440.

[4] *Progress of Education in Bengal.* J. W. Holme, M.A. Sixth Quinquen l Review.

ately uphill attempt to bestow literacy upon the women India, represents, first and foremost, a steady and patie effort of persuasion on the part of the British Governmen second, the toil of British and American missionaries; an third, the ability of the most progressive Indians to concei and effect the transmission of thought into deed. But it estimated that, without a radical change in performance the part of the Indians themselves, ninety-five more years such combined effort will be required to wrest from hostili and inertia the privilege of primary education for as much 12 per cent. of the female population.[1]

The Seva Sadan Society, pioneer Indian women's orga ization to provide poor women and girls with training primary teaching and useful work, was started in 1908, Poona, near Bombay. By the latest report at hand, it h about a thousand pupils. This society's success shows wh the happier women of India could do for the rest, were th so minded. But its work is confined wholly to Bomb Presidency; and unfortunately, it has no counterpart, sa the official report, in any other part of India.

As will be shown in another chapter, the administratic of education as a province of Government has of late yea rested in Indian hands.

In 1921–2, British India possessed 23,778 girls' schoo inclusive of all grades, from primary schools to arts and pr fessional colleges. These schools contained in the prima stage 1,297,643 pupils, only 24,555 in the Middle Schoc and a still smaller number – 5,818 – in the High Schools

[1] Cf. *Village Schools in India.* Mason Olcott, Associated Press, Calcut 1926, p. 90.

[2] The figures in this paragraph are drawn from *Progress of Education India*, 1917–22. Vol. II.

'Although,' says the report, 'the number of girls who roceed beyond the primary stage is still lamentably small · 30,000 in all India out of a possible school-going popu-ıtion of 15,000,000 – still it shows an increase of 30 per ent. over the attendance in 1917.'[1]

In Bombay Presidency, in 1924–5 only 2·14 per cent. of he female population was under instruction of any kind,[2] hile in all India, in 1919, ·9 per cent. of the Hindu female opulation, and 1·1 per cent. of the Muhammadan females, vere in school.[3]

'It would be perfectly easy to multiply schools in which ittle girls would amuse themselves in preparatory classes, nd from which they would drift away gradually during the ɔwer primary stage. The statistical result would be im-ressive, but the educational effect would be *nil* and public noney would be indefensibly wasted.'[4]

But, in the fight for conserving female illiteracy, as in hose for maintaining the ancient midwifery and for con-inuing the cloistering of women, the great constant factor n the side of Things-As-They-Were will be found in the lder women themselves. Out of sheer loyalty to their gods of heaven and their gods of earth they would die to keep heir daughters like themselves.

As that blunt old Sikh farmer-soldier, Captain Hira Singh Brar, once said, speaking from his seat in the Legislative Assembly on a measure of reform:[5]

[1] *Progress of Education in India*, 1917–22. Vol. I, p. 135.

[2] *Bombay*, 1924–25. Government Central Press, Bombay, 1926, pp. XV–XVI.

[3] *Progress of Education in India*, 1917–22. Vol. I, p. 126.

[4] *Ibid.*, pp. 138–9.

[5] *Legislative Assembly Debates*, 1925. Vol. V, Part III, p. 2830.

'So many Lalas and Pandits get up on the platforms an say, "Now the time has come for this reform and that." Bu what happens? When they go home and when we meet the next morning they say, "What can we do? We are helpless When we went back home, our ladies would not allow us t do what we wanted to do. They say they do not care wha we talk, but they would not allow us to act accordingly."

Abreast of these priestesses of ancient custom in pre serving the illiteracy of women, stands another mighty in fluence – that of economic self-interest; a man must marr his daughter or incur an earthly and eternal penalty that fe will face. He can rarely marry her without paying a dowr so large that it strains his resources; to which must be adde the costs of the wedding – costs so excessive that, as a rule they plunge him deep into debt. This heavy tax he com monly incurs before his daughter reaches her teens. Why then, should he spend still more money on her, to educat her; or why, if he be poor and can use her labour, should h go without her help and send her to school, since she is s early to pass for ever into another man's service? The ide has been expressed by Rai Harinath Ghosh, Bahadur, Fellow of Calcutta University.[1]

'People naturally prefer to educate their boys, well know ing that in future they will make them happy and confortabl in their old age, and glorify their family, whilst the girls after marriage, will be at the mercy of others.'

To the average Indian father, of whatever estate, thi range of reasoning appears conclusive. And so the momen tous opportunities of the motherhood of India continue t be entrusted to the wisdom and judgment of illiterate babies.

[1] *Calcutta University Commission Report*, Vol. XII, p. 425.

Given such a public sentiment toward even rudimentary chooling for girl children, the facts as to more advanced arning may be easily surmised. Mr. Mohini Mohan hattacharjee, of the Calcutta University faculty, expressed in these words:[1]

'The higher education of Indian women . . . may almost e said to be beyond the scope of practical reform. No Iindu or Muhammadan woman of an orthodox type has ver joined a college or even read up to the higher classes in school. The girls who receive university education are ither Brahmo[2] or Christian. . . . The time is far distant hen the University will be called upon to make arrange-ients for the higher education of any large or even a decent umber of girls in Bengal.'

By the latest available report, the women students in arts nd professional colleges, in all British India, numbered nly 961. But a more representative tone than that of Mr. hattacharjee's rather deprecatory words is heard in the rank statement of Rai Satis Chandra Sen, Bahadur:[3]

'Amongst advanced communities in the West, where vomen are almost on a footing of equality with men and vhere every woman cannot expect to enter upon married life, igh education may be a necessity to them. But . . . the Vestern system . . . is not only unsuitable, but also demoral-zing to the women of India . . . and breaks down the ideals nd instincts of Indian womanhood.'

[1] *Calcutta University Commission Report*, Vol. XII, p. 411.

[2] The Brahmo or Brahmo Samaj is a sect numbering 6,388 persons, as hown in the *Census of India* of 1921, p. 119.

[3] *Calcutta University Commission Report*, Vol. XII, p. 449.

There remains, then, the question of education after marriage. Under present conditions of Indian thought, this may be dismissed with a word – 'impracticable.'[1] Directly she enters her husband's home, the little wife, whatever her rank, is at once heavily burdened with services to her husband, to her mother-in-law and to the household gods. Child-bearing quickly overwhelms her and she has neither strength nor leave for other activities. Further, she must be taught by women, if taught at all, since women, only, may have access to her. And so you come to the snake that has swallowed his tail.

For, as we have just seen, the ban that forbids literacy to the women of India thereby discourages the training of women teachers who might break the ban. Those who have such training barely and feebly suffice for the schools that already exist. *Zenana* teaching has thus far languished, an anæmic exotic – a failure, in an undesiring soil.

Returning to the conviction of the uselessness of spending good money on a daughter's education, this should not be supposed a class matter. Nobles and rich men share the sentiment with their lesser compatriots.

The point is illustrated in Queen Mary's College in Lahore. This institution was founded years ago by two English ladies who saw that the fractional percentage of Indian girls then receiving education came chiefly if not wholly from the low castes, whilst the daughters of princes, the wives and mothers of princes to come, the future regents, perhaps, for minor sons, were left in untouched darkness. The undertaking that the two ladies began enlisted the

[1] The Seva Sadan Society in Bombay has among its pupils a certain percentage of married women of the labouring class who come for two or three hours' instruction daily.

pproval of Government. The reigning princes, spurred on y the visit of Queen Mary to India, subscribed a certain um. This sum Government tripled. Suitable buildings ere erected and equipped, and there the liberality of the rinces practically ceased.

For, as will be found in every direction in which the trait an be expressed, the raising of a building as a monument to is name, be it school, hospital, or what not, interests the ealthy Indian; but for its maintenance in service he can arely if ever be induced to give one penny. In this case it as necessary, in order to combat initial indifference, to resent schooling practically free. To-day, the charges have een advanced to stand approximately thus: day scholars, unior, *6s. 3d.* per month; senior, *12s. 6d.* per month; oarding scholars, £2 *2s.* to £4 *4s.* per month, inclu-ive of all tuition, board, laundry, and ordinary medical reatment.

These terms contemplate payment only for the time ctually spent at college. And still some of the fathers are oth slow and disputatious over the settlement of accounts. You send a bill of two rupees [*2s. 9d.*] for stationery, all used p in your school by my two daughters in only two months. consider this bill excessive. They should not be allowed to se so much costly material; it is not right. It should not e paid,' protests one personage; and the representative of nother conducts a three weeks' correspondence of inquiry, emonstrance, and reproach over a charge for two yards of ibbon to tie up a little girl's bonnie black locks.

Partly because of the original policy of nominal charges dopted by Government to secure an entering wedge, partly ecause of their traditional dissociation of women and letters, he rich men of India as a whole remain to-day still convinced at heart that, if indeed their daughters are to b schooled at all, then Government should give them schoolin free of charge.

Queen Mary's College, a charming place, with clas rooms, dormitories, common rooms and gardens suitab and attractively designed, is staffed by British ladies university training. The curriculum is planned to suit th needs of the students. Instruction is given in the sever languages of the pupils – Arabic, Urdu, Hindi, etc., an against the girls' pleas, native dress is firmly required – le the elders at home take fright of a contagion of Western idea Throughout the school's varied activities, the continuo effort is to teach cleanliness of habit; and marks are give not only on scholarship but on helpfulness, tidiness, truth fulness, and the sporting spirit.

Outdoor games in the gardens are encouraged to th utmost possible degree, and a prettier sight would be har to find than a score or so of these really lovely little gazell eyed maidens playing about in their floating gauzes of blu and rose and every rainbow hue.

'They have not ginger enough for good tennis,' one c the teachers admits, 'but then, they have just emerged fro the hands of grandmothers who think it improper for littl girls even to walk fast. Do you see that lively small thing i pink and gold? When she first came two terms ago, sh truly maintained that her "legs wouldn't run." Now she i one of the best at games.

'But what a pity it is,' the teacher continues, 'to think o the life of dead passivity to which, in a year or two at best they will all have relapsed!'

'Will they carry into that after-life much of what the have learned here?' I ask.

'Think of the huge pervading influence that will encom-ass them! The old palace *zenana*, crowded with women owed under traditions as fixed as death itself! Where ould these delicate children find strength to hold their own one, through year upon year of that ancient, changeless, nothering domination? Our best hope is that they may, omehow, transmit a little of tonic thought to their chil-ren; that they may send their daughters to us; and that so, ich generation adding its bit, the end may justify our work.'

Queen Mary's is the only school in all India instituted specially for ladies of rank. Not unnaturally, therefore, ome of the new Indian officials, themselves without rank ther than that which office gives, covet the social prestige f enrolling their daughters in Queen Mary's. The question f enrolment rests as yet with an English Commissioner, and ne Commissioner lets the young climbers in. With the esult that the princes, displeased, are sending fewer of their hildren than of yore.

'Shall our daughters be subjected to the presence of aughters of *babus* – of upstart Bengali politicians!' they xclaim, leaving no doubt as to the reply.

And some of the resident faculty, mindful of the original urpose of the school, anxiously question:

'Is it wise to drive away the young princesses? Their uture influence is potentially so much further-reaching than hat of other women, however intelligent. Should we not train all points to get and to hold them?'

But to this question, when asked direct, the Commis-ioner himself replied:

'In British India we are trying to build a democracy. As or the Native States, undoubtedly it would be well to ducate the future *Maharanis*; I say to their fathers, the

Princes: "If you want to keep for your daughters a scho for their own rank, it can easily be done – but not on Gover ment funds. You must pay for the school yourselves." B this, invisible as the cost would be to men of their fortune they are not apt to do.'

Another centre of interest in Lahore is the Victoria Schoo occupying the palace of a grandson of the famous Ranj Singh, in the heart of the old city, just off the bazaar. Th head of this institution is an extremely able Indian lady, Mi K. M. Bose, of the third generation of an Indian Christia family. Miss Bose's firm and powerful character, her liber and genial spirit, her strong influence and fine mind, indica the possibilities of Indian womanhood set free.

In Victoria School are 500 girl pupils. 'Some are ric some poor,' says Miss Bose, 'but all are of good caste, and a are daughters of the leading men of the city. If we took low caste children here, it would increase expense to an impo sible degree. The others would neither sit nor eat wit them. Separate classes would have to be maintained, a almost double teaching staff employed, and so on throug innumerable embarrassments.

' "The tuition fees?" Merely nominal; we Indians wi not pay for the education of our daughters. In days but ju gone by, the richest refused to pay even for lesson book Books, teaching, and all, had at first to be given free, or w should have got no pupils. This school is maintained b Government grant and by private subscriptions fro England.'

Many rooms on many floors honeycomb the old barre rabbit-warren of a palace, each chamber filled with childre from mites of four or five in Montessori classes up to big hearty Muhammadan girls of fifteen or sixteen, not yet give ı marriage. Like Queen Mary's, this is a strict *purdah* :hool. The eye of man may not gaze upon it. When it is ecessary to introduce some learned pundit to teach his undit's specialty, he is separated from the class he teaches y a long, deep, thick, and wholly competent curtain. And e is chosen, not only for learning, but also for tottering age.

'I am responsible for these schools,' says the Commis- oner, smiling ruefully, 'and yet, being a man, I may never ıspect them!'

Work, in Victoria School, is done in six languages – Jrdu, Persian, Hindi, Punjabi, and Sanskrit, with optional ;nglish.

'We give no books to the children until they can really :ad,' says Miss Bose. 'Otherwise they merely memorize, :arning nothing.'[1] And the whole aim and hope of the :heme is to implant in the girls' minds something so efinitely applicable to their future life in the *zenana* that ɔme part of it may endure alive through the years of dark nd narrow things so soon to come.

Reading, writing, arithmetic enough to keep simple ousehold accounts; a little history; sewing – which art, by he way, is almost unknown to most of the women of India; little drawing and music; habits of cleanliness and sanitary bservance – both subjects of incredible difficulty; first aid, ɔ save themselves and their future babies as far as may be rom the barbarities of the domestic code – these are the ıain studies in this practical institution. Added to them is

[1] The Muslim Indian boy may be letter-perfect in long sections of the ırabic Koran without understanding one word that he speaks; similarly the oung Hindu, so both English and Indian teachers testify, easily learns by ɔte whole chapters of text whose words are mere meaningless sounds to is mind.

simple cooking, especially cooking for infants and invalids using always the native type of stove and utensils; and th handling and serving of food, with particular emphasis o keeping it clean and off the floor.

'Their cooking, in later life, they would never by natur do with their own hands, but would leave entirely to filth servants, whence come much sickness and death,' says th instructress. 'Our effort here is to give them a conviction o the use and beauty of cleanliness and order in all things.'

Miss L. Sorabji, the Indian lady-principal of the Ede High School for girls at Dacca, thus discreetly suggests th nature of the teacher's struggle:[1]

'Undesirable home influences are a great hindrance t progress. Unpunctuality, sloth, untidiness, carelessnes regarding the laws of health and sanitation, untruthfulness irresponsibility, absence of any code of honour, lack of hom discipline, are some of the difficulties we have to conten with in our schools. Character-building is what is mos needed.'

And – the patient upbuilding of a public opinion that eventually, may create and sustain a genuine and practica Indian movement toward self-help.

At present one beholds a curious spectacle: the daughter of rich landlords; of haughty Brahman plutocrats; of militan nationalist politicians, ferocious denouncers of the white ma and all his works, fed and lodged by the dimes and sixpence of dear old ladies in Illinois and Derbyshire, and taught th a-b-c of responsible living by despised Christians and out caste apostates.

[1] *Calcutta University Commission Report*, Vol. XII, p. 453.

Part Three: The Brahman

ATTLING south by rail, out of Bengal into Madras. Square
ısses of elephant-coloured rock piled up to build rect-
gular hills, sitting one upon another in segments, like
ephant Gods on pedestals. – Miles and more miles of it.
On and on. Then a softer country, where the earth is
ınge and the only trees are small-topped palms scratched
ıg across the sky like penstrokes ending in a splutter.

Much cultivation, rice fields marked off in slips and
gments by hand-high earth-ridges to hold the precious
ter. Little dark people with cherry-coloured garments,
nost black people, with big, bristling mops of curly black
ir, drawing water out of wells as they drew it a thousand
ars ago, or threshing grain under the circling feet of
llocks. Stands of sugar-cane, high and four-square.
ıall clay villages, each small clay house eclipsed under a
ʒ round palm-leaf roof like a candle-snuffer. Flocks of
ange-coloured goats. Patches of orange, on the ground –
lm-nuts for betel chewing, spread out to dry. Big orange
wks with proud, white heads. Orange after-glow of sun-
t, flooding orange over the stubble fields of rice. An
ange world, punctuated by black human bodies with
erry-coloured splashes.

Madras, citadel of Brahmanic Hinduism. Citadel also
the remnant of the ancient folk, the dark-skinned Dravid-
ıs. Brahmanic Hinduism broke them, cast them down
d trampled upon them, commanded them in their multi-
illions to be pariahs, outcastes, ignorant and poor. Then
me the Briton, for whatever reason, establishing peace,
der, and such measure of democracy as could survive in
e soil.

Gradually the Dravidian raised his eyes, and then, mo timidly, his head. With him, also, the multitudes of tl low castes of the Brahman's world. And now all thes become an Anti-Brahman party, had developed streng enough, for the time at least, to snatch from the Brahma his political majority in the Legislative Council of Madr Presidency.[1] Which, in itself, constituted an epoch i Indian history.

With one of these low-caste men become rich, respecte and politically powerful, I sat in private conference, in tl city of Madras. A little, vivacious person he was, full heat and free of tongue. 'Will you draw me your picture the Brahman?' I asked. He answered – and these are h actual words, written down at the moment:

'Once upon a time, when all men lived according to the choice, the Brahman was the only fellow who applied himse to learning. Then, having become learned, and being b nature subtle-minded, he secretly laid hold upon the sacre books, and secretly wrote into those books false texts th declared him, the Brahman, to be lord over all the peopl Ages passed. And gradually, because the Brahman onl could read and because he gave out his false texts that fo bade learning to others, the people grew to believe him tl Earthly God he called himself and to obey him accordingl So in all Hindu India he ruled the spirit of man, and no dared dispute him, not till England came with schools fc all.

'Now, here in this Province, Madras, we fight the Bral man. But still he is very strong, because the might thousands of years breaks slowly, and he is as shrewd as

[1] In the autumn elections of 1926, the Brahmans regained the majori in the Legislative Council of Madras Presidency.

ost of demons. He owns the Press, he sways the Bench, holds eighty per cent. of the public offices, and he terror-es the people, especially the women. For we are all perstitious and mostly illiterate. The "Earthly God" has en to that. Also, he hates the British, because they keep m from strangling us. He makes much "patriotic" outcry, manding that the British go. And we – we know that if ey go now, before we have had time to steady ourselves, will strangle us again and India will be what it used to be, cruel despotism wielded by fat priests against a mass of aves, because our imaginations are not yet free from him. isten:

'Each Hindu in India pays to the Brahman many times ore than he pays to the State. From the day of his birth the day of his death, a man must be feeding the Earthly od. When a child is born, the Brahman must be paid; herwise, the child will not prosper. Sixteen days after-ard, to be cleansed of "birth pollution," the Brahman must paid. A little later, the child must be named; and the rahman must be paid. In the third month, the baby's ir must be clipped; and the Brahman must be paid. In e sixth month, we begin to feed the child solids; and the rahman must be paid. When the child begins to walk, e Brahman must be paid. At the completion of the first ar comes the birthday ceremony and the Brahman must paid. At the end of the seventh year the boy's education gins and the Brahman must be paid well. In well-to-do milies he performs the ceremony by guiding golden writ-g-sticks placed in the boy's hand; and the sticks also go to e Brahman.

'When a girl reaches her first birthday, her seventh, or r ninth, or when a boy is one and a half, or two years old, or anywhere up to sixteen, comes the betrothal, and big pa to the Brahman. Then, when puberty comes, or earlier, the marriage is consummated earlier, rich pay to the Bral man. At an eclipse, the Brahman must be paid heavil And so it goes on. When a man dies, the corpse can b removed only after receiving the blessing of the Brahma for which he is paid. At the cremation, again a lot of mone must be paid to many Brahmans. After cremation, ever month for a year, the dead man's son must hold a feast fo Brahmans – as great a feast as he can – and give the clothes, ornaments, food and whatever would be dear t the dead. For whatever a Brahman eats, drinks or uses enjoyed by the dead. Thereafter, once a year, during th son's life, he must repeat this observance.

'All such ceremonies and many more the Brahman cal his "vested rights," made so by religious law. Whoev neglects them goes to eternal damnation. During the pe formance of each rite we must wash the Brahman's fe with water and then we must drink some of that water fro the palm of our hand. The Brahman is indolent, produc nothing, and takes to no calling but that of lawyer Government official. In this Province he numbers one and half million, and the rest of us, over forty-one millions, fee him.

'Now do you understand that, until we others are able hold our own in India, we prefer a distant King beyond th sea, who gives us peace, justice, something back for o money and a chance to become free men, to a million and half masters, here, who eat us up, yet say our very touc would pollute them?'

CHAPTER XI

LESS THAN MEN

HE conundrums of India have a way of answering themves, when one looks close.

Long and easily we have accepted the catch word 'mysteris India.' But 'mystery,' as far as matters concrete are conned, remains such only as long as one persists in seeking a ·sterious cause for the phenomena. Look for a practical ıse, as you would do in any bread-and-butter country not ·elled 'inscrutable,' and your mystery vanishes in smoke.

'Why, after so many years of British rule, do we remain per cent. illiterate?' reiterates the Hindu politician, im·ing that the blame must be laid at the ruler's door.

But in naming his figure, he does not call to your attenn a fact which, left to yourself, you would be slow to ess: he does not tell you that of the 247,000,000 inhabiıts of British India, about 25 per cent. – 60,000,000 – ve from time immemorial been specially condemned to teracy, even to sub-humanity, by their brother Indians. rely, if there be a mystery in India, it lies here – it lies in Hindu's ability anywhere, under any circumstances, to use any man, any society, any nation, of 'race prejudice,' long as he can be reminded of the existence in India of 000,000 fellow Indians to whom he violently denies the nmon rights of man.[1]

Indian politicians have for some time been directing a loud and conous fire upon the British Home Government for not finding means to ce the Government of the Union of South Africa into a complaisant ude towards British Indian immigrants in that country. It is worthy of

In the beginning, it is explained, when the light-skinne ancestors of the present Hindus first came to India, th found there a darker, thicker-featured native race, the Dra idians, builders of the great temples of the South. And t priests of the new-comers desired that the blood of the people be not mixed with the native stock, but be kept one strain. So they declared Dravidians to be unclea 'untouchable.'

Then the old lawmakers, gradually devising the cas system, placed themselves at the head thereof, under t title of 'earthly gods' – Brahmans. Next beneath them th put the Kshattryas, or fighting men; after the fighters, t Vaisyas, or cultivators, upon whom the two above look dow and finally, the fourth division, or Sudra caste, born solely be servants to the other three. Of these four divisions, the selves to-day much subdivided, was built the frame of Hin society. Outside and below all caste, in a limbo of sco earned by their sins of former existences, must for e grovel the Untouchables.

A quotation from the rule by which the unfortuna were nailed to their fate will suffice to show its natu the *Bhagavata*,[1] treating of the murder of a Brahm decrees:

note that of the original 130,000 British Indian immigrants to South Afr one-third were 'Untouchables,' mostly from Madras Presidency, wh condition in India is indicated in this chapter, and who would find th selves again in such status were they to return to Hindu India. The Bri Indians in South Africa in 1922 numbered, as shown in the official Y Book, a little over 161,000. This figure includes a later immigration 10,000 traders, and the natural increase of the combined body.

[1] Chief of the eighteen *Puranas*, sacred books of India. The transla here given is that of the Abbé Dubois, *Hindu Manners, Customs and C monies*, p. 558.

'Whoever is guilty of it will be condemned at his death to e the form of one of those insects which feed on filth. ng reborn long afterwards a Pariah [Untouchable], he l belong to this caste, and will be blind for more than four es as many years as there are hairs on the body of a cow. can, nevertheless, expiate his crime by feeding forty usand Brahmans.'

Thus, at one sweep, is explained the Untouchable's stence as such; are justified the indignities heaped upon 1; is emphasized his unspeakable degradation; and is eguarded the oppressor from the wrath of him oppressed. en as the Hindu husband, by the horrors imposed upon lowhood, is safeguarded from a maddened wife's revolt.

If a Brahman kills a Sudra,[1] it will suffice to efface the sin gether if he recites the *gayatri* [a prayer] a hundred times,' tinues the scripture, by opposites driving home its point.

Leaving the ancient roots of things, and coming down to year A.D. 1926, we find the orthodox Hindu rule as to touchables to be roughly this:

Regarded as if sub-human, the tasks held basest are erved for them; dishonour is associated with their name. ne are permitted to serve only as scavengers and removers night soil; some, through the ignorance to which they are demned, are loathsome in their habits; and to all of them privilege of any sort of teaching is sternly denied. They y neither possess nor read the Hindu scriptures. No hman priest will minister to them; and, except in rarest tances, they may not enter a Hindu temple to worship or y. Their children may not come to the public schools.

[1] A member of the fourth division, lowest Hindu caste, yet far above the ouchable.

They may not draw water from the public wells; and if tl habitation be in a region where water is scarce and sour far apart, this means, for them, not greater considerat from others, but greater suffering and greater toil.

They may not enter a court of justice; they may not en a dispensary to get help for their sick; they may stop at inn. In some provinces they may not even use the pul road, and as labourers or agriculturists they are continu: losers, in that they may not enter the shops or even p through the streets where shops are, but must trust to a h hazard chain of hungry go-betweens to buy or sell tl meagre wares. Some, in the abyss of their degradation, permitted no work at all. These may sell nothing, not e their own labour. They may only beg. And even for t purpose they dare not use the road, but must stand far unseen, and cry out for alms from those who pass. If al be given, it must be tossed on the ground, well away fr the road, and when the giver is out of sight and the ro empty, then, and not till then, the watcher may creep snatch, and run.

Some, if not all, pollute, beyond caste men's use, food upon which their shadow falls. Food, after such def ment, can only be destroyed.

Others, again exude 'distant pollution' as an effluvi from their unhappy bodies. If one of these presumes approach and linger by a high-road, he must measure distance to the high-road. If it be within two hundred yar he must carefully place on the road a green leaf weigh down with a handful of earth, thereby indicating that he, unclean, is within pollution distance of that point. T passing Brahman, seeing the signal, halts and shouts. T poor man forthwith takes to his heels, and only when ıs fled far enough calls back, 'I am now two hundred yards vay. Be pleased to pass.'

Still others – the Puliahs of the Malabar Coast – have :en forbidden to build themselves huts, and permitted to ›nstruct for houses nothing better than a sort of leaf vning on poles, or nests in the crotches of big trees. These .ay approach no other type of humanity. Dubois recorded ıat, in his day, a Nair (high-caste Hindu) meeting a Puliah the road, was entitled to stab the offender on the spot.[1] 'o-day the Nair would hesitate. But still, to-day, the Puliah .ay approach no caste man nearer than sixty or ninety feet.

Under such conditions of preordained misery, certain ›mmunities among the Untouchables have developed a ısiness in the practice of crime. These communities ›ecialize, one in pocket-picking, another in burglary, yet hers in forging, in highway robbery, in murder, etc., 'ten combining their special trade with prostitution as a :cond industry. Scattered all over India and known as the riminal Tribes, they number to-day about four and a ılf million persons.

Now it must not be forgotten that the matter of Un- uchability, like almost all other Hindu concerns, is woven, arp and woof, into the Hindu religion; and that the Hindus e a tremendously religiose people. To quote the words of ıat prominent Indian, Sir Surendranath Banerjea:[2]

'You cannot think of a social question affecting the Hindu ›mmunity that is not bound up with religious considera-

[1] *Hindu Manners, Customs and Ceremonies*, pp. 60–1. See also *Three yages of Vasco da Gama*, Gaspar Correa, Hakluyt Society, London, 1869, 155.

[2] *A Nation in Making*. London, Humphrey Milford, 1925, p. 396.

tions; and when divine sanction, in whatever form, is i voked in aid of a social institution, it sits enthroned in t popular heart with added firmness and fixity, having i roots in sentiment rather than in reason.'

And dire experience shows to what lengths of bloo drenched madness the people can be goaded by a whisp that their caste is threatened or that insult is offered to the gods. That this was from the beginning understood Government, is shown in an unequivocal clause in t Queen's Proclamation of December 2, 1858:

'We do strictly charge and enjoin all those who may be authority under us that they abstain from all interferen with the religious belief or worship of our subjects, on pa of our highest displeasure.'

Nevertheless the immediate impulse of the Briton India was to espouse the cause of the social victim. T Directors of the East India Company, as early as 185 recommended that 'no boy be refused admission to a Gover ment school or college on ground of caste,' and stuck to t principle until their authority was sunk in that of the Crow Thenceforward it was continually re-affirmed, yet push with a caution that might seem faint-hearted to one u familiar with the extreme delicacy of the ground. Little nothing was to be gained in any attempt to impose a forei idea, by force, on unready and non-understanding millio

Nor must the workings of caste be confused with sno bery. A man's caste is the outward sign of the history of soul. To break caste by infringing any one of the multitu inous caste laws brings down an eternal penalty. If, as Hindu, in obeying these laws, you inflict suffering up ıother, that is merely because his soul-history has placed m in the path of pain. You have no concern in the matter; either will he, thinking as a good Hindu, blame you. For oth you and he are working out your god-appointed destiny.

To-day almost all that can be accomplished by civil law r the Untouchable has been secured. Government have eely opened their way, as far as Government can determine, every educational advantage and to high offices. And overnment's various land-development and co-operative hemes, steadily increasing, have provided tremendous deeming agencies and avenues of escape.

But for Provincial Governments to pass legislation asserting the rights of every citizen to enjoy public facilities, such public schools, is one thing; to enforce that legislation er enormous countrysides and through multitudinous nall villages without the co-operation and against the will the people, is another. Witness that paragraph in the Iadras Government Order of March 17, 1919, reading:

'Children of Panchamas [Untouchables] are admitted ıly into 609 schools out of 8,157 in the Presidency, though the regulations state that no boy is to be refused lmission merely on the ground of caste.'

Yet, rightly read, the announcement proclaims a signal lvantage won. Six hundred and nine schools in a most thodox province admitting outcastes, as against only irteen times that number who refuse!

In the Bombay Legislative Council, one day in August, 926, they were discussing a resolution to coerce local ıards to permit Untouchables to send their children to hools, to draw water from public wells, and to enjoy other ımmon rights of citizenship. Most of the Hindu members approved in principle. 'But if the resolution is put ir effect we would be faced with a storm of opposition,' c murred one member, representative of many others. 'Ortl dox opinion is too strong, and while I sympathize with t resolution I think that . . . given effect, it may have dis trous effect.' [1] And he submits that the path of wisdom, f friends of the Untouchables, is not to ask for action, b instead, to content themselves with verbal expressions sympathy, such as his own.

A second Hindu member, with characteristic nimblene pitchforks the load toward shoulders broad enough to be it: [2]

'I think the British Government have followed a ve timid policy in this presidency. They have refused to ta part in any social legislation. Probably, being an ali Government, they were afraid that they would be accused tampering with the religion of the various communities. spite of the Proclamation of Queen Victoria about equali between the different classes and communities, Governme have not given practical effect to it.'

It remains, however, to a Muhammadan, Mr. No Mahomed, of Sind, to strike the practical note: [3]

'I think the day will not be distant when the people w are placed by the tyranny of the higher classes into the low grade of society . . . will find themselves driven to oth religious folds. There will then be no reason at all for t Hindu society to complain that Mahomedan or Christi missionaries are inducing members of depressed classes

[1] *Bombay Legislative Council Debates*, 1926. Vol. XVIII, Part IX, p. 7
[2] *Ibid.*, p. 728. [3] *Ibid.*, August 5, p. 721.

change the religion of their birth. . . . If the Hindu society refuses to allow other human beings, fellow creatures at that, to attend public schools, and if . . . the president of a local board representing so many lakhs [1] of people in this House refuses to allow his fellows and brothers the bare elementary human right of having water to drink, what right have they to ask for more rights from the bureaucracy? . . . Before we accuse people coming from other lands, we should see how we ourselves behave toward our own people. . . . How can [we] ask for greater political rights when [we ourselves] deny elementary rights of human beings?'

Regulations may prevail to bring the outcaste to the school door, but his courage may not suffice to get him across the threshold, for his self-assertion was done to death centuries ago. So that his admission to the school will mean, at best, permission to sit on the veranda and pick up from that distance whatever he can by his unaided ears.

Says the Village Education Commission: [2]

'Speaking generally, it is still the case that the caste man not only does nothing for the enlightenment of the outcaste, but puts positive obstacles in his way, knowing that if he is enlightened he can no longer be exploited. Outcastes who have the temerity to send their children to school – even if the school be in their quarter, so that there can be no complaint of defiling caste children by contact – find themselves subject to such violence and threatening that they yield and withdraw their children. If the outcastes want not only education but Christian teaching, the persecution, for a time, is

[1] A lakh is one hundred thousand.

[2] *Village Education in India*. London, Oxford University Press, 1922, p. 21.

all the fiercer, for the caste people are afraid that if the out castes become Christians they will no longer be available fo menial service.'

An exceedingly small percentage of the outcastes are ye in school, but he of their number who pursues education pas all the dragons that bar the door is likely to be one of the bes of his kind. And, in spite of his immemorial history of de gradation, the seed of the power to rise is not dead withi him. The Namasudras of Bengal, an Untouchable clas there numbering about 1,997,500, have, under the encour agement of the new light, made a vigorous, steady, an successful fight for self-elevation, and have organized to sup port schools of their own. By the last report they had i Bengal over 49,000 children under tuition, of whom 1,02 had reached the High School and 144 the Arts Colleges,[1] where, because of caste feeling, Government has been oblige to set aside special hostels for their lodging. This com munity is rapidly raising its status.

In the Punjab, where Government irrigation work i destroying many ancient miseries, appears evidence of weakening of the ban that bars the outcaste from the com mon schools; although some of the Punjab municipalitie have displayed a genius in tricking these most needy of thei citizens out of the privileges of education.[2] Bombay's educa tional reports also indicate a significant advance in the per centage of Untouchables receiving tuition, largely unde mission auspices. And the net results point to some interest ing surmises.

[1] *Progress of Education in Bengal*, Sixth Quinquennial Review, p. 83.

[2] Cf. *Report on the Progress of Education in the Punjab*, 1924–25. Lahore, 1926, p. 71.

Thus, the 'depressed classes' have begun holding annual conferences of delegates to air their wrongs and to advance their rights. Their special representatives, now appointed to legislatures and to local bodies, grow more and more assertive. Their economic situation, under Government's steady effort, is, in some communities, looking up. With it their sense of manhood is developing in the shape of resentment of the degradation to which until now they have bowed. Among them a few men of power and parts are beginning to stand out.

Finally, their women, as Christian converts, furnish the main body of Indian teachers for the girls of India of all castes, and of trained nurses for the hospitals; both callings despised and rejected by the superior castes, both necessitating education, and both carrying the possibility of increasing influence.

The first time that I, personally, approached a realizing sense of what the doctrine of Untouchability means, in terms of man's inhumanity to man, was during a visit to a child-welfare centre in a northerly Indian city.

The place was crowded with Indian women who had brought their babies to be examined by the English professional in charge, a trained public-health nurse. Toward her their attitude was that of children toward a wise and loving mother – confiding, affectionate, trusting. And their needs were inclusive. All morning I had been watching babies washed and weighed and examined, simple remedies handed out, questions answered, advice and friendly cautions given, encouragement and praise. Just now I happened to be looking at a matronly high-caste woman with an intelligent, clean-cut face. She was loaded with heavy gold and silver jewelry and wore a silken mantle. She sat down on the floor to show her baby, unrolling him from the torn fragment of an old quilt, his only garment. This revealed his whole little body caked in a mass of dry and half-dry excreta.

'She appears unconcerned,' I remarked to the Sister. The Sister replied:

'We try to get such women to have napkins for their babies, but they won't buy them, they won't wash them themselves, and they won't pay washers to wash them although they are quite able to do so. This woman is well born. Her husband is well educated – a technical man – and enjoys a good salary. Sometime it may please her to hang that bit of quilt out in the sun in her court-yard, and when it is dry, to brush off what will come off. That's all. This, incidentally, helps to explain why infantile diarrhœa spreads through the families in a district. They will make no attempt whatever to keep things clean.'

As the Sister spoke, a figure appeared before the open doorway – a young woman so graceful and with a face so sweet and appealing as to rivet attention at once. She carried an ailing baby on her arm, but came no farther – just stood still beyond the doorway, wistfully smiling. The Sister, looking up, smiled back.

'Why does she not come in?' I asked.

'She dare not. If she did, all these others would go. She is an Untouchable – an outcaste. She herself would feel it wicked to set foot upon that sill.'

'She looks at least as decent as they,' I remarked.

'Untouchables may be as intelligent as anyone else – and you see for yourself that they couldn't be dirtier,' said the Sister. 'But such is the custom of India. Since we can't alter it, we just plod on, trying to help them all, as best we can.'

And so the gentle suppliant waited outside, among

rowd of others of her kind, till Sister could go to them, ringing to this one ointment for baby's eyes, to that one a iixture for baby's cough, and hearing the story of another.

But they might not bring their little ones in, to the mercy f the warm bath, as the other women were doing at will. 'hey might not come to the sewing class. They might not efile the scales by laying their babies in its basket, to see 'hat the milk-dole was doing. For they were all horrible nners in æons past, deserving now neither help nor sympathy while they worked out their curse.

CHAPTER XII

BEHOLD, A LIGHT

MUCH is said of the inferiority of character that has result from the Untouchables' long degradation. But evidence the survival of virtues, through all the crushing of the ce turies, is by no means lacking. The Mahars, for exampl outcastes used by caste villagers as are the Palers of Madra practically as slaves [1] and for the basest tasks, are now en ployed by Government as couriers. In that capacity they a said to be entirely trustworthy, transporting hundreds rupees without abstracting the smallest coin. The Dhed Untouchables from whom, in the Bombay region, mo Britons' servants are drawn, and whom few high-cas Indians would tolerate near their persons, are, as a rul honest, sober, and faithful.

As to the rating of converts to Christianity – there a now about 5,000,000 of them – opinions differ; but in an case the fact stands that these converts are set free, as far they can grasp freedom, from caste bonds. The faces of th Hindus are fixed against them, to be sure. But of the co verts of the third generation many persons are found to sa that they are the hope of India.

So much, thus far, Britain, greatly aided by the Christia Missions, has accomplished for the outcaste, by patient, u hill work, teaching, persuading, encouraging, on either si

[1] *Joint Select Committee on the Government of India Bill*, 1919, Vol. *Minutes of Evidence*, p. 188, Rai Bahadur, K. V. Reddi, 'They are t slaves of the Nation.'

the social gulf. And the last few years have seen the rise new portents in the sky.

One of these is the tendency, in the National Social Conrence and in Hindu political conventions, to declare penly against the oppression of the outcaste. But these clarations, though eloquent, have as yet borne little fruit her than words. A second phenomenon is the appearance Indian volunteer associations partially pledged against ntouchability. These include the Servants of India,[1] owedly political; Lord Sinha's society for the help of the itcastes of Bengal and Assam; the Brahmo Samaj, and hers. Their work, useful where it touches, is sporadic, and finitesimal compared to the need, but notable in comparin with the nothingness that went before.

For no such conception is native to India. 'All our Indian ocial work of to-day,' the most distinguished of the Brahmo amaj leaders said to me, 'is frankly an imitation of the nglish and an outgrowth of their influence in the land.' gain and again I heard the gist of that statement from the ps of thoughtful Indians, in frank acknowledgment of the ource of the budding change.

'The curse of Untouchability prevails to this day in all arts of India,' said Sir Narayan Chandravarkar,[2] adding, with the liberalizing forces of the British Government, the roblem is leaping into full light. Thanks to that Government, it has become . . . an all-India problem.'

Mr. Gandhi has been less ready to acknowledge benecent influence from such a source – has, in fact, described

[1] *A Brief Account of the Work of the Servants of India Society*, Aryaushan Press, Poona, 1924, pp. 60–1.

[2] Hindu reformer, Judge of the High Court of Bombay, quoted in *India 1920*, p. 155.

the whole administrative system in India as 'vile beyor description.' But for the last five years his own warfare c Untouchability has not flagged, even though his one u faltering co-worker therein has been the British Goveri ment, aided pre-eminently by the Salvation Army. In i course he reprinted from the Indian vernacular Press learned Brahman pundit's recent statement on the subjec including this passage:[1]

'Untouchability is a necessity for man's growth.

'Man has magnetic powers about him. This *sakti*[2] is lil milk. It will be damaged by improper contacts. If one ca keep musk and onion together, one may mix Brahmans ar Untouchables.

'It should be enough that Untouchables are not denie the privileges of the other world.'

Says Mr. Gandhi, in comment on the pundit's creed:

'If it was possible to deny them the privileges of the oth world, it is highly likely that the defenders of the monst would isolate them even in the other world.'

'Among living Indians,' says Professor Rushbroc Williams,[4] 'Mr. Gandhi has done most to impress upon h fellow countrymen the necessity for elevating the depresse classes. . . . When he was at the height of his reputatio the more orthodox sections of opinion did not dare to cha lenge his schemes.'

But to-day the defenders of Untouchability are myria

[1] *Young India*, July 29, 1926, p. 268. Mr. Gandhi's phrase quoted a fe lines above will be found in *Gandhi's Letters on Indian Affairs*, Madra V. Narayanah & Co., p. 121.

[2] Energy, or the power of the Supreme personified.

[3] *Young India*, July 29, 1926.

[4] *India in 1924–25*, p. 26

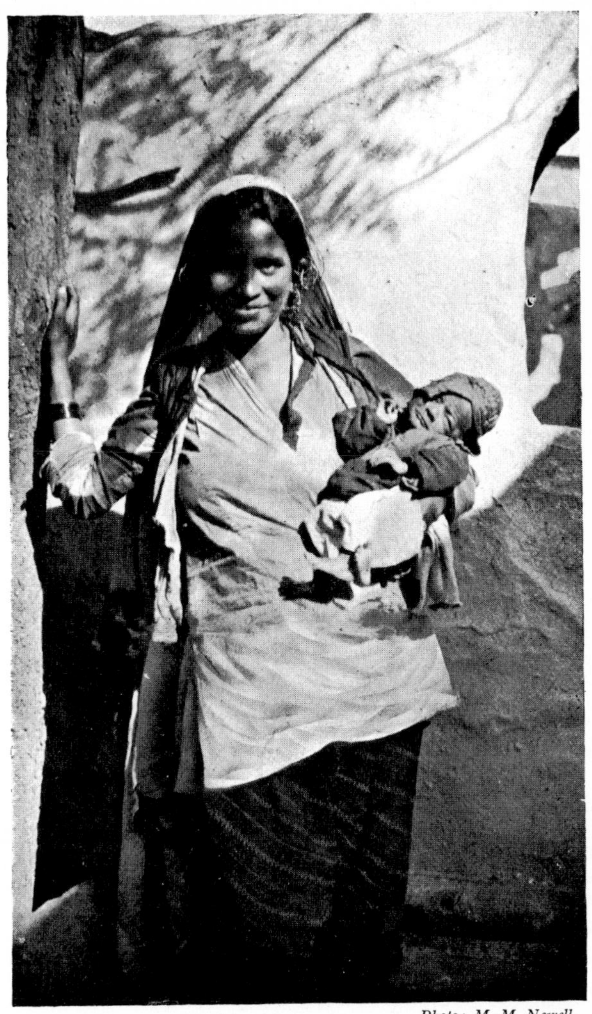

Photo: M. M. Newell.

THE UNTOUCHABLE

l, though Mr. Gandhi lives his faith, but few of his supters have at any time cared to follow him so far.

On January 5, 1925, a mass meeting of Hindus was held Bombay to protest against Mr. Gandhi's 'heresy' in ıcking Untouchability. The presiding officer, Mr. Manahandas Bamji, explained that Untouchability rests on a ne with the segregation of persons afflicted with conious diseases. Later he interpreted the speaker who ntedly suggested lynching for 'heretics' who 'threaten the ruption of Hindu society,' to mean only that Hindus are epared to sacrifice their lives for the Hindu religion in er to preserve its ancient purity.' The meeting closed r appointing a committee specially to undermine Mr. ndhi's propaganda.

And it is fair to say that the discussions of Untouchlity evoked by successive introductions of the subject in great Hindu conventions show mainly by the heat of the tem's defenders that ground has been won.

'You saw,' said Mr. Gandhi, 'the squabble that arose over in the Hindu *Mahasabha*.[1] But Untouchability is going, spite of all opposition, and going fast. It has degraded lian humanity. The "Untouchables" are treated as if less n beasts. Their very shadow defiles in the name of God. m as strong or stronger in denouncing Untouchability as m in denouncing British methods imposed on India. ntouchability for me is more insufferable than British rule. Hinduism hugs Untouchability, then Hinduism is dead l gone.'[2]

A hot and disorderly demonstration directed against those who would x the pains of the Untouchables had persisted in the session of this great ndu Convention of 1926.

Verbal statement to the author. Revised by Mr. Gandhi.

Meantime another and a curious development has co to the Untouchables' aid. With the rapid Indianization Government services, with the rapid concessions in Ind autonomy that have characterized British administrat since the World War, an intense jealousy has arisen betw the Hindu three-quarters and the Muhammadan fourth the population. This subject will be treated elsewhe Here it will suffice merely to name it as the reason why Untouchables, simply because of numbers, have sudde become an object of solicitude to the Hindu world. T. W. Holderness, writing in 1920, put the point thus

'The "depressed classes" in India form a vast multitu . . . A question that is agitating Hinduism at the pres moment is as to whether these classes should be counted Hindus or not. Ten years ago the answer would have b emphatically in the negative. Even now the conservat feeling of the country is for their exclusion. But the c science of the more advanced section of the educated Hin is a little sensitive on the point. It is awkward to be minded by rival Muhammadan politicians that more t one-third of the supposed total Hindu population is accepted by Hindus as a part of themselves, is not allov the ministration of Brahman priests, is excluded fr Hindu shrines. It is obviously desirable, in presence of s an argument, to claim the "depressed castes" as within pale of Hinduism. But if they are to be so reckoned, lo demands that they should be treated with greater conside tion than at present. Educated Hindus see this, and uplifting of these castes figures prominently on the p

[1] *Peoples and Problems of India*, Revised Edition. London, Williams Norgate, 1920, pp. 101–2.

nmes of Indian social conferences. But the stoutest-rted reformer admits to himself that the difficulties in the · of effective action in this matter are great, so strong is hold that caste has on the Indian mind.'

Βut here a fresh element comes in – another disturbing t of the intrusion of the West – a likelihood that, stimu-d by the strange new foreign sympathy, the Untouchable y not much longer leave his religious status to be deter-ıed at the leisure and pleasure of the Hindu caste man. m, utterly democratic, will readily receive him into full tnership in the fold. Christianity not only invites him, will educate and help him. The moment he accepts ıer Islam or Christianity, he is rid of his shame. The stion, then, is chiefly a question of how long it takes a n, ages oppressed, to summon courage, spirit, and energy stand up and shake off the dust.

In the autumn of 1917, the then Secretary of State for India, . E. S. Montagu, chief advocate of the speedy Indianiza-ı of the Government, sat in Delhi receiving deputations m such elements of the Indian peoples as were moved to lress him on that subject. All sorts and conditions of men peared, all sorts of documentary petitions were submitted, sorts of angles and interests. Among these, not meanly resented, loomed an element new on the Indian political ge – the Untouchables, awake and assertive, in many ganized groups entreating the Secretary's attention.

Without one divergent voice they deprecated the thought Home Rule for India. To quote them at length would be petition. Their tenor may be sufficiently gathered from excerpts:

The Panchama Kalvi Abivirthi-Abimana Sanga, a

Madras Presidency outcastes' association,[1] 'deprec
political change and desires only to be saved from
Brahman, whose motive in seeking a greater share in
Government is . . . that of the cobra seeking the charg
a young frog.'

The Madras Adi Dravida Jana Sabha, organized to rep
sent 6,000,000 Dravidian aborigines of Madras Presiden
said:[2]

'The caste system of the Hindus stigmatizes us as
touchables. . . . Caste Hindus could not, however, get
without our assistance. We supplied labour and they
joyed the fruit, giving us a mere pittance in return. (
improvement in the social and economic scale began w
and is due to the British Government. The Britishers
India – Government officers, merchants, and last, but
least, Christian missionaries – love us, and we love them
return. Though the general condition of the communit
still very low, there are some educated men amongst
But these are not allowed to rise in society on account of
general stigma attached by the Hindus to the commun
The very names by which these people refer to us brea
contempt.

'We need not say that we are strongly opposed to Ho
Rule. We shall fight to the last drop of our blood
attempt to transfer the seat of authority in this country fr
British hands to so-called high caste Hindus who have
treated us in the past and would do so again but for the p
tection of British laws. Even as it is, our claims, nay,

[1] *Addresses Presented in India to His Excellency the Viceroy and the R Honourable the Secretary of State for India.* London, 1918, p. 87.

[2] *Ibid.*, pp. 60–1.

ry existence, is ignored by the Hindus; and how will they omote our interests if the control of the administration sses into their hands?'

'We love them,' said these spokesmen of the outcaste – d the expression strikes home with a certain shock. But e is forced to remember that the sorrows of these particu- under-dogs have never before, in all their dim centuries history, elicited from any creature a thought or a helping nd. Here is a tale, as told to me, to show that even the gradation of ages cannot kill that in a man which lifts up s heart to his friend.

It concerns a command of Madrassi Sappers – coal-black ravidians from around Bangalore – Untouchables all, or most all. And it happened in the World War, at the king of Kut.

'The river,' said the witness, 'is about 300 yards wide at at point and swift. Our job was to cross in pontoons in the m first grey of the morning, hoping to surprise the Turk. he duty of the sappers was to take the boats up the night fore, under cover of darkness, and to make them ready; en to stand back while the combatant troops rowed them-lves across.

'The sappers did their job. But just as the moment came embark our men, the Turk waked up and opened fire. Our rprise was a washout. But we carried on, all the same.

'Now, the troops could lie flat in the bottom of the boats, it their rowers must sit on the thwarts and pull – 300 yards, antwise, in point-blank rifle range. Why, they hadn't a iance!

'What happened? What but those little Madrassis, push-g forward, all eagerness, begging: "Sahibs, you want rifles over there. *Rifles*, Sahibs, *rifles*! We are only sappers. I *us* row!"

'So the troops, rushing down, sprang into the boats a stretched flat. And the sappers jumped into the thwarts a pulled. And then – the Turk's machine-guns!

'When the boats came back, out of seventy rowers scarc a man was left unhurt and many were dead. But those lit sapper fellows ashore, they swarmed down, hove their de out on the bank, jumped into their places, and, as each b filled with men, shoved off into their comrades' fate. Tha how the rifles got over to Kut. And those were coal-bla Dravidians, mind you – "Untouchables," unless they h turned Christian – which a fair lot of them had.'

When the Prince of Wales sailed to India, late in 192 Mr. Gandhi, then at the height of his popularity, proclaim to the Hindu world that the coming visit was 'an ins added to injury,' and called for a general boycott.[1]

Political workers obediently snatched up the torch, rus ing it through their organizations, and the Prince's landi in Bombay became thereby the signal for murderous riot a destruction. No outbreak occurred among the responsit part of the population, nor along the line of progress, whi was, of course, well guarded. But in the remoter areas of t city, hooliganism ran on for several days, with some killings and 400 woundings, Indian attacking Indian, whi arson and loot played their ruinous part.

Meanwhile the Prince, seemingly unmoved by the fi unfriendly reception of all his life, proceeded to carry out h officially arranged programme in and about the city. C the evening of November 22 it was scheduled that he shou depart for the North.

[1] *Gandhi's Letters on Indian Affairs*, pp. 96–7.

ʌs he left Government House on the three- or four-mile ve to the Bombay railway station, his automobile ran unırded save for the pilot police car that went before. When entered the city, however, a cordon of police lined the eets on both sides. And behind that cordon pressed the ple – the common poor people of the countryside in their countable thousands; pressed and pushed until, with the way station yet half a mile away, the police line bent and ke beneath the strain.

Instantly the crowd surged in, closing around the car, uting, fighting each other to work nearer – nearer still. hat would they do? What was their temper? God knew! ndhi's hot words had spread among them, and God alone, v, could help. Some reached the running-boards and ng. Others shoved them off, for one instant to take their ces, the next themselves to be dragged away. And what s this they shouted? At first nothing could be made of it, the bedlam of voices, though those charged with the safety the progress strained their ears to catch the cries.

Then words stood out, continuously chanted, and the rds were these:

'*Yuvaraj Maharaj ki jai!*' 'Hail to the Prince!' And: et me see my Prince! Let me see my Prince! Let me ly see my Prince just once before I die!'

The police tried vainly to form again around the car. oving at a crawl, quite unprotected now, through an nost solid mass of shouting humanity, it won through to railway station at last.

There, within the barriers that shut off the platform of the yal train, gathered the dignitaries of the Province and the ty, to make their formal farewells. To these His Royal ighness listened, returning due acknowledgments. Then, clipping short his own last word, he turned suddenly to aide beside him.

'How much time left?'

'Three minutes, sir,' replied the aide.

'Then drop those barriers and let the people in' – indi ing the mobs outside.

'Our hearts jumped into our mouths,' said the men v told me the tale, 'but the barriers, of course, went dov

Like the sweep of a river in flood the interminable mu tudes rolled in – and shouted and adored and laughed a wept, and, when the train started, ran alongside the rc carriage till they could run no more.

After which one or two super-responsible officials w straight home to bed.

So the Prince of Wales moved northward. And as moved much of his wholesome influence was lost, throu the active hostility of the Indian political leader.

But if Gandhi's exhortations travelled, so did the new the Prince's aspect – travelled far and fast, as such things amongst primitive peoples.

And when he turned back from his transit of the Gr North Gate – the Khyber Pass itself – a strange th awaited him. A swarm of Untouchables, emboldened news that had reached them, clustered at the roadside to him reverence.

'Government *ki jai*!' 'Hail to the Government!' th shouted, with cheers that echoed from the barren hills.

And when the Prince slowed down his car to return th greetings, they leapt and danced in their excitement.

For nowhere in all their store of memory or of legend h they any history of an Indian magnate who had noticed Untouchable except to scorn him. And here was a grea ıan all India contained – the son of the Supreme Power, to ıem almost divine, who deigned not only to receive but ·en to thank them for their homage! Small wonder that ıeir spirits soared, that their eyes saw visions, that their ›ngues laid hold upon mystic words.

'Look! Look!' they cried to one another. 'Behold, the ight! the Light!'

And such was their exaltation that many of them someow worked through to Delhi to add themselves to the 5,000 of their kind who there awaited the Prince's coming. 'he village people from round about flocked in to join them the simple people of the soil who know nothing of politics ut much of friendship as shown in works. And all together aunted the roadside, waiting and hoping for a glimpse of is face.

At last he came, down the Grand Trunk Road, toward he Delhi Gate. And in the centre of the hosts of the Jntouchables, one, standing higher than the rest, unfurled flag.

'*Yuvaraj Maharaj ki jai! Raja ke Bete ki jai!*' 'Hail to he Prince! Hail to the King's Son!' they all shouted ogether, to burst their throats. And the Prince, while the ıigh-caste Indian spectators wondered and revolted within hemselves at his lack of princely pride, ordered his car o be stopped.

Then a spokesman ventured forward, to offer in a humble ittle speech the love and fealty of the 60,000,000 of the Jnclean and to beg the heir to the throne to intercede for hem with his father the King Emperor, never to abandon hem into the hands of those who despised them and would ceep them slaves.

The Prince heard him through. Then – whether he

realized the magnitude of what he did, or whether he acte merely on the impulse of his natural friendly courte toward all the world – he did an unheard-of thing. H stood up – stood up, for them, the 'worse than dogs,' spok a few words of kindness, looked them all over, slowly, an so, with a radiant smile, gave them his salute.

No sun that had risen in India had witnessed such a sigh As the car started on, moving slowly, not to crush then they went almost mad. And again their eastern tongue clothed their thought. 'Brother – that word was truth tha our brothers brought us. Behold, the Light is there indeed The Light – the Glory – on his face!'

CHAPTER XIII

GIVE ME OFFICE OR GIVE ME DEATH

ᴇᴅᴜᴄᴀᴛɪᴏɴ, some Indian politicians affirm, should be driven ıto the Indian masses by compulsory measures. 'England,' ıey say, 'introduced compulsory education at home long ʒo. Why does she not do so here? Because, clearly, it suits ɛr purpose to leave the people ignorant.'

To this I took down a hot reply from the lips of the aja of Panagal, then anti-Brahman leader of Madras residency.

'Rubbish!' he exclaimed. 'What did the Brahmans do for ur education in the 5,000 years before Britain came? I ɛmind you: They asserted their right to pour hot lead into ıe ears of the low-caste man who should dare to study ooks. All learning belonged to them, they said. When the Iuhammadans swarmed in and took us, even that was an nprovement on the old Hindu regime. But only in Britain's ay did education become the right of all, with state schools, ɔlleges, and universities accessible to all castes, communi-es, and peoples.'

'[The Brahmans] saw well enough,' says Dubois,[1] 'what moral ascendancy knowledge would give them over the ther castes, and they therefore made a mystery of it by ıking all possible precautions to prevent other classes from btaining access to it.'

But the Brahmans, whatever their intellectual achieve-ıent in earliest times, rested quiescent upon these laurels

[1] *Hindu Manners, Customs and Ceremonies*, p. 376.

through the succeeding centuries. They were content, whi denying light to the remainder of their world, to abid themselves, in the ever-fading wisdom of the ever-dimm past. Says the Abbé Dubois again, writing in the beginnin of the nineteenth century:[1]

'I do not believe that the Brahmans of modern times ar in any degree, more learned than their ancestors of the tim of Lycurgus and Pythagoras. During this long space c time many barbarous races have emerged from the darkne of ignorance, have attained the summit of civilization, an have extended their intellectual researches . . . yet all th time the Hindus have been perfectly stationary. We do n find amongst them any trace of mental or moral improv ment, any sign of advance in the arts and sciences. Ever impartial observer must, indeed, admit that they are no very far behind the peoples who inscribed their names lon after them on the roll of civilized nations.'

This was written some half-century before the Britis Crown assumed the government of India.

During that fifty years a new educational movemer sprang up in the land. The design of Warren Hastings an later of the East India Company, impelled by the Britis Parliament, had been to advance Indian culture, as such toward a native fruition. It remained for a private citize one David Hare, an English merchant domiciled in Indi to start the wheels turning the opposite way.

David Hare, no missionary, but an agnostic, was a ma with a conviction. Under its impulse he gave himself an his all to 'the education and moral improvement of th natives of Bengal.' Parallel to him worked the famou

[1] *Hindu Manners, Customs and Ceremonies*, pp. 376–7.

ndu, Raja Ram Mohan Roy, a solitary soul fired to action the status of his own people in the intellectual and social-ical world. And these two, one in purpose, at length ned to create a secular Hindu College, whose object they nounced as 'the tuition of the sons of respectable Hindus the English and Indian languages, and in the literature d science of Europe and Asia.'

The project, however, only roused the wrath and distrust the orthodox Hindu. This was in 1817.

A year later three Baptist missionaries, Carey, Marshman d Ward, founded a still-extant school near Calcutta. In 20 the Anglican Church opened a college. In 1830 exander Duff, again with the help of Ram Mohan Roy, tituted a fourth college for the giving of western science India. A network of primitive vernacular schools at that ne existed throughout Bengal, but it was Raja Ram ohan Roy himself who continuously urged upon the itish authorities the necessity, if 'the improvement the native population' were contemplated, of doing ay with the old code and system, of teaching western ences, and of conducting such teachings in the English nguage.[1]

While these influences were still combating the earlier itude of the British with its basic tenet that Indian educa-n should run along Indian lines, came a new force into the ld – one Thomas Babington Macaulay, to be Chairman a Committee of Public Instruction. Lord Macaulay clared, and with tremendous vigour, on the side of the stern school. In the name of honour and of humanity the ll light of western science must, he felt, be given to the

[1] *A Biographical Sketch of David Hare*. Peary Chand Mittra. Calcutta, 77. Raja Ram Mohan Roy's Letter to Lord Amherst.

Indian world. And he demanded,[1] with fervour, to know what right, when

'. . . we can patronize sound philosophy and true history, shall countenance, at the public expense, medical doctrir which would disgrace an English farrier, – astronomy, wh would move laughter in girls at an English boarding scho – history, abounding with kings thirty feet high, and rei thirty thousand years long, – and geography, made up seas of treacle and seas of butter? . . . What we spend the Arabic and Sanskrit colleges is not merely a dead loss the cause of truth; it is bounty money paid to raise champions of error.'

This new advocate, welcomed with acclaim by a modernist Hindus facing the condemnation of their co munity, finally cast the expenditures of public educatio monies from oriental into western channels. Departme of Public Instruction were now set up in each province practical steps taken to stimulate private effort in the est lishment of schools and colleges.

All this was done with a definitely stated object – to g into the hands of the peoples the key to health and pr perity and social advance, and to rouse them to 'the devel ment of the vast resources of their country, . . . and gra ally, but certainly, confer upon them all the advanta which accompany the healthy increase of wealth and co merce.'[2]

It should not, however, be understood either that Gove ment now discouraged oriental learning as such or tha excluded the vernacular. On the contrary, it insisted on

[1] *Minute on Education*. T. B. Macaulay, Feb. 2, 1835.

[2] Despatch of Sir Charles Wood, 1854.

pper teaching of the vernacular in all schools, looking forrd to the day when that vehicle should achieve a developnt sufficient to convey the ideas of modern science.[1] eantime, it chose to teach in English rather than in either the two classic Indian languages, for the reasons that any e of the three would have to be learned as a new language all save the most exceptional students, and that the cessary books did not exist in either Eastern tongue.

Centres of teaching now gradually multiplied. In the rty years following 1857, five universities were estabhed – in Calcutta, Bombay, Madras, Lahore, and Allabad. Aside from literacy courses, instruction in practical, n-literary branches was urged upon the attention of all nded to learn.

But the difficulty then as now was that commerce, scienti- agriculture, forestry, engineering, teaching, none of these enues for service smiled to Indian ambition. India as a tional entity was ever an unknown concept to the Indian. d thoughts for the country at large holds little or no part native ethical equipment.

This last-named fact, damaging as it is from our viewint, should be thoughtfully taken as a fact and not as an cusation. It is the logical fruit of the honestly held ctrines of fate and transmigration and of the consequent ocentric attitude.

For present purposes, the history of modern India's ucational progress may be passed over, to reach statistics to-day.

In 1923–4 thirteen universities of British India put forth total of 11,222 graduates. Of these, 7,822 took their

[1] See *Calcutta University Commission Report*, Vol. I, Chapter III; and Vol. Chapter XVIII; also *The Educational Despatch of 1854*.

degrees in arts and sciences, 2,046 in law, 446 in medicir 140 in engineering, 546 in education, 136 in commerce, a: 86 in agriculture. At the same time, the universities show an enrolment of 68,530 undergraduates, not dissimilar apportioned.[1] The high figures consistently stand oppos the arts and law courses, while such vital subjects as agric ture, hygiene and sanitation, surgery, obstetrics, veterina science and commerce, under whatever ægis offered, s attract few disciples.

For example, the agricultural school maintained by t American Presbyterian Mission near Allahabad, althou equipped to receive 200 scholars, had in 1926 only 50 m in residence.

'We don't care to be coolies,' the majority say, turni away in disgust when they find that the study of agricult demands familiarity with soil and crops.

'If,' says the director, 'we could guarantee our graduate Government office, we should be crowded.'

One hears of few technical schools, anywhere in Ind that are pressed for room.

The representative Indian desires a university Arts gree, yet not for learning's sake,[2] but solely as a means public office. To attain this vantage-ground he will gri cruelly hard, driven by the whip and spur of his own and family's ambition, and will often finally wreck the poor lit body that he and his forebears have already so merciles maltreated.

Previous chapters have indicated the nature of this m

[1] *Statistical Abstract for British India*, 1914–15 to 1923–24, p. 27

[2] *Cf.* Mr. Thyagarajaiyer (Indian), Census Superintendent of Mys *Census of India*, Vol. I, p. 182: 'The pursuit of letters purely as a means intellectual growth is mostly a figment of the theorists.'

tment. One of its consequences is to be seen in the
ден mental drooping and failure – the 'fading,' as it has
ɩe to be called, that so frequently develops in the brilliant
ian student shortly after his university years.

Meantime, if, when he stands panting and exhausted,
ree in hand, his chosen reward is not forthcoming, the
le family's disappointment is bitter, their sense of injury
injustice great.

Then it is that the young man's poverty of alternatives
ds most in his light and in that of Mother India. A
rich in opportunities for usefulness pleads for the ser-
of his brain and his hands, but tradition and 'pride' make
blind, deaf and callous to the call.

s Sir Gooroo Dass Banerjee mildly states it:[1]

The caste system . . . has created in the higher castes a
udice against agricultural, technological, and even com-
cial pursuits.'

The university graduate in these latter days may not be a
ı-caste man. But if he is not, all the more is he hungry to
me high-caste customs, since education's dearest prize
s promise of increased *izzat* – prestige. Whatever their
h, men disappointed of office are therefore apt flatly to
se to turn their energies in other directions where their
rior knowledge and training would make them in-
ely useful to their less favoured brothers. Rather than
employment which they consider below their newly
ired dignity, they will sponge for ever, idle and un-
med, on the family to which they belong.

am a Bachelor of Arts,' said a typical youth simply;
ave not been able to secure a suitable post since my

[1] *Calcutta University Commission Report*, Vol. III, p. 161.

graduation two years ago, so my brother is supporting r He, having no B.A., can afford to work for one-third wages that my position compels me to expect.'

Nor had the speaker the faintest suspicion that he mi be presenting himself in an unflattering light. Even attempt to capture a degree is held to confer distinction. man may and does write after his name, 'B.A. Plucked' 'B.A. Failed,' without exciting the mirth of his public.[1]

A second case among those that came to my perso attention was that of a young university graduate, appointed of Government employment, who petitioned American business man for relief.

'Why do you fellows always persist in pushing in wh you're not needed, and then being affronted and outra because there's no room?' asked the American, with Am can bluntness. 'How can you possibly all be Governm clerks? Why on earth don't any of you ever go home to y villages, teach school, or farm, or do sanitation and give poor old home town a lift, out of what you've got? Coul you make a living there all right, while you did a jot work?'

'Doubtless,' replied the Indian patiently. 'But you for That is beneath my dignity now. I am a B.A. Theref if you will not help me, I shall commit suicide.'

And he did.

Lord Macaulay, over ninety years ago, observed the s phenomenon in the attitude of the Indian educated Government expense. Regarding a petition presented to

[1] The terms are actually used in common parlance as if in themsel title, like M.A. or Ph.D. – as: 'The school . . . is now under an enthus B.A. plucked teacher.' *Fifteenth Annual Report of the Society for the Imp ment of the Backward Classes. Bengal and Assam.* Calcutta, 1925, p. 1

ımittee by a body of ex-students of the Sanskrit College, ;ays:[1]

Γhe petitioners stated that they had studied in the college or twelve years; that they had made themselves ɹainted with Hindu literature and science; that they received certificates of proficiency; and what is the fruit ll this! . . . "We have but little prospect of bettering condition . . . the indifference with which we are generlooked upon by our countrymen leaving no hope of ɔuragement and assistance from them." They therefore that they may be recommended . . . for places under Government, not places of high dignity or emolument, such as may just enable them to exist. "We want ns," they say, "for a decent living, and for our progresimprovement, which, however, we cannot obtain ıout the assistance of Government, by whom we have ı educated and maintained from childhood." They can:e by representing, very pathetically, that they are sure it was never the intention of Government, after behavso liberally to them during their education, to abandon n to destitution and neglect.'

'he petition amounts to a demand for redress brought nst a Government that has inflicted upon them the injury liberal education. 'And,' comments Macaulay:

doubt not that they are in the right . . . [for] surely we ht, with advantage, have saved the cost of making these ons useless and miserable; surely, men may be brought o be burdens to the public . . . at a somewhat smaller ·ge to the State.'

[1] *Minute on Education*, Feb. 2, 1835.

Sanskrit scholars of a century ago or B.A.'s of to-c whether plucked or feathered, the principle remains same, though the spirit has mounted from mild compl to bitterness.

All over India, among politicians and intelligent Government is hotly assailed for its failure to provide offi for the yearly output of university graduates. With ranc and seeming conviction, Indian gentlemen of the higl political leadership hurl charges from this ground.

'Government,' they repeat, 'sustains the univers Government is responsible for its existence. What doe mean by accepting our fees for educating us and then giving us the only thing we want education for? Cursed the Government! Come, let us drive it out and make pla for ourselves and our friends.'

Nor is there anywhere that saving humour of pu opinion whose Homeric laugh would greet the Ameri lad, just out of Yale or Harvard or Leland Stanford, w should present his shining sheepskin as a draft on Treasury Department, and who should tragically refuse form of work save anti-government agitation if the d were not promptly cashed.

CHAPTER XIV
WE BOTH MEANT WELL

TWEEN the years 1918 and 1920, compulsory education
's for primary grades were, indeed, enacted in the seven
jor provinces of India. This was largely the effect of an
lian political opinion which saw, in principle, at least, the
:d of a literate electorate in a future democracy.

The laws, however, although operative in some few locali-
s, are permissive in character and have since remained
gely inactive[1] – a result partly due to the fact that the
iod of their passage was the period of the 'Reforms.'
yarchy' came in, with its increased Indianization of
vernment. Education itself, as a function of Government,
ame a 'transferred subject' passing into the hands of
lian provincial ministers responsible to elected legislative
incils. The responsibility, and with it the unpopularity
be incurred by enforcement of unpopular measures, had
v changed sides. The Indian ministers, the Indian muni-
al boards, found it less easy to shoulder the burden than
ad been to blame their predecessors in burden-bearing.
elected officer, anywhere, wanted either to sponsor the
ning up of budgets or to dragoon the children of a resent-
public into schools undesired.

For example: 'The Bengal Legislature . . . passed an Act introducing the
iciple of compulsory primary education in May, 1919; but it does not
ear that a single local authority in the province has availed itself of the
on for which the Act provides.' 'Primary Education in Bengal,' London
ies, Educational Supplement, Nov. 13, 1926, p. 484.

A recent official report prepared by Mr. Govindbhai H. Desai, Naib

Compulsory education, moreover, should mean f education. To build schools and to employ teachers enou to care for all the children in the land without cha would mean money galore – which must be taxed out the people.

In one province – the Punjab – the Hindu element in Legislature tried to meet one aspect of the crux by saddli the compelling act with a by-law exempting from sch attendance all 'Untouchables,' otherwise known as ' pressed classes.' This idea, pleasant as it was for the él withered in the hands of unsympathetic British author As with the Maharajas,[1] so at the other end of the so scale, it would sanction no class monopoly of public edu tion.

Thus Government spoke. But negative weapons, e India's most effective arms, remained unblunted. How Punjab cities used them is revealed as follows:[2]

'The percentage of boys of compulsory age at school risen with the introduction of compulsion in Multan fr 27 to 54 and in Lahore from 50 to 62. Since no provis has been made at either place for the education of the c dren belonging to the depressed classes and no proceedi have yet been taken against any defaulting parent, it is probable that a much higher percentage of attendance ca expected in the near future.'

Dewan of Baroda, by order of the reigning Prince, shows that alth that State has had compulsory education for twenty years, its proportic literacy is less than that of the adjoining British districts where educ began much earlier than in Baroda, but where compulsion scarcely ex

[1] See *ante*, p. 143.

[2] *Progress of Education in India.* Eighth Quinquennial Review, V p. 108.

owing that there are more ways than one to keep the under g in his kennel!

In all British India, the total number of primary schools, ether for boys or girls was, by latest official report,[1] 8,013. Their pupils numbered approximately 7,000,000. t there are in British India about thirty-six and a half llion children of primary school age,[2] 90 per cent. of om are scattered in groups averaging in school attendance children each.[3] The education of these children presents the difficulties that beset education of difficult folk in other ficult countries, plus many that are peculiar to India alone, ile offsetting advantages are mainly conspicuous by their sence.[4]

We of America have prided ourselves upon our own ucational efforts for the Philippines, and in India that formance is frequently cited with wistful respect. rallels of comparison may therefore be of interest.

We recall that in the Philippines our educational work been seriously burdened by the fact that the islanders ak eighty-seven dialects[5] and have no common tongue. ainst this, set the 222 vernaculars spoken in India,[6] with common tongue.

In the Philippines again, no alphabet or script aside from own is used by the natives. In India 50 different scripts employed, having anywhere from 200 to 500 characters

Statistical Abstract for British India, 1914–15 to 1923–24, pl. 263
Ibid., p. 24.
Progress of Education in India, 1917–22. Vol. II, p. 119.
Cf. *Village Education in India*, pp. 176–7.
Population of the Philippine Islands in 1916. H. Otley Beyer. Manila, 7, pp. 19–20.
Census of India, 1921. Vol. I, Part I, p. 193.

each; and these are so diverse as to perplex or defeat unde standing between dialects.

In the Philippines and in India alike, little or no curre literature exists available or of interest to the masses, whi in both countries many dialects have no literature at a In the Philippines and in India alike, therefore, lack of hon use of the shallow-rooted knowledge gained in the scho produces much loss of literacy – much wastage of cost ar effort.

In the Philippines, no social bars exist – no caste distin tions except the distinction between *cacique* and *tao* – ri man and poor man – exploiter and exploited. In India som thing like 3,000 castes [1] split into mutually repellent grou the Hindu three-quarters of the population.

In the Philippines, whatever may be said of the quality the native teachers especially as instructors in English, the good-will suffices to carry them, both men and women, fro the training schools into little and remote villages and to ke them there, for two or three years at least, delving on the job. In India, on the contrary, no educated man wants serve in the villages. The villages, therefore, are starved f teachers.

In the Philippines the native population hungers ar thirsts after education and is ready to go all lengths acquire it, while rich Filipinos often give handsomely o of their private means to secure schools for their own loca ties. In India, on the contrary, the attitude of the mass toward education for boys is apathy. Toward education f girls it is nearer antagonism, with a general unwillingne on the part of masses and classes alike to pay any education cost.

[1] *Oxford History of India,* p. 37

The British Administration in India has without doubt ıade serious mistakes in its educational policies. As to the ature of these mistakes, much may be learned by reading ıe Monroe Survey Board's report [1] on education in the 'hilippine Islands. The policies most frequently decried as ritish errors in India are the very policies that we ourselves, ıd for identical reasons, adopted and pursued in our ttempt to educate our Filipino charges. Nothing is easier ıan to criticize from results backward, though even from ıat vantage-point conclusions vary.

Queen Victoria, in 1858, on the assumption by the Crown f the direct Government of India, proclaimed the royal will ıat: [2]

'So far as may be, our subjects, of whatever race or creed, e freely and impartially admitted to office in our service, ıe duties of which they may be qualified by their education, bility, and integrity duly to discharge.'

Similarly President McKinley, in his instructions to the Ion. William H. Taft, as President of the first Philippines 'ommission, laid down that: [3]

'The natives of the islands . . . shall be afforded the pportunity to manage their own local affairs to the fullest xtent of which they are capable, and . . . which a careful udy of their capacities and observation of the workings of ative control show to be consistent with the maintenance of w, order, and loyalty.'

[1] *A Survey of the Educational System of the Philippines*. Manila, Bureau of inting, 1925.

[2] Foreshadowed in Lord Hardinge's Resolution of 1844.

[3] Letter from the Secretary of War, Washington, April 7, 1900.

On both congeries of peoples the effect of these pro nouncements was identical. Their small existing intell gentsia, ardently desiring office, desired, therefore, that typ of education which prepares for office-holding.

Britain, as we have seen, began with another idea – th of developing Indian education on native lines. But unde Indian pressure she soon abandoned her first policy;[1] th more readily because, counting without the Indian' egocentric mentality, she believed that by educating th minds and pushing forward the men already most cultivate she would induce a process of 'infiltration,' whereb through sympathetic native channels, learning converte into suitable forms would rapidly seep down through th masses.

America, on her side, fell at once to training Filipin youths to assume those duties that President McKinley ha indicated. At the same time, we poured into the empt minds of our young Asiatics the history and literature c our own people, forgetting, in our ingenuous altruism, th confusion that must result.

Oblivious of the thousand years of laborious natior building that linked Patrick Henry to the Witenagemo drunk with the new vocabulary whose rhythm and thunde they loved to roll upon their nimble tongues, but whos contents they had no key to guess, America's new charge at one wild leap cleared the ages and perched trium phant at Patrick Henry's side: 'Give us liberty or giv us death!'

'Self-government is not a thing than can be "given" t any people. . . . No people can be "given" the self-contro

[1] *The Heart of Aryavarta*. The Earl of Ronaldshay. London, 192 Chapters II and III.

of maturity,' said President Wilson,[1] commenting on the situation so evoked. But such language found no lodgment in brains without background of racial experience. For words are built of the life-history of peoples.

And between the Filipino who had no history, and the Hindu, whose creative historic period, as we shall see, is effectively as unrelated to him as the period of Pericles is unrelated to the modern New York Greek, there was little to choose, in point of power to grasp the spirit of democracy.

Schools and universities, in the Philippines and in India, have continued to pour the phrases of western political-social history into Asiatic minds. Asiatic memories have caught and held the phrases, supplying strange meanings from their alien inheritance. The result in each case has been identical. 'All the teaching we have received . . . has made us clerks or platform orators,' said Mr. Gandhi.[2]

But Mr. Gandhi's view sweeps further still:[3]

'The ordinary meaning of education is a knowledge of letters. To teach boys reading, writing and arithmetic is called primary education. A peasant earns his bread honestly. He has ordinary knowledge of the world. He knows fairly well how he should behave towards his parents, his wife, his children and his fellow villagers. He understands and observes the rules of morality. But he cannot write his own name. What do you propose to do by giving him a knowledge of letters? Will you add an inch to his happiness? . . .

[1] *Constitutional Government in the United States.* Woodrow Wilson. New York, 1908, pp. 52–3.

[2] Statement to the author. Ahmedabad, March, 1926.

[3] *Indian Home Rule.* M. K. Gandhi. Ganesh & Co., Madras, 1924, pp. 97–8, 100, 113.

'It now follows that it is not necessary to make this education compulsory. Our ancient school system is enough. . . We consider your [modern] schools to be useless.'

On such views as this, the Swarajist leader, Lala Lajpa Rai, makes caustic comment:[1]

'There are some good people in India who do, now an then, talk of the desirability of their country leading a retired, isolated, and self-contained life. They pine for goo old days and wish them to come back. They sell book which contain this kind of nonsense. They write poems an songs full of soft sentimentality. I do not know whethe they are idiots or traitors. I must warn my countrymen mo solemnly and earnestly to beware of them and of that kin of literature. . . . The country must be brought up to th level of the most modern countries . . . in thought and life

But whose shoulder is being put to the wheel in th enormous task of bringing 92 per cent. of the populac of British India – 222,000,000 Indian villagers – 'up to th level of the most modern countries,' even in the one deta of literacy? Who is going to do the heavy a-b-c work c creating an Indian electorate on whose intelligence the wor of a responsible government can be based?

A little while ago a certain American Mission Boar being well replenished in means from home and about t embark on a new period of work, convened a number c such Indian gentlemen as were strongest in citizenship an asked their advice as to future efforts. The Indian gentlemen, having consulted together, proposed that all highe

[1] *The Problem of National Education in India.* George Allen and Unwi London, 1920, pp. 79–80.

lucation (which is city work), and also the administration ' all funds, be at once turned over to them, the Indians.

'Does that, then, mean that you see no more use for mericans in India?'

'By no means! You Americans, of course, will look after ıe villages.'

'To you, perhaps, it sounds dubious,' said a British Civil ervant of thirty years' experience, to whom I submitted my oubts, 'but we who have spent our lives in the work know ıat the answer is this: We must just plod along, giving the eople more and yet more education, as fast as we can get ıem to take it, until education becomes too general to rogate to itself, as it does to-day, a distinction by rights ue only to ability and character.'

CHAPTER XV

'WHY IS LIGHT DENIED?'

THE illiteracy of India is sometimes attributed to h
poverty – a theory as elusive as the famous priority disp
between the hen and the egg. But Indian political criti
are wont to charge the high illiteracy rate to the inefficienc
even to the deliberate purpose, of the sovereign pow
Thus, Lala Lajpat Rai, the Swaraj political leader, refers
the Viceregal Government as having 'so far refused ev
elementary instruction in the three R's to our masses.
And Mr. Mahomed Ali Jinnah [2] accusingly asks, 'Why
light denied?'

But, before subscribing to the views of either of the
legislative leaders, before accepting either India's poverty
Britain's greed as determining the people's darkness, it m
be well to remember the two points recently examined, a
to record a third.

First, of British India's population of 247,000,000 pe
sons about 50 per cent. are women. The people of Indi
as has been shown, have steadfastly opposed the educati
of women. And the combined efforts of the British Gover

[1] *The Problem of National Education in India*, p. 67. In 1923–
India's total expenditure of public funds on education, including municip
local, Provincial and Central Government contributions, reached 19·9 cro
of rupees, or £13,820,000. This sum is much too small for the work to
done. Nevertheless, when taken in relation to the total revenue of Brit
India, it compares not unfavourably with the educational allotments
other countries. See *India in 1924–25*, p. 278; and *Statistical Abstract*
British India, p. 262.

[2] Leader of the Nationalist party in the Legislature of 1925–26.

ent, the few other-minded Indians, and the Christian issions, have thus far succeeded in conferring literacy on less than 2 per cent. of the womenkind. Performing e arithmetical calculation herein suggested, one arrives at approximate figure of 121,000,000, representing British dia's illiterate women.

Secondly, reckoned in with the population of British dia [1] are sixty million human beings called 'Untouchles.' To the education of this element the great Hindu ajority has ever been and still is strongly, actively and fectively opposed. Subtracting from the Untouchables' tal their female half, as having already been dealt with in e comprehensive figure, and assuming, in the absence of thoritative figures, 5 per cent. of literacy among its males, e arrive at another 28,500,000, representing another lot Indians condemned to illiteracy by direct action of the ajority will.

Now, neither with the inhibition of the women nor with e inhibition of the Untouchables has poverty anything hatever to do. As to the action of Government, it has disayed from the first, both as to women and as to outcastes, steadfast effort in behalf of the inhibited against the dictum their own people.

Expressed in figures, the fact becomes clearer:

Illiterate female population of British India	121,000,000
Illiterate male Untouchables	28,500,000
	149,500,000
Total population of British India	247,000,000

[1] *Census of India*, 1921. Vol. I, Part I, p. 225.

Percentage of the population of British India kept illiterate by the deliberate will of the orthodox Hindu	60.53 per cent.

Apart from these two factors appears, however, a thi of significance as great, to appreciate whose weight one mu keep in mind that the total population of British India is 9 per cent. rural – village folk.

As long, therefore, as the villages remain untaught, th all-India percentage of literacy, no matter what else hap pens, must continue practically where it is to-day – huggin the world's low-record line.

But to give primary education to one-eighth of the huma race, scattered over an area of 1,094,300 square miles, i 500,000 little villages, obviously demands an army teachers.

Now, consider the problem of recruiting that army whe no native women are available for the job. For the villag school ma'am, in the India of to-day, does not and cann exist.

Consider the effect on our own task of educating th children of rural America, from Canada to the Gulf, fro the Atlantic to California, if we were totally debarred fro the aid of our legions of women and girls.

No occidental country has ever faced the attempt educate its masses under this back-breaking conditio The richest nation in the world would stand aghast at th thought.

As for the reason why India's women cannot teach India children, that may be re-stated in few words. Indian wome of child-bearing age cannot safely venture, without speci protection, within reach of Indian men.

t would thus appear clear that if Indian self-government e established to-morrow, and if wealth to-morrow rushed succeeding poverty in the land, India, unless she reversed own views as to her 'Untouchables' and as to her women, st still continue in the front line of the earth's illiterates.

As to the statement just made concerning women's un-ilability as teachers in village schools, I have taken it vn, just as it stands, in the United Provinces, over the njab, in Bengal and Bombay Presidencies, and across dras, from the lips of Hindu and Muhammadan officials l educators, from Christian Indian educators and clergy, m American and other Mission heads, and from re-nsible British administrators, educational, medical, and ice. So far as I know, it is nowhere on official record, nor it been made the subject of important mention in the islatures. It is one of those things that, to an Indian, natural matter of course. And the white man administer- India has deliberately adopted the policy of keeping nce on such points – of avoiding surface irritations, ile he delves at the roots of the job.

I should not have thought of telling you about it,' said an lian gentleman of high position, a strong nationalist, a -long social reformer. 'It is so apparent to us that we e it no thought. Our attitude toward women does not mit a woman of character and of marriageable age to ve the protection of her family. Those who have ven-ed to go out to the villages to teach – and they are usually ristians – lead a hard life, until or unless they submit to incessant importunities of their male superiors; and their ole career, success and comfort are determined by the nner in which they receive such importunities. The same uld apply to women nurses. An appeal to departmental chiefs, since those also are now Indians, would, as a ru merely transfer the seat of trouble. The fact is, we India do not credit the possibility of free and honest women. ' us it is against nature. The two terms cancel each othe

The Calcutta University Commission, made up, as will recalled, of British, Muhammadan, and Hindu professio men, the latter distinguished representatives of their resp tive communities, expressed the point as follows:[1]

'The fact has to be faced that until Bengali men genera learn the rudiments of respect and chivalry toward wom who are not living in *zenanas*, anything like a service women teachers will be impossible.'

If the localizing adjective 'Bengali' were withdrawn, Commission's statement would, it seems, as fairly apply all India. Mason Olcott[2] is referring to the whole fi when he says:

'On account of social obstacles and dangers, it is pra cally impossible for women to teach in the villages, unl they are accompanied by their husbands.'

Treating of the 'almost desperate condition' of m education in rural parts, for lack of women teachers, the Director of Public Instruction of the Central Provin says:[3]

'The general conditions of *mofussil* [rural] life and Indian attitude toward professional unmarried women such that life for such as are available is usually intolerab

[1] *Calcutta University Report*, Vol. II, Part I, p. 9.

[2] *Village Schools in India*, p. 196.

[3] *The Education of India*. Arthur Mayhew. London, Faber and Gw 1926, p. 268.

No Indian girl can go alone to teach in rural districts. he does, she is ruined,' the head of a large American ssion college in northern India affirmed. The speaker was idely experienced woman of the world, characterized by matter-of-fact a freedom from ignorance as from pre-ice. 'It is disheartening to know,' she went on, 'that not of the young women that you see running about this ıpas, between classroom and classroom, can be used on great job of educating India. Not one will go out into villages to answer the abysmal need of the country. Not dare risk what awaits her there, for it is no risk, but a tainty. And yet these people cry out to be given *self-*ernment.'[1]

Unless women teachers in the *mofussil* are provided with tected residences, and enabled to have elderly and near tives living with them, it is more than useless, it is almost el, to encourage women to become teachers,' concludes Calcutta University Commission after its prolonged vey.[2]

And the authors of an inquiry covering British India, of whom is the Indian head of the Y.M.C.A., Mr. nakarayan T. Paul, report:[3]

'The social difficulties which so militate against an ade-ate supply of women teachers are well known, and are mensely serious for the welfare of the country. All the mary school work in the villages is pre-eminently men's work, and yet the social conditions are such that no gle woman can undertake it. . . . The lack of women

Statement to the author, February, 1926.

Calcutta University Report, Vol. II, Part I, p. 9.

Village Education in India, the Report of a Commission of Inquiry. Oxford iversity Press, 1922, p. 98.

teachers seems to be all but insuperable, except as the res of a great social change.'

That a social stigma should attach to the woman wl under such circumstances, chooses to become a teacher, perhaps inevitable. One long and closely familiar w Indian conditions writes:[1]

'It is said that there is a feeling that the calling cannot pursued by modest women. *Prima facie*, it is difficult to s how such a feeling could arise, but the Indian argument support it would take, probably, some such form as th "The life's object of woman is marriage; if she is married l household duties prevent her teaching. If she teaches, s can have no household duties or else she neglects them. she has no household duties she must be unmarried, and t only unmarried women are no better than they should b If she neglects her household duties, she is . . . no bet than she should be."'

This argument might seem to leave room for the deplo ment of a rescue contingent drafted from India's 26,800,o widows, calling them out of their dismal cloister and ir happy constructive work. The possibility of such a move indeed, discussed; some efforts are afoot in that directio

[1] *Census of India*. E. A. H. Blunt, C.I.E., O.B.E., I.C.S. 1911, Vol. X pp. 260–1.

[2] *Census of India*, 1911, Vol. XV, p. 229. 'It is safe to say that after age of seventeen or eighteen no females are unmarried who are not prostitu or persons suffering from some bodily affliction such as leprosy or blindn the number of genuine spinsters over twenty is exceedingly small and an maid is the rarest of phenomena.' These age figures are set high in order include the Muhammadan women and the small Christian and Brah Samaj element, all of whom marry later than the Hindu majority.

d a certain number of widows have been trained. Their efulness, however, is almost prohibitively handicapped, in e great school-shy orthodox field, by the deep-seated re- ;ious conviction that bad luck and the evil eye are the dow's birthright. But, as writes an authority already ıoted:[1]

'A far more serious objection is the difficulty . . . to safe- ıard these ladies who take up work outside the family rcle. Their employment without offence or lapse seems ›ssible only in mission settlements and schools under close ıd careful supervision. In a general campaign [widows] n play only an insignificant part.'

In other words, the young widow school-teacher would eet in the villages the same temptations from within, the me pressure, exaction of complaisance, and obloquy from ithout, that await the single girl.

Thus is reached the almost complete ban which to-day ·ands teaching as socially degrading, and which, as an ıdian writer puts it,[2] condemns women to be economi- lly dependent upon men, and makes it impossible for em to engage in any profession other than that of a house- ife.'

The rule has, however, its exceptions. In the year 1922, ıt of British India's 123,500,000 women, 4,391 were udying in teachers' training schools. But of that 4,391, :arly half – 2,050 – came from the Indian Christian com- unity,[3] although this body forms but 1·5 per cent. of the

[1] *The Education of India* Arthur Mayhew, p. 268.

[2] *Reconstructing India.* Sir M. Visvesvaraya. London, P. S. King and ns, 1920, p. 243.

[3] *Progress of Education in India*, 1917–22. Vol. II, pp. 14–15.

total population. And exceedingly few of the few who a trained serve their country's greatest need.

Says a professional educator:[1]

'It is notoriously difficult to induce Indian women of goo position, other than Christians and Brahmos, to underg training for the teaching profession; and even of those wh are trained . . . the majority refuse to go to places when th are wanted.'

Now it chanced, in my own case, that I had seen a goo deal of Indian village life before opportunity arose to visit th women's training schools. When that opportunity came, met it, therefore, with rural conditions fresh in mind ar with a strong sense of the overwhelming importance of rur needs in any scheme for serving the body politic.

'What are you training for?' I asked the students.

'To be teachers,' they generally replied.

'Will you teach in the villages?'

'Oh, no!' as though the question were curiously un intelligent.

'Then who is to teach the village children?'

'Oh – Government must see to that.'

'And can Government teach without teachers?'

'We cannot tell. Government should arrange.'

They apparently felt neither duty nor impulse urgin them to go out among their people. Such sentiments, in deed, would have no history in their mental inheritance whereas the human instinct of self-protection would sub consciously bar the notion of an independent life from crossing their field of thought.

It would seem, then, taking the several elements of th

[1] *Quinquennial Review of Education in Eastern Assam and Bengal.*

se into consideration, that utterances such as Mr. Jinnah's ɩd Lala Lajpat Rai's[1] must be classified, at best, as relating the twig-tips, rather than to the root and trunk, of their eadly upas tree.'

Coming now to the villager himself – the cultivator or the *ot*, as he is called – one finds him in general but slightly ncerned with the village school. Whenever his boy can be eful to him – to watch the cattle, to do odd jobs – he un- sitatingly pulls him out of class, whereby is produced a mplete uncertainty in the matter of attendance. Often the *ot* is too poor to keep his little family alive without the help the children's labour and of such wages as they can earn. ckness, too, plays a large part in keeping school-going own – hookworm, malaria, congenital weakness. Or, often, e village astrologer, always a final authority, discovers in e child's horoscope periods inauspicious for school-going. nd in any case, the Indian farmer, like the typical farmer all countries, is sceptically inclined toward innovations. is fathers knew nothing of letters. He knows nothing of tters himself.[2] Therefore who is to tell him that letters are ood? Will letters make the boy a better bargainer? A etter hand at the plough?

'The school curriculum is not sufficiently practical,' say any of the British who work to better it. 'Show the *ryot* that s boy will be worth more on the land after a good schooling, d he will find means somehow to send the boy to school.' nd such a writer as the Hindu Sir M. Visvesvaraya does ot hesitate to accuse Government of deliberately making

[1] See *ante*, p. 184.

[2] Adult education, in connection with Government's rural co-operative edit movement, is now doing signal work among the peasant farmers of the injab.

economic education unattractive in order to keep In[dia]
dependent.[1] The report of Mr. Kanakarayan T. Pau[l's]
committee, based upon its India-wide inspection, giv[es,]
however, different testimony, saying:[2]

'It is often assumed that the education given in the villa[ge]
school is despised because it is not practical enough. [In]
many cases, however, the parent's objection is just t[he]
opposite. He has no desire to have his son taught agric[ul]ture, partly because he thinks he knows far more about th[at]
than the teacher, but still more because his ambition is th[at]
his boy should be a teacher or a clerk. If he finds that su[ch]
a rise in the scale is improbable, his enthusiasm for educati[on]
vanishes. Of the mental and spiritual value of educati[on]
. . . he is ignorant.'

'*It is not change in the curriculum in this early stage*,' pursu[es]
the authority just quoted, 'that is going to affect the e[ffi]ciency of the school or the length of school attendance, *b[ut]
the ability and skill of the teaching staff*.'

[1] *Reconstructing India*, p. 258.

[2] *Village Education in India*, p. 20.

CHAPTER XVI

A COUNSEL OF PERFECTION

IT was one of the most eminent of living Indians who gave me this elucidation of the attitude of a respected Hindu nobleman toward his own 'home town.'

'Disease, dirt and ignorance are the characteristics of my country,' he said in his perfect English, sitting in his city-house library where his long rows of law-books stand marshalled along the walls. 'Take my own village, where for centuries the head of my family has been chief. When I, who am now head, left it seventeen years ago, it contained some 1,800 inhabitants. When I revisited it, which I did for the first time a few weeks since, I found that the population had dwindled to fewer than 600 persons. I was horrified.

'In the school were 70 or 80 boys apparently five or six years old. "Why are you teaching these little children such advanced subjects?" I asked.

' "But they are not as young as you think," the schoolteacher replied.

'They were stunted – that is all; stunted for lack of intelligent care, for lack of proper food, and from malaria, which, say what you like about mosquitoes, comes because people are hungry. Such children, such men and women, will be found all over western Bengal. They have no life, no energy.

'My question, therefore, is plain: *What have the British been doing in the last hundred years that my village should be like this?* It is true that they have turned the Punjab from a desert to a garden, that they have given food in abundanc to millions there. But what satisfaction is that to me whe they let my people sit in a corner and starve? The Britis say: "We had to establish peace and order before we coul take other matters up"; also, "this is a vast country, we hav to build bridges and roads and irrigation canals." But surely surely, they could have done more, and faster. And they le my people starve!'

Now this gentleman's village, whose decadence he s deplored, lies not over four hours by railroad from the city i which he lives. He is understood to be a man of large wealth and himself informed me that his law practice was highl lucrative, naming an income that would be envied by a eminent lawyer in New York. Yet he, the one great man o his village, had left that village without help, advice, leader ship, or even a friendly look-in, for seventeen years, thoug it lay but a comfortable afternoon's ride away from his home And when at last he visited it and found its decay, he coul see no one to blame but a Government that has 500,000 such villages to care for, and which can but work through huma hands and human intelligence.

Also, he entirely neglected to mention, in accounting fo the present depopulation of his birthplace, that a large in dustrial plant lately erected near it had drawn away a heavy percentage of the villagers by its opportunities of gain.

It would be a graceless requital of courtesy to name the gentleman just quoted. But perhaps I may without offence name another, Sirdar Mohammed Nawaz Khan, lord o twenty-six villages in Attock District, northern Punjab.

This young Muslim went for his early education to the College for Punjab Chiefs, at Lahore, and thence to the Royal Military College at Sandhurst, to earn a commission ı the Indian Army. During his stay in England, being from me to time a guest in English country houses, his attention 'as caught and fixed by the attitude of large English land-wners toward their tenants.

Coming as a living illustration of the novel principles of ındowners' duties laid down by the English head master of is college in Lahore, the thing struck root in his mind and oon possessed him. Dashing young soldier that he made, fter eighteen months' service with a Hussar regiment, opular with officers and men, he resigned his commission nd returned to his estates. 'For I see where my place is ow,' he said.

There he spends his time, riding from village to village, 'orking out better conditions, better farming methods, etter sanitation, anything that will improve the status of his eople. Twenty-seven years old and with an annual income f some four lakhs of rupees (say £25,000), he is an enthusıstic dynamo of citizenship, a living force for good, and ıe sworn ally of the equally enthusiastic and hard-working ;nglish Deputy Commissioner.

Curiously enough, he strongly objects to Government's ew policy of rapid Indianization of the public services, ıkes no interest in Swaraj politics, and less than none in riticism of Government's efforts to clean up, educate, and nrich the people. His whole time goes to vigorous co-peration with Government betterment schemes, and to igorous original effort.

If the good of the people is the object of government, then ıultiplication of the type of Sirdar Mohammed Nawaz Khan, rather than of the talkers, would produce the strongest rgument for more rapid transfer of responsibility into ndian hands.

Meantime, of those who remain in the little towns an hamlets, 'the upper classes and castes,' says Olcott,[1] 'ar often not only indifferent to the education of the less for tunate villagers, but are actively opposed to it, since it i likely to interfere with the unquestioning obedience an service that has been offered by the lowest castes through th ages.'

'There is in rural India very little public opinion in favou of the education of the common folk,' says the Commissio of Inquiry, and 'the wealthy landowner or even the well-to-d farmer has by no means discovered yet that it is to hi interest to educate the agricultural labourer.'[2]

The village school-teacher is in general some dreary in competent, be he old or young – a heavy wet-blanket sloppe down upon a helpless mass of little limp arms and legs an empty, born-tired child noddles. Consequently anythin duller than the usual Indian village school this world wil hardly produce. Fish-eyed listlessness sits upon its brow and its veins run flat with boredom.

But I, personally, could find nothing to justify the belie that melancholy as distinct from the view-point produced b the Hindu religion, is a necessary inborn trait of the Indian The roots of joy certainly live within young and old. A smile, I found, brings forth a ready smile, a joke, a laugh, a object of novelty evokes interest from all ages, in any villag gathering; and serious philosophical consideration crowne with ripe speech awaits new thoughts. The villagers ar dignified, interesting, enlisting people, commanding affec tion and regard and well worthy the service that for the las sixty-odd years they have enjoyed – good men's best effort

[1] *Village Schools in India*, p. 93.

[2] *Village Education in India*, p. 26.

ithout their active and intelligent partnership, no native ›vernment better than an oligarchy can ever exist in India. But it is only to the Briton that the Indian villager of ·day can look for steady, sympathetic and practical interest d steady, reliable help in his multitudinous necessities. It the British Deputy Commissioner, none other, who is s father and his mother,' and upon the mind of that :puty Commissioner the villagers' troubles and the lagers' interests sit day and night.

In my own experience, it was an outstanding fact that in ery one of the scores of villages I visited, from one end of dia to the other, I got from the people a friendly, confiding, ppy reception. King George and the young god Krishna, ›king down from the walls of many a mud cottage, seemed link the sources of benefit. All attempts to explain myself an American proving futile, since a white face meant only ngland to them, an 'American' nothing at all – I let it go that, accepting the welcome that the work of generations d prepared.

Yet there are so few Britons in India – fewer than 200,000 unting every head, man, woman and child – and there are ›0,000 British Indian villages!

'Would not your educated and brilliant young men of dia,' I once asked Mr. Gandhi, 'be doing better service to dia, if, instead of fighting for political advantage, social ace and, in general, the limelight, they were to efface emselves, go to the villages, and give their lives to the ople?'

'Ah, yes,' Mr. Gandhi replied, 'but that is a counsel of rfection.'

To four interesting young Indian political leaders in lcutta, men well considered in the city, I put the same question: 'Would not you and all like you best serve yo beloved Mother India by the sacrifice to her of your pe sonal and political ambitions – by losing yourselves in yo villages, to work there for the people, just as so many Britis both men and women, are doing to-day? In twenty yea time, might not your accomplishment be so great that tho political powers you now vainly and angrily demand wou fall into your hands simply because you had proved you selves their fit custodians?'

'Perhaps,' said the three. 'But talk, also, is work. Talk now the only work. Nothing else can be done till we pu the alien out of India.'

'If I were running this country, I'd close every universi to-morrow,' said the chief executive of a great Americ business concern, himself an American long resident India, deeply and sympathetically interested in the India 'It was a crime to teach them to be clerks, lawyers an politicians till they'd been taught to raise food.'

'After twenty-odd years of experience in India,' said a American educator at the head of a large college, 'I hav come to the conclusion that the whole system here is wron These people should have had two generations of prima schools all over the land, before ever they saw a gramm school; two generations of grammar schools before th creation of the first high school; and certainly not before th seventh or eighth generation should a single Indian unive sity have opened its doors.'

Part Four: Mr. Gandhi

SMALL stone house, such as would pass unremarked in · small town in America. A wicket gate, a sun-baked den, a bare and clean room flooded with light from a ad-side of windows. In the room, sitting on a floor hion with his back to a blank wall, a man. To his right younger men, near a slant-topped desk perhaps eighteen hes high. To his left, a backless wooden bench for the of western visitors. If there are other objects in the m, one does not see them for interest in the man with his k to the wall.

His head is close-shaven, and such hair as he has is turn- grey. His eyes, small and dark, have a look of weariness, ost of renunciation, as of one who, having vainly striven, v withdraws from striving, unconvinced. Yet from time time, as he talks, his eyes flash. His ears are large and spicuously protruding. His costume, being merely a cloth, exposes his hairy body, his thin, wiry arms, and bare, thin, interlaced legs, upon which he sits like Buddha h the soles of his feet turned up. His hands are busy h a little wooden spinning-wheel planted on the ground ore him. The right hand twirls the wheel while the left lves a cotton thread.

"What is my message to America?" ' he repeated, in light, dispassionate, even voice. 'My message to America he hum of this spinning-wheel.'

Then he speaks at length, slowly, with pauses. And as speaks the two young men, his secretaries, lying over ir slant-topped desk, write down every word he says. The wheel hums steadily on. And the thread it spins for ıerica appears and reappears in the pages of this book,

CHAPTER XVII

THE SIN OF THE SALVATION ARMY

'Why, after so many years of British rule, is India s so poor?' the Indian agitator tirelessly repeats.

If he could but take his eyes from the far horizon a direct them to things under his feet, he would find answer on every side, crying aloud for honest thought a labour.

For example, the cattle question, by itself alone, mi determine India's poverty.

India is being eaten up by its own cattle. And even at t the cattle are starving.

The Live-Stock Census taken over British India 1919–20 showed a total of 146,055,859 head of bov cattle. Of these, 50 per cent., at a flattering estimate, reckoned unprofitable. Because of their uneconomic va the food they consume, little as it is, is estimated to rep sent an annual loss to the country of £117,600,000, or o four times more than the total land revenue of Brit India.[1]

The early Hindu leaders, it is surmised, seeing importance of the cow to the country, adopted the expedi of deifying her, to save her from and for the people. Acco ingly, Hindu India to-day venerates the cow as holy. In Legislative Assembly of 1921, a learned Hindu mem

[1] See *Proceedings of Board of Agriculture of India, at Bangalore*, Jan. 1924, and following days. Also see *Round Table*, No. 59, June, 1925.

'ased the point in a way that, probably, no Hindu would pute:[1]

'Call it prejudice, call it passion, call it the height of re-on, but this is an undoubted fact, that in the Hindu mind hing is so deep-rooted as the sanctity of the cow.'

To kill a cow is one of the worst of sins – is to be a deicide. s Highness the late Maharaja Scindia of Gwalior once l the misfortune to commit that sin. He was driving a loco-tive engine on the opening run over a railway that he had t built. The cow leaped upon the track. The engine ran down before the horrified Prince could forestall his fate. hink,' he told a friend, years after, 'that I shall never sh paying for that disaster, in penances and purifications, l in gifts to the Brahmans.'

Prince or peasant, the cow is his holy mother. She should present when he dies, that he may hold her tail as he athes his last. Were it only for this reason, she is often ot inside the house, to be in readiness. When the late haraja of Kashmir was close upon his end, the appointed , it is said, refused all inducements to mount to his mber; wherefore it became necessary to carry the Prince he cow, and with a swiftness that considered the comfort his soul only.

Also, the five substances of the cow – milk, clarified ter (*ghee*), curds, dung, and urine, duly set in a row in little pots, petitioned in prayer for forgiveness and assoil-nt and then mixed together and swallowed, surpass in

Legislative Assembly Debates, 1921. Rai Bahadur Pandit J. L. Bhargava, I, Part I, p. 530. See also *Commentaries of the Great Afonso Dalbo-ue*, translation of Walter de Gray. London, Hakluyt Society, 1877. II, p. 78.

potency all other means of purifying soul and body. T combination, known as *panchagavia*, is of grace sufficien wipe out even the guilt of sin intentionally committed. S the Abbé Dubois:[1]

'Urine is looked upon as the most efficacious for purify any kind of uncleanness. I have often seen . . . Hindus lowing the cows to pasture, waiting for the moment w they could collect the precious liquid in vessels of brass, carrying it away while still warm to their houses. I have seen them waiting to catch it in the hollow of their har drinking some of it and rubbing their faces and heads w the rest. Rubbing it in this way is supposed to wash away external uncleanness, and drinking it, to cleanse all inter impurity.'

Very holy men, adds the Abbé, drink it daily. And ort dox India, in these fundamentals, has changed not a w since the Abbé's time.

We of the West may reflect at our leisure that to t eventual expedient are we driving our orthodox Hir acquaintances when, whether in India or in America, cow-eaters insist on taking them in greeting by the ha One orthodox Prince, at least, observes the precaution, wl going into European society, always to wear gloves. Bu is told of him that, at a certain London dinner party, wl he had removed his gloves, the lady beside him chan to observe a ring that he wore.

'What a beautiful stone, your Highness!' she remark 'May I look at it?'

[1] *Hindu Manners, Customs and Ceremonies*, p. 43. See also pp. 152, 195 529.

Certainly,' said he, and, removing the ring from his ;er, laid it by her plate.

The lady, a person of rank, turned the jewel this way and t, held it up to the light, admired it as it deserved, and, h thanks, laid it beside the plate of the owner. The latter n, by a sidewise glance, indicated the ring to his own ndant who stood behind his chair.

Wash it,' ordered the Prince, and, undisturbed, resumed conversation.

This seeming digression from the chapter's original text y help to make clear the nature of the cow's hold upon ia. And, as you see them of mid-mornings, trooping in idreds out from the cities and villages on their slow, ile way to jungle pasturage, you might well fancy they w and are glad of their place in the people's mind. ght strings of beads – blue, coral, red – adorn their necks. l in their eyes and the eyes of the bullocks, their sons, a look of slumbrous tranquillity.

That tranquil, far-off gaze is, indeed, often remarked and aimed by the passing traveller as an outward sign of an er sense of surrounding love. In Holland, in England, may observe an extraordinary tranquillity, peacefulness, ndliness, even in pastured bulls, which may reasonably be ibuted to the gentle handling to which they are accus- ed, to good food and much grooming, and to the freedom y enjoy. But in India, after examining facts, one is en to conclude that the expression in the eyes of the s is due partly to low vitality, partly to the close quarters h humanity in which they live, and for the rest, simply to curious cut of the outer corner of the lid, subtly beautiful an Aubrey Beardsley woman's.

Fifty years ago, the political Indians say, India had

pasturage enough for all her cattle. However that may h been, judged by a Western definition of 'enough,' the f to-day are otherwise. One of Mr. Gandhi's Indian writ Mr. Desai, sees the matter in this way:[1]

'In ancient times and even during the Musalman peri cattle enjoyed the benefit of common pastures and had the free run of the forests. The maintenance of the cattle their owners practically nothing. But the British Gove ment cast a greedy eye upon this time-honoured propert the cattle, which could not speak for themselves and wh had none else to speak on their behalf, and confiscated sometimes with an increase in the land-revenue in view, at other times in order to oblige their friends, such as missionaries.'

This writer then supports his last-quoted phrase by statement that the Salvation Army was once allowed Government to take up 560 acres of public grazing-gro in Gujarat for farm purposes. He continues:

'The result of this encroachment upon grazing areas been that at the present day in India the proportion of gr ing grounds to the total area is the smallest of all countr . . . It is not, therefore, a matter for surprise that our ca should have rapidly deteriorated under British rule.'

And he cites figures for the United States as leading list of happier peoples whose grazing areas are large.

But unfortunately, in choosing his American statist Mr. Desai omits those which carry most value for ne India. We have, it is true, great grazing areas – but rotate them and protect them from over-grazing – a ma

[1] *Young India*, June 3, 1926. V. G. Desai, p. 200.

onceived by the Indian. And even in the section where ; area is widest, our semi-arid and arid western range ntry, we devote three-fifths of our total cultivated ground ·aising feed for our cattle. Our cotton belt gives 53 per t. of its crop area to live-stock feed, as corn, cow-peas, ns, peanuts, against 10 per cent. used to grow food for n; our corn and winter wheat belt uses 75 per cent. of its tivated land to grow similar forage for its cattle; our corn t gives 84 per cent. of its crop-land to forage-growing, l only 16 per cent. to man's food; and the North and East 'ote about 70 per cent. of their crops to fodder. Sevenths of our total crop area is devoted to harvested forage. : have 257,000,000 acres in crops for cattle's feed, against 000,000 acres in crops for human food, and we have one king cow to every family of five.[1]

Γhese are figures that should concern the Indian sinely interested in the welfare of his great agricultural ıntry, and I confess to placing them here at such length the hope that they may challenge his eye.

Still pursuing the question of India's cattle, Mr. Gandhi oked the counsel of an Italian-trained specialist, domiciled India. From him came the impatient reply of the pracıl man who sees small beauty in the spared rod where ldish folly is wasting precious substance. If the Indian ·e not callous, and so unintelligent as to the needs of his tle – if he were only compelled to rotate crops and to grow der as Italians do in circumstances no better than the Inns', his troubles were done, says this witness, continuing:[2]

U.S. Department of Agriculture Bulletin No. 895, 'Our Forage Rc· ces,' Government Printing Office, 1923, pp. 312–26.

Young India, May 13, 1926. Mr. Galletti-di-Cadilhac, 'The Cattle olem,' p. 177.

'Rotated crops require no more expenditure of money tl unrotated crops. In Java the Dutch forced paddy rotat on the people a century ago, by the *sjambok* [rhinoceros-h whip]. The population of Java has increased from 2 mill to 30 million during their rule, and the yield of the rice a sugar fields has increased proportionately. The change v brought about not by capital expenditure but by an inte gent government using force. In India there is no quest of using the *sjambok*. We wish to convince, not to comp

The writer continues:[1]

'Where the cow is a valuable possession [as in Italy], sh tended with care and love, and crops are grown for her a palaces are built for her. Here [where] she is merely object of veneration, she is left to stand and starve in public standing- and starving-grounds, which are miscal grazing-grounds in India. India should abolish these pla of torture and breeding-grounds of disease and abortion, a every Indian should devote three-fifths of his land to grow grass and fodder for his cattle.'

No one who has seen the public pasturage will be likel dispute the accuracy of the last-quoted witness. 'Pul standing- and starving-grounds' they are, nor is there faintest reason, despite the celebrants of the past, for s posing that they were ever materially better. Bernier, French traveller of the Musalman period, testifies:[2]

'Owing to the great deficiency of pasture land in Indies, it is impossible to maintain large numbers of cat . . . The heat is so intense, and the ground so parch

[1] *Young India*, p. 178.
[2] *Travels in the Mogul Empire*, p. 326.

ɹring eight months of the year, that the beasts of the field, ady to die of hunger, feed on every kind of filth, like so any swine.'

And one's own eyes and common sense, together with the story of men and forests, are enough to satisfy one's ind.

Further, the general conditions under which Indian ıimals had lived and propagated might have been ›ecially devised for breeding down to the worst possible pe.

Cattle experts know that if 120 cows are put without other od on pasturage that will keep alive only 100, the 20 that :rish will be the 20 best milkers; for the reason that a good ilch cow throws her strength to her milk production, leav- g herself a diminished maintenance reserve. The Indian actice of selection by starvation, therefore, works the breed ›wnhill, through the survival of the least useful strain. gain, in India the bull runs with the herds, which may ımber 300 cows. Though he were of the best, such :travagance must exhaust him. But, on the consistent ›ntrary, he is so far from the best as to be deliberately of e worst that can be found.

When a man needs specially to placate the gods, as upon .e death of his father, he may vow a bull to the temple. And nce one bull will do as well as another, he naturally chooses s feeblest, his most misshapen. Or, if he buys the offering, : buys the cheapest and therefore the poorest to be had. he priests accept the animal, which, receiving the temple and, thereupon becomes holy, goes where he pleases, and rves as sire to a neighbouring herd. Straying together, arving together, young and old, better and worse, the poor creatures mingle and transmit to each other and to the young their manifold flaws and diseases. Half of India cattle,[1] if given the food consumed by the worse half, wou produce, it is affirmed, more than India's present total mi supply.

In eastern Bengal, one of the most fertile countries of t world, pasturage scarcely exists, the country being entire taken up with rice-paddy and jute. They grow no fodd crops for their cattle and feed a bit of chopped rice-stra or nothing. In western Bengal, some districts report t loss of 25 per cent. of the cultivated crops by depredatio of hungry stock. The country being everywhere witho fences or hedges, a man may easily turn his cows into h sleeping neighbours' crops. The sin is small – the cows a holy as well as hungry, and the neighbour's distress is bo his illusion and his fate.

I have seen the cow driven by starvation so far from h natural niceness as to become a scavenger of human excr ment. The sight is common.

In certain districts some green fodder is grown, to be sur and during the rains and the earlier cold weather a poor so of grass exists on the grazing-grounds of all but the mo desert sections. By January, however, the grey cracked eart is eaten bare, so to remain until the late spring rains set in and starvation begins in earnest.

Mr. Gandhi's correspondent has shown us in the cow hunger one of the evil effects of British rule. And Britis rule is indeed largely responsible for the present disastro condition.

[1] Samuel Higginbottom, Director of the Allahabad Agricultu Institute. Testimony before the Indian Taxation Enquiry Committe 1924–25.

Up to the advent of the British in India, raids great and nall, thieving, banditry and endless internal broils and warres kept the country in chronic distress; and a sure butt of ery such activity was the cattle of the attacked. Conseuently, with a spasmodic regularity whose beneficent effect more easily appreciated to-day than can well have been ossible at the time, the cattle of any given area were killed f or driven away, the grazing-grounds of that area, such they were, got an interval of rest, and, for the moment, breeding stopped, for new animals had to be slowly cumulated.

Upon this order broke the British with their self-elected mmitment, first of all, to stop banditry, warfare and desuction and to establish peace. The task was precisely the me that America set for herself in the Philippines. As we hieved it in the Philippines, so did the British achieve it India – in a greater interval of time commensurate with e greater area and population to be pacified. About fifty ars ago Britain's work in this respect, until then allsorbing, stood at last almost accomplished. Life and operty under her controlling hand had now become as arly safe as is, perhaps, possible. Epidemics, also, were ecked and famine largely forestalled. So that, shielded om enemies that had before kept down their numbers, men d cattle alike multiplied. And men must be fed. Therere Government leased them land [1] in quantity according to eir necessities, that they might raise food for themselves d not die.

They have raised food for themselves, but they will not ise food for their mother the cow. So the cow starves.

[1] By ancient law all land ownership is vested in Government

And the fault – is the greed of Britain or of the Salv tion Army.[1]

[1] Government has largely entrusted to the Salvation Army, because its conspicuous success therewith, the reformation of the Criminal Trib nomads, whose first need is domestication in a fixed habitat where they m be trained to earn an honest and sufficient livelihood by agriculture, cattl raising and handiworks. For this purpose and to further its excellent work the Untouchables in general, the Salvation Army has received from Gover ment the use of certain small and scattered tracts of uncultivated land Gujerat and elsewhere. It is to this step that Mr. Gandhi's organ objec *See ante*, p. 206. *See*, further, *Muktifauj*, by Commissioner Booth-Tuck Salvationist Publishing and Supplies, London.

CHAPTER XVIII

THE SACRED COW

[URNING from the people and the cattle within their ates to Government's experimental work on Government ırms, we find one world-contribution. They have solved a ıain domestic problem of low latitudes – how to get milk ɔr the babies.

Only those who have lived in the tropics are likely to ppreciate what this means, in terms of family security, ealth and happiness. In the Philippines our own hopeful vork was nipped in the bud by the Filipinization of the ıgricultural Department. From that day, cattle-breeding ecame a farce, played out in office chairs by vague young nen spinning webs of words learned by rote in one or nother American college, while a few rough and neglected nimals wearied out a beggar's existence in the corral. And o, as far as colonial America is concerned, the old notion till reigned – that the cow can neither be bred nor led to ;ive real milk, in real quantity, in the tropics.

In other words, our work in that field is yet to do.

But the British in India have given us a tremendous lift ınd encouragement to effort. On the Imperial Dairy Farm .t Bangalore their breeding experiments have conclusively ›roved that, with skill, care and persistence, a cow can be leveloped that will stand up against the tropical climate for ifteen lactations and still produce well, doing her duty as a ıuman life-saver. In the Government Military Dairy Farm ıt Lucknow, I saw 'Mongia,' a half-bred cow sired by an mported American Friesian on a native dam of the Punjab

Hariana stock. Mongia, with her eighth calf, had give 16,000 pounds[1] of milk in a lactation period of 305 day With her seventh calf she gave 14,800 pounds. 'Edna another of the herd, had reached a production of 15,324 i 305 days. Butter-fat, with these sturdy half-breeds, rur from 4·05 per cent. in full lactation to about 5·05 per cen during hottest weather, which is beyond even our America home requirements.

Again, these cows' milk production drops scarcely at a in hot weather. Edna began her 1925 lactation in Augus starting off at a steady seventy-pound daily yield. Edna an Mongia are, to be sure, admittedly stars; but the averag daily production of the Lucknow herd of 105 milking cow of Indo-Western crosses was twenty-one pounds per capita and the work is yet young.

The best milch breed native to India is the Saniwal, o the Punjab, which averages only 3,000 pounds a lactatio period, and is too small to be usefully cross-bred with ou big western milch stock. But Government within the las ten years have developed on their farm in Pusa a cross-bree of Saniwal with Montgomery, a second Punjabi strain, tha has more than doubled the previous Saniwal record, whil further interesting experiments, as of crossing native Sind stock with imported Ayrshires, are in course of developmen at other Government breeding stations.

The significance of all this may be measured in part b the fact that over 90 per cent. of the cows in India give les than 600 pounds of milk a year, or less than a quart a day.

Government began experiments in the year 1912. The came the Great War, preventing the bringing of animal

[1] 2·15 pounds of milk make a quart.

[2] *The Gospel and the Plough*, London, 1921, Samuel Higginbottom, p. 69

om abroad. Directly the war was over, Government imorted from America, for the Lucknow farm, two more riesian bulls, 'Segis' and 'Elmer.' Other experimental ations were similarly supplied, and the work went on.

Enough has now been accomplished to prove that stamina oes with the half-breed, and that, beyond the fifty-fifty oint, imported blood weakens the result, creating extraisceptibility to the many diseases of the country. Every ow over half-blood, therefore, is now bred back to a native ull.

Thus, by selective breeding, by crossing, and by better eding and housing, slowly and steadily the results of enturies of inbreeding, starvation, infection, and of breeding om the worst are being conquered; definite pedigree types re being fixed; and the foundations of distinct breeds are uilding.

The trail is opened, the possibilities revealed. When the eople of India are ready to accept it, their profit is ready to ieir hand.

Cattle-lovers, at this point, will be interested in the fact iat India demands a dual-purpose cow, but that 'dual urpose,' in India, signifies, not the combination upon which ome of us in America look askance – milk and beef, but – iilk and muscle!

The sale of cattle as beef is small; the price of beef i Lucknow in 1926 was 1*d.* a pound. The Indian's use or a cow, aside from her religious contribution earlier desribed, is to produce, first, milk and butter; second, dung to e used as fuel or to coat the floors and walls of their dwelligs; and, third, to produce draught animals for the cart and lough. To breed for milk and for draught might seem a elf-cancelling proposition. But such is the demand of the country, and the concern of Government is to get on wi the job and strike the best possible compromise.

On the Government farms, foreign fodder crops, such Egyptian clover, have also been introduced; much emphas is laid on fodder developments; and the use of silage, ecor omically stored in pits, is demonstrated. Men are sent out deliver illustrated lectures and to install silage pits in th villages. And young pedigreed herd bulls, whether as loan or as gifts, or to purchase, are offered to the people.

All the fine animals produced at Lucknow, Pusa, Ba galore and the other Government plants, are conscientious watched over by British breeders. In points of general con petence, of cleanliness and order, and of simple practicalit the plants stand inspection. But all such matters a utterly foreign to the minds of the Indian peasant, an for those who might best and quickest teach the peasant the Indian aristocrat, the Indian intelligentsia – rarely d peasant or cattle carry any appeal.

With the exception of certain princes of Indian States wh have learned from England to take pride in their herds, an again with the exception of a mere handful of estate-holder scattered over the country, cattle-breeding is left entirely t a generally illiterate class known as *gvalas*, who lack ente prise, capital and intelligence to carry on the work.

I saw little, anywhere, to suggest a real appreciation of th importance of change and much of opposite import, suc for example, as the spectacle of a fine pedigreed herd bul lent by Government for the improvement of the cattle of village and returned a wreck from ill-usage. He was brough into a Government Veterinary Hospital during my visit i the place, and it needed no testimony other than one's eye to see that he had been starved, cruelly beaten and crippled ile the wounds on one leg, obviously inflicted by blows, re so badly infected that healing seemed scarcely possible. What will you do?' I asked the British official in charge. Fine the head man of the village, probably. But it does le good. It is a human trait not to appreciate what one sn't pay for. And they won't pay for bettering their tle.'

Further, to take at random another point, it is difficult to intelligent selective breeding work out of a people who, example, refuse to keep record of the milk-yield of a cow the ground that to weigh or to measure the gift of God is pious. 'We will not do it!' the milkers of the Punjab lare. 'If we did, our children would die.'

Meantime, aside from the selection of the worst, by starion and by breeding from the worst through sacred runt ls, a third force works to remove the best milch cows m a land whose supply of milk is already tragically short. vernment, at Karnal, has amply demonstrated the feasity of producing milk in the country and transporting it he city in bulk, even as far as a thousand miles. And the lcutta co-operative dairies have shown the possibilities of al service from suburb to town. But the Indian milk puror in general sees naught in that. His practice is to buy best up-country young milch cows he can find, bring m to the city in calf, keep them during their current tation, to prolong which he often removes their ovaries, l then to sell them to the butcher. This happens on the nd scale, kills off the best cows, and thereby constitutes teady drain on the vital resources of the country.

The Indian holds that he cannot afford to maintain an mal in the city during her dry season, and he has no plan keeping her elsewhere. Therefore he exterminates her after her lactation; most of the cost of her raising goes waste and her virtues die with her.[1]

Government, all over India, have learned to prepare trouble on the annual Muhammadan feast, one of the featu of which is the sacrificial killing of cows. Hindu feeling that period, rises to the danger pitch, and riots, bloodsl and destruction are always the likely outcome. For is not embodied Sacrosanctity that lies at the root of Hindui being done to death by the infidel in the very arms of adorers?

Given this preliminary reminder, nothing is more char teristic of the Indian mentality than the balancing fa pointed out in Mr. Gandhi's *Young India* of November 1925:

'We forget that a hundred times the number of cows kil for *Kurbani*[2] by the Musalmans are killed for purposes trade. . . . The cows are almost all owned by Hindus, a the butchers would find their trade gone if the Hin refused to sell the cows.'

Four weeks after the publication of the leading art above quoted, Mr. Gandhi returns to the subject, cit what he describes as 'illuminative extracts' from a repor the Indian Industrial Committee sitting in Bengal and Central Provinces.[3] The hearing is on the commer slaughter of cows for beef and hides. The investigat committee asks, concerning the attitude of the surround Hindu populace toward the industry:

[1] W. Smith, Imperial Dairy Expert, in *Agricultural Journal of In* Vol. XVII, Part I, January, 1922.

[2] The annual Muhammadan feast above mentioned.

[3] *Young India*, Nov. 26, 1925, p. 416.

Have these slaughterhouses aroused any local feeling in matter?'

The witness replies:

They have aroused local feelings of greed and not of in-ıation. I think you will find that many of the municipal nbers are shareholders in these yards. Brahmans and ıdus are also found to be shareholders.'

If there is any such thing as a moral government in the verse, we must answer for it some day,' Mr. Gandhi's ımentor helplessly laments.

This example of the selling of the cow by the Hindu for ıghter – he who will rise in murdering riot if a Muham-lan, possibly not too averse to the result, kills a cow out-: a Hindu temple door – opens a topic that should per-s be examined for other than its face value.

We of the West are continually in danger of misunder-ıding the Indian through supposing that the mental ure produced by a given word or idea is the same in ght and significance to him and to us. His facility in glish helps us to this error. We assume that his thought ke his tongue. He says, for example, that he venerates all and is filled with tenderness for all animals. Lecturing America, he speaks of the Hindu's sensitive refinement in direction and of his shrinking from our gross unspirit-ty, our incomprehension of the sacred unity of the vital rk.

But if you suppose, from these seemingly plain words, that average Hindu in India shows what we would call ımon humaneness toward animal life, you go far astray. To the highly intelligent Brahman foreman of the Government farm at Bangalore, I one day said: 'I regret that all o India you torture most bullocks and some cows by the jointing of their tails. Look at the draught bullocks in t cart over there. Every vertebra in their tails is dislocat As you are aware, it causes exquisite pain. Often the is broken short off.'

'Ah, yes,' replied the young Brahman, indifferently, 'i perfectly true that we do it. But that, you see, is necess The animals would not travel fast enough unless their t nerves are wrenched.'

You may stand for hours on the busy Howrah Bridg Calcutta, watching the bullock-carts pass, without disco ing a dozen animals whose tails are not a zig-zag string breaks. It is easier, you see, for the driver to walk with animal's tail in his hand, twisting its joints from time time, than it is to beat the creature with his stick. If you r in the bullock-cart, however, with the driver riding bef you, you will discover that, from this position, he has anot way of speeding the gait. With his stick or his long hard t nails he periodically prods his animals' genital glands.

And only the alien in the land will protest.

It is one of the puzzles of India that a man whose bull is his best asset will deliberately overload his animal, then, half starved as it is, will drive it till it drops dead. T steep hillsides of Madras are a Calvary for draught bulloc One sees them, branded from head to tail, almost raw fr brands and blows, forced uphill until they fall and die. a British official sees this or any other deed of cruelty, acts. But the British are few in the land. Yet far fewer the Indians whose sensibilities are touched by the suf ings of dumb beasts, or whose wrath is aroused by pain abuse inflicted upon defenceless creatures.

Che practice of *phúká* is common in most parts of India. : object is to increase and prolong the milk production of 's. It is committed in several ways, but usually consists in ısting a stick on which is bound a bundle of rough straw • the vagina of the cow and twisting it about, to produce :ation. The thing gives intense pain to the cow, and also duces sterility – a matter of indifference to the dairyman, :e he will in any case sell her for slaughter when she :s. Mr. Gandhi cites authority [1] that out of 10,000 cows Calcutta dairy sheds, 5,000 are daily subjected to this cess.

Mr. Gandhi quotes another authority on the manufacture ι dye esteemed by Indians and known as *peuri.*[2]

By feeding the cow only on mango leaves, with no other n of feed nor even water to drink, the animal passes in form of urine a dye which is sold at high rates in the aar. The animal so treated does not last long and dies in ny.'

Che young milch cow is usually carrying her calf when she rought to the city. The Hindu dairyman does not want calf, and his religion forbids him to kill it. So he finds er means to avoid both sin and the costs of keeping. In ıe sections of the country he will allow it a daily quarter-ıalf-cup of its mother's milk, because of a religious teach- that he who keeps the calf from the cow will himself fer in the next life. But the allowance that saves the ner's soul is too small to save the calf, who staggers ut after the mother on her door-to-door milk route as long ts trembling legs will carry it. When the end comes, the ner skins the little creature, sews the skin together, stuffs

[1] *Young India*, May 6, 1926, pp. 166–7. [2] *Ibid.*, p. 167.

it crudely with straw, shoves four sticks up the legs, a
when he goes forth on the morrow driving his cow, car
his handiwork over his shoulder. Then, when he stops
customer's door to milk, he will plant before the mother
thing that was her calf, to induce her to milk more fre
Or again, in large plants, the new-born calves may
simply tossed upon the morning garbage carts, at the da
door, and carried away to the dumps where they brea
their last among other broken rubbish.

The water buffalo – the carabao of the Philippines – is
India an immensely useful creature. The best of the De
blood give yearly from 6,000 to 10,000 pounds of m
carrying from 7·5 to 9 per cent. butter-fat. The buffalo b
makes a powerful draught animal for cart and plough. But
species is large, and expensive to raise. Therefore it is us
for milk dealers to starve their buffalo calves outright. *Yo
India*[1] quotes testimonies showing various phases of t
practice. One of these draws attention to

'. . . the number of buffalo calves . . . being abandoned
die of starvation in public streets, and often when they
down through sheer exhaustion, being mutilated by tra
motor-cars and carriages. These animals are generally dri
out from the cattle stables at night . . . simply to save
the milk the mother has, for sale.'

Otherwise, the calf is tied to a stake anywhere about
place and left without food or water till it dies.

The water buffalo, having no sweat-glands, suff
severely in the hot sun and should never be compelled
endure it unprotected. Therefore, says another of *Yo*

[1] *Young India*, May 6, 1926, p. 167.

ia's authorities, 'one finds that [the starving buffalo es] are usually tied in the sunniest part of the yard. The ymen appear systematically to use these methods to kill the young stock.'

And then, turning from city dairymen to country owners country regions, Mr. Gandhi gives us this picture: [1]

In Gujarat [northern Bombay Presidency] the he-calf is ply starved off by withholding milk from him. In other s he is driven away to the forests to become the prey of l beasts. In Bengal he is often tied up in the forest and without food, either to starve or be devoured. And yet people who do this are those who would not allow an nal to be killed outright even if it were in extreme ering!'

n this, one is reminded of the fate of the villagers' cows, ch, when they are too diseased or too old to give further rice, are turned out of the village, to stand and starve till y are too weak to defend themselves with heel or horn and n are pulled down and devoured by the starving village s.

Surely no Westerner, even the most meteoric tourist, has sed through India without observing those dogs. They nt every railway platform, skulking along under the car dows. Bad dreams out of purgatory they look, all bones sores and grisly hollows, their great, undoglike eyes full error and furtive cunning, of misery and of hatred. All r the land they exist in hosts, for ever multiplying. In the ns they dispute with the cows and goats for a scavenger's ng among the stalls and gutters of the bazaars. Devoured h disease and vermin, they often go mad from bites

[1] *Ibid.*

received from mad jackals of the packs that roam even c parts by night.

And, according to the Hindu creed, nothing can be d for them. Their breeding may not be stopped, their num may not be reduced, and since a dog's touch defiles, th wounds and sores and broken bones may not be attend

In this connection an interesting discussion has recer developed in the pages of *Young India*.[1] The incident t gave it birth was the destruction of sixty mad dogs, collec on the premises of an Ahmedabad mill-owner. The m owner himself, though a Hindu, had ordered their killi This act aroused much ill feeling in the town, and the Hir Humanitarian League referred the question to Mr. Gand as a religious authority, asking:

'When Hinduism forbids the taking of the life of a living being, . . . do you think it right to kill rabid do . . . Are not the man who actually destroys the dogs, as a the man at whose instance he does so, both sinners? . . . T Ahmedabad Municipality . . . is soon going to have bef it a resolution for the castration of stray dogs. Does religi sanction the castration of an animal?'

Mr. Gandhi's reply is full of light on Hindu thinking

'There can be no two opinions on the fact that Hindui regards killing a living being as sinful. . . . Hinduism l laid down that killing for sacrifice is no *himsa* [violenc This is only a half-truth. . . . But what is inevitable is

[1] *Young India*, October and November, 1926. The issue of November 1926, gives the following figures for cases of hydrophobia treated in the C Hospital of the town of Ahmedabad: Jan. to Dec., 1925, 1,117; Jan. to Se 1926, 990.

garded as a sin, so much so that the science of daily practice s not only declared the inevitable violence involved in kill- g for sacrifice as permissible but even regarded it as meri- rious. . . . [But the man] who is responsible for the pro- ction of lives under his care and who does not possess the rtues of the recluse [to heal by spirit], but is capable of stroying a rabid dog, is faced with a conflict of duties. If kills the dog he commits a sin. If he does not kill it, he mmits a graver sin. So he prefers to commit the lesser one. . It is therefore a thousand pities that the question of stray gs, etc., assumes such a monstrous proportion in this cred land of *ahimsa* [non-violence]. It may be a sin to stroy rabid dogs and such others as are liable to catch bies. . . . It is a sin, it should be a sin, to feed stray dogs.'

In the land of *ahimsa*, the rarest of sins is that of allowing crumb of food to a starving dog, or, equally, of putting him t of his misery. Mr. Gandhi's approval of the latter step, en as to animals gone mad, has brought down upon him ch an avalanche of Hindu protest that he sighs aloud under burden upon his time.

And since the only remaining resource, castration, lies der religious ban because it interrupts the ordained stages life, the miseries of the dog, like many another misery of dia, revolves in a circle.

CHAPTER XIX

THE QUALITY OF MERCY

'WE will pose as protectors of the cow, and quarrel w Musalmans in her sacred name, the net result being that l last condition is worse than the first,' [1] laments the faith. accuser on Mr. Gandhi's staff, and again:

'In spite of our boasted spirituality, we are still sa(backward in point of humanity and kindness to the low animals.' [2]

Legislation for the prevention of cruelty to animals w enacted in the early years of Crown rule in India. But su legislation, anywhere, must rest for effectiveness on pub opinion, and the opinion of Mr. Gandhi's paper is, in tl matter, as a voice crying in the wilderness, awakening b the faintest of echoes. If the people feel no compassion; the police, themselves drawn from the people, private consider the law a silly, perhaps an irreligious law, who greatest virtue lies in the chance it gives them to fill the pockets; and if little or no leaven of another sentiment exis in the higher classes, Government's purpose, as far as means immediate relief, is handicapped indeed.

Laws in India for the prevention of cruelty to anima have uniformly originated as Government Bills. Whether the Central or of the Provincial Administrations, measur for the protection of animals from cruelty have been passe over the indifference, if not over the pronounced hostility, the Indian representation.

[1] *Young India*, May 6, 1926. V. G. Desai, p. 167.

[2] *Ibid.*, August 26, 1926, p. 303.

Thus, a Bill to limit the driving of water buffaloes, heavily len, through the hottest hours of the day in the midst of e hottest season of the year, was introduced in the Bengal gislative Council by Government, on March 16, 1926. the streets of Calcutta the sufferings of buffaloes so driven d long been, to Western susceptibilities, a public scandal. t this proposal for the animals' relief was finally enacted o law despite the resistance of the leading Indian merants, who saw in it merely a sentimentality inconvenient their trade.

The practice of *phúká*, the deliberate daily torture of the w in order that the worth of a few more pennies may be ung from her pain, has been forbidden and heavily penaled by the Governor-General-in-Council and by successive ovincial laws. Mr. Gandhi finds room, in the columns of *oung India*,[1] to print an Englishman's protest against *úká*. But if any mass of Hindu feeling exists against it, e vitality of that feeling is insufficient to bring it forth to deeds.

In 1926, the Government of Bombay Presidency introced in the Bombay Legislative Council a measure[2] amendg the Police Act of the City of Bombay so that police icers should have power to kill any animal found in such a ndition, whether from hurt or from disease, that it would sheer cruelty to attempt to remove it to a dispensary. In der to safeguard the owners' interests in the matter, the nendment further provided that, if the owner is absent, or he refuses to consent to the destruction of the suffering imal, the police officer must secure, before he can proceed

[1] *Young India*, May 13, 1926, p. 174.

[2] *Bill No. V of* 1926, 'A Bill Further to Amend the City of Bombay Police t, 1902.'

under the law, a certificate from one of several veterinaria whom the Governor-in-Council should appoint.

No small part of the necessity for a law such as this wo arise from the Indian's habit, already described, of turni diseased and dying cows, and calves that he is in process starving to death, into the streets to wander until they what he calls 'a natural death.' As their strength fails, th become less and less able to guide their movements, and, the end, are often caught and crushed by some vehic against whose wheels they fall.

The debates evoked by the Bombay Government's pr posal of relief throw so much general light on Indian mod of thought that their quotation at some length may justified. On the introduction of the measure, a Hin member, Mr. S. S. Dev, came at once to his feet with:[1]

'The principle of the bill is revolting to an Indian min . . . If you will not shoot a man in similar circumstanc how can you shoot an animal, in the name of preventi cruelty to animals? . . . Further, the bill, if it becomes la may in actual operation give rise to fracas in public street

Then follows Mr. B. G. Pahalajani, of Western Sin Says he:[2]

'This section makes no exception whatever whether t animal is a cow or a horse or a dog. The policeman with t certificate of the veterinary practitioner can destroy a animal. The official [British] members of the Council oug to know – some of them have remained here for over 3 years – that no Hindu would allow a cow to be destroyed whatsoever condition it is. There are *pinjrapoles*[3] in whic

[1] *Bombay Legislative Council Debates,* Official Report, 1926. Vol. XVI Part VII, pp. 579–80.

[2] *Ibid.,* p. 580.

[3] Animal asylums, later to be described

e worst diseased animals are nursed and fed. . . . [This easure] proceeds on the assumption that animals have no ul, and they deserve to be shot if they are not in a con- ion to live. The Hindu idea of soul is quite different om that held by Westerners. . . . A measure of this kind uld wound the religious susceptibilities of Hindus.'

To this declaration Mr. A. Montgomerie, Secretary to vernment, responds, with a picture from the daily life of e city:[1]

'I can hardly think that the honourable member means at he says. Is it a decent sight to see some poor animal sembowelled, legs broken and bleeding, in the streets of mbay? The only humane thing . . . is to put the beast t of misery. It is inhumanity to allow this animal to suffer d remove it with the probability that it may break to pieces ile being so moved.'

But Hindu after Hindu decries the measure, and on ounds of offended sentiment alone, save that one of their mber, Mr. R. G. Soman, takes thought that a question of pense is involved. For the Bill empowers Government to point a few district veterinarians, to be locally handy to e police. This charge upon public funds, Mr. Soman feels, es beyond any suffering animal's proper claim. As he ts it:[2]

'If any generous-minded practitioners come forward tc lp the police officers, so much the better. But if any new sts are to be created, which are to be maintained at public pense, I would like certainly to oppose the bill.'

[1] *Bombay Legislative Council Debates*, p. 581.

[2] *Ibid.*, March 2, 1926, p. 583.

And the debate, for the day, closes on the note of fa Says Rao Sahib D. P. Desai, member from Kaira:[1]

'All the trouble arises from having two conflicting ideals mercy. The framers of the bill think that shooting an anin which is diseased and which could not be cured is mu better. We on the other hand think that God Himself h ordained what is to come about.'

On the resumption of the reading of the Bill, over thr months later,[2] the Honourable J. E. B. Hotson, Ch Secretary to Government, assumes the labour of trying win Indian support. He pleads:[3]

'The one object of this bill is to make it possible to de with injured animals which are lying in the street or in a other public place in a state of suffering and pain, for whi there is no relief for them. It is open to the owners of su animals to remove them, [or] to have them taken away other charitable persons to a *pinjrapole* or to any other pla where animals are received and cared for. It is only in cas where the animal is neglected in its misery, where, as thin are now, the animal has to lie in the public streets of Bomb for many hours, perhaps until death brings relief, that t power . . . will be exercised. That such an animal should l in such a condition in a public place where there are mar passers-by in a great city like Bombay . . . causes pain observers of all classes and it is desirable not only that tl animal should be relieved . . . but that the feelings of tl passers-by should be saved from the extreme discomfo

[1] *Bombay Legislative Council Debates*, March 2, 1926, p. 585.
[2] *Ibid.*, July 26, 1926.
[3] *Bombay Legislative Council Debates*, Vol. XVIII, Part I, pp. 70–1.

ısed by such sights. That is all that this bill seeks to ain.'

But the Hindu position remains unshaken. The old ;uments [1] come forward until, presently, they arouse the ›nourable Ali Mahomed Khan Dehlavi, Muhammadan, inister of Agriculture in the Bombay Government. Says , expressing himself as 'rather anxious in the interests of :iculturists': [2]

'It was argued at the last session that every animal having oul should not be destroyed. I have been tackled severely this House by honourable members on the opposite nches for not taking sufficient precaution and for not :nding sufficient money to kill elephants, [wild] pigs and s in the interests of agriculturists. And if this is a question killing a soul, I think an elephant has a bigger soul than a ;, and the latter a bigger soul than a rat. If that principle re applied to the agricultural department, I shall be asked stop killing the animals I have mentioned. The result will that the agriculturists in the country will suffer very much. ay, Sir, there is absolutely no difference at all between the ;e of an animal in the streets of cities like Bombay, or in : jungles or fields in the country outside.'

The concern of the Minister of Agriculture for the culti- :ors, his special charges, again uncovers the usual attitude the Indian politician toward that body of humanity which ıstitutes over 72 per cent. of the people of India. Says o Sahib D. P. Desai, frankly tossing off their case: [3]

'The agriculturists should not be taken as the whole of

[1] Cf. *Bombay Legislative Council Debates*, Vol. XVIII, Part I, pp. 72–3.
[2] *Ibid.*, p. 73.
[3] *Ibid.*, p. 76.

Indian society. . . . But even if the agriculturist thinks t
it is desirable that any animals that are dangerous to agric
ture should be destroyed, it should not be taken that t
whole Hindu society agrees with that view of the agric
turists, and I think that no weight should be given su
views in this House.'

Out of the remainder of the day's debate emerge mu
sterile criticism and accusation of Government's effort a
no fresh thought excepting that of the old Muhammad
member from the Central Division, Moulvi Rafiudc
Ahmad, who counsels, Nestorwise:[1]

'It is not the intention in the remotest degree of the Gc
ernment to injure the susceptibilities of any classes of H
Majesty's subjects in India. . . . If [anything] can be do
by any other means than by the provisions of this bill, I thi
Government will be only too pleased to adopt them, and
far as I know – and I have been in this house long enough
there has never been any question of sentiment which Gc
ernment have not taken into consideration, and I do adm
them for that. . . . In this House Hindus and Muhamn
dans have joined to oppose Government if in any remote c
gree they thought that Government were mistaken and
many occasions Government have conceded. . . . It is
use coming here with empty heads, there must be some su
gestions offered, it is easy to criticize, but it is at the sa
time our duty also to suggest better measures. I appeal to
those persons that have raised objections. . . . Governme
is quite open to reason.'

'Are you authorized to speak on behalf of Governmen
a Hindu hotly interrupts.

[1] *Bombay Legislative Council Debates*, pp. 77–8.

I am authorized to speak on behalf of every person with m this Council is concerned. I do say this, this objection ltogether unreasonable,' the other returns.

ut his appeal wins no response. On the contrary, a du member grimly suggests that if by chance a Muham-lan were to be appointed veterinary and were to approve killing of a sick cow, the peace of the city as between dus and Muhammadans would go up in smoke.

nd the discussion ends by the referring of the Bill to a t committee of the House, composed of nine Indians – du, Muhammadan, and Parsi, and of two British.

n the second reading of this Bill,[1] we find the Chief etary of Government, Mr. Hotson, presenting the select mittee's report with the comment that the committee gone so far in the desire to avoid giving offence to any of brethren' that the usefulness of the Bill has been im-ed – a mild and diplomatic phrasing of the emasculation has taken place.

ows and bulls are now excepted from the proposed law, temple precincts are put beyond its reach; anything may oen there. Yet, without a single constructive proposal of sort, the Hindu opposition keeps up. Members urge legislation be delayed if not abandoned, that Govern-t is indiscreet in urging any action; that 'the agonies of animals' are not so great that sympathy need pass the t of theory; that, in any event, Hindu policemen should xempt from the duty of shooting animals, since to do so ntrary to their religion; that to avoid invidious distinc-s Muhammadan officers may likewise claim exemption; because Indian officers bungle with fire-arms, British e sergeants 'whose marksmanship is perfect' be

[1] August 5, 1926.

charged with the duty. Says Mr. Surve, Hindu mem from Bombay City, advocating the last suggestion:

'To kill a disabled animal which is just about to die, t kind of butchery we are incapable of . . . that is not chivalry.' [1]

So failed, for this time at least, Government's attemp defend the cow from her worshippers. With its inten chief beneficiary left out, the Bill passed. Yet, Gove ment's argument, so patiently and courteously pursued, as it continued, educe a certain amount of Indian supp And in view of the fact that the principle involved is a co plete exotic in minds committed to the expiatory journe the soul, each bit of ground so gained speaks of rewa however distant.

It was in 1890 that the Governor-General-in-Cou passed the Act for the Prevention of Cruelty to Animals which Act the fifth section prohibited the killing of animal in an unnecessarily cruel manner. In 1917 it found necessary to clarify the intentions of Section expressly directing it upon persons cruelly killing a go or having in their possession the skin of a goat so kill Provincial Governments have enacted the same laws. A yet the offence against which these measures are aimed c tinues in the land.

It is the skinning of goats alive.

The skin stripped from a living goat can be stretche little larger, and therefore brings a little higher price, t one removed after killing.

It will scarcely be necessary to amplify this point. In Province of Behar and Orissa in the year 1925, thirty-f cases of the flaying alive of goats were brought to court

[1] *Bombay Legislative Council Debates*, August 5, 1926, p. 716.

police. But light fines, meted out by Indian judges se sentiment is not shocked, are soon worked off in the a price fetched by the next batch of flayed-alive skins. risk of prosecution is small; and 'there is every reason,' :ludes the Provincial Police Administration report, 'to ›ose that the number of reported cases is no criterion of ›revalence of this outrage.' Many skins so stripped have ı shipped to America.

ritain, by example and by teaching, has been working nearly three-quarters of a century to implant her own s of mercy on an alien soil. In this and in uncounted ·r directions she might perhaps have produced more ›le results, in her areas of direct contact, by the use of e. But her administrative theory has been that small con- ctive value lies in the use of force to bring about surface pliance where the underlying principle is not yet grasped. l, given a people still barbarian in their handling of their women, it is scarcely to be expected that they should yet : taken on a mentality responsive to the appeal of dumb tures.

Jnhappily for the helpless animal world, Prevention of elty to Animals is, under the current Indianization ·ement, a 'transferred subject' of Government. That is ıy: in each province working the 'Reforms' the adminis- on of this branch has been transferred by the British iament into the hands of an Indian minister. Dumb tion pays with its body the costs of the experiment.

CHAPTER XX

IN THE HOUSE OF HER FRIEN

'THIS country is the cruellest in the world, to anim said an old veterinarian, long practising in India. It wo perhaps be fairer to repeat that the people of India fol their religions, which, save with the small sect called Ja produce no mercy either to man or to beast, in the sense we of the West know mercy.

Mr. Gandhi himself writes: [1]

'In a country where the cow is an object of worship t should be no cattle problems at all. But our cow-worship resolved itself into an ignorant fanaticism. The fact tha have more cattle than we can support is a matter for ur treatment. I have already suggested the taking over of question by cow protection societies.'

Cow Protection Societies maintain *gaushalas*, or asylums. These asylums, like the *pinjrapoles*, or asylum all animals, are maintained by gifts, and have access, thro rich Hindu merchants, to almost unlimited funds. Government of India promise to stop the killing of cow India and they can have all the money they can use – pl war with the Muhammadan,' an experienced old Hi official once told me.

A strong claim to the bounty of the gods is believed t established through saving the life of a cow. Yet as a Hi you are not disturbed in conscience by selling your good to a butcher, because it is he, not you, who will kill the

[1] *Young India*, Feb. 26, 1925.

en, taking the money he gives you, you may buy of him, a fraction of that sum, the worst cow in his shambles, turn over to the *gaushala* to care for, and thereby acquire gious merit, profiting your soul and your purse in one ısaction.

Having personally visited a number of *gaushalas* and *irapoles*, I cannot but wonder whether those who support m so lavishly, those who commit animals to their care, those who, like Mr. Gandhi, so strongly advocate their intenance and increase, ever look inside their gates. I t heard of them through a Western animal lover long niciled in India. He said:

The Hindu who, as an act of piety, buys a cow of the cher and places her in the *gaushala*, always buys a poor ased animal because he gets her cheap. When he places in the *gaushala* he does not give money with her, or, at t, not money enough for her decent keep. And even if he , the keeper would pocket most of it. The suffering in se places is terrible. In one of them I recently saw an old lying helpless, being consumed by maggots which had un at her hind quarters. It would take them ten days to eat to her heart and kill her. Till then she must lie as she lay.

"Can't you do something for her?" I asked the keeper.

"Why?" he replied, honestly enough. "Why should What for?" '

My second informant was an American cattle specialist ng in India, a highly-qualified practical man. He said:

I was asked to visit some of these *gaushalas* and give ice. And because the political unrest since the War has ined many of these people to shut their minds to the ncil of British officials, I hoped that, as an American and outsider, I could be of use. But I found in every place that I visited either intentional dishonesty or gross m management. In all cases the animals imprisoned there w the least of anybody's concern. My advice was not welco When they found I would not give them a rubber-sta approval, they had no use for me at all.'

I next consulted a notable religious leader, the *Guru*[1] Dial Bagh. His words were:

'I have visited two of these places, both times taking th by surprise. The sights that I saw there were so horri that for two days afterward I could not take food.'

Finally, I recorded the testimony of an Indian trained the Western school of cattle-breeding and dairying and n occupying a position of considerable responsibility in t line. Describing the *pinjrapole* as 'a lane or square full animals' pens,' he went on:

'Religious sentiment puts the creatures there, but ther stops. They are much neglected and suffer torments thro neglect. Rich merchants and bankers subscribe annu tons of money for their care, but the money all goes to g and waste. The creatures in most of the asylums are worse off than they were when they scavenged in the gutt for a living, with a happy chance of getting killed by pass cars. They are miserable, dying skeletons. The caretak have no knowledge of the care of animals and no previ training or experience. The money spent in such big su is not spent on them! There *are* good animal asylums India, but they are few!'

The first *gaushala* that I saw for myself was in the subu of a central Indian city. Over the entrance gate was a cha ing painting of the blue god Krishna in the forest, piping white cows.

[1] Religious master.

nside the high walls at a distance lay a large pleasant den of fruit-trees and vegetable beds encircling a pleasant ıgalow – the keeper's house. On the hither side of the den was the place of the cows. This was a treeless, shrub-, shelterless yard of hard-trodden, cracked, bare clay, ch, in the rains, would be a wallow of foul mud, in-ited by animals whose bones, in some cases, were literally ting through their skins. Some lay gasping, too weak to ıd. Some had great open sores at which the birds, ched on their hipbones or their staring ribs, picked and :. Some had broken legs that dangled and flopped as they red. Many were diseased. All were obviously starved.

Bulls as wretched as the cows stood among them, and in ttle pen at the side were packed some 250 small calves. m these last arose a pitiful outcry, at the sound of roaching steps; and as I looked down over the pen-wall their great brown eyes, their hollow sides and their king legs, it occurred to me to ask how they were fed. answer, frankly given by the *gaushala* attendant, was each calf gets the equivalent of one small tea-cupful of k a day, until it dies – which as a rule, and happily, it rtly does – the rest of the milk being sold in the bazaar by keeper of the *gaushala*.

Asking next to see the daily ration of a cow, I was shown granary – a bin measuring perhaps 5 by 3 by 2 feet, con-ing small seeds heavily mixed with husks. Of this each -grown animal got one half-pound daily. Nothing else ıtever was fed, excepting a little dry chopped straw. ıw contains no food values, but would serve for a time to p the creatures' two sides from touching. No paddock provided, and no grazing of any sort. The animals 'ely stood or lay as I saw them until the relief of death.

One cow had but three legs, the hind leg having b amputated below the knee, 'because she kicked when t milked her.'

In other *gaushalas* I saw cripples who had been made in the process of creating monsters. For this purpose t cut a leg from one calf and graft it anywhere on the body another, to exhibit the result for money as a natural porte The maimed calf, if it does not bleed or starve or rot to dea may be bought for a song and sent to a *gaushala*. No c satisfaction seemed to be felt as to this history.

In the heart of the city of Ahmedabad, within a few m of Mr. Gandhi's pleasant and comfortable home in which writes his earnest pleas for the support of cow shelters a *pinjrapoles*, I visited a large *pinjrapole* whose descripti after what has already been said, need not be inflicted u the reader's sensibilities. I hope that every animal that I s in it is safely dead.

But from such memories it is a pleasure to turn to the exception that my personal experience revealed, an establi ment maintained by 'The Association for Saving Mi Cattle from Going to the Bombay Slaughter House.'

This society is composed practically entirely of r Indian merchants and merchants' associations. Its lat report[1] affords some interesting reading. It begins wit statement incorporating the estimate that, during the years from April 1, 1919, to March 31, 1924, 229,257 c were slaughtered in Bombay City, and that 97,583 cal and young buffaloes were 'tortured to death in the stabl

The report proceeds with an appeal against all slaugh even of bullocks, sheep and goats, for which the figures

[1] *An Appeal by Shree Ghatkopar Sarvajanika Jivadaya Khata*, Mahabir Building, Bombay.

ɔ given. Then it concerns itself with the question of the •rtage of milk:

'We Hindus claim to protect the cow. If this claim were t, India should be a land flowing with milk. But as a tter of fact this is not the case. Milk in cow-protect- · Bombay, for instance, is nearly as dear as in cow-killing ndon or New York. Good milk cannot be had for love or ney and the direct consequence of this state of things is a lly terrible mortality among infants and a heavy death rate ong adults. . . .'

Γhe 'dairy' plant that the Association itself maintains in country on the outskirts of Bombay consists of a decent of cowsheds, substantially and practically built for shelter, and sanitation, and reasonably clean. The superintendent d he was feeding fifteen pounds of hay, with eight pounds grain and oil cake, per head, daily. And the cattle, such as y were, did not look hungry. The herd consisted of 277 .d, whose aggregate milking came to about 130 quarts a , which, sold to some 130 families, gave a daily income about £4 14*s*. to the establishment. Fresh cows were sold of the plant on condition that the purchaser should never them to be killed.

Γhe staff, entirely Indian, impressed me as being eager l interested as to their work. Said the chief:

If this place were merely commercial there would not be many non-commercial cattle here. We have to buy out of slaughter-house; but where once we bought the poorest l cheapest, now we have learned to buy the best. And ides, the idea of any sort of commercial element, in a *shala*, is new to India. Up to the present we have not put · private milkmen out of business, or appreciably reduced the city's slaughter. But we hope to do so, in the long ru On my staff here I have two or three Bachelors of Ag culture – young men trained on the Government Breedi and Dairy farms to understand cattle. And that you w never find in any other *gaushala* or *pinjrapole* in all Ind We, here, believe in scientific care.'

Looked at from the point of view of an American farm the whole thing was too primitive to discuss. Looked from the Indian background, it was a shining light, and o felt almost guilty in noticing that all the staff were cousi nephews, or close relatives of the superintendent.

But it was a British-trained Indian in Governme employ under the direction of a British chief, who rescu this *gaushala* from a bad start, devised the present advanc scheme and persuaded the Association to adopt it.

Meantime, the Indian politicians, at home and abroa curse 'the criminal negligence of the Government,' [1] beat t air with words, spurn agriculture and the agriculturist, an when publicity dictates, send small contributions to the oth kind of *gaushala*.

[1] *Young India*, May 13, 1926, p. 174.

CHAPTER XXI

HOME OF STARK WANT

NE hears a great deal from the new Indian intelligentsia ut the glories of the 'Golden Age' – a period in the dowy past when the land smiled with health and plenty, dom, beauty and peace, and when all went well with India. is happy natural condition was done to death, one is given understand, by the mephitic influence of the present vernment.

The argument for the Golden Age is wont to take typical ms, such as this:

'You admit that the Emperor Chandragupta lived? And t he was the man who fought Seleucus, who fought xander? Very well: In Chandragupta's day a girl of rteen, beautiful and loaded with jewels, could walk oad in perfect safety. And there was perfect peace, no verty, no famine, no plague. But Britain ruined our lden Age.'

Or again, the accuser first paints a picture of an idyllic d, distinguished by science, philosophy and pastoral ce, then suddenly confronts his hearer with the challenge: n you show me, in all India, any remnant of that life? No? actly. Then, if it exists nowhere, does it not follow that tain must have destroyed it?'

But the period of Chandragupta, whatever its quality, was noved from that of England's first acquisition of foothold India by over nineteen hundred years.[1] Chandragupta's nasty having disappeared into mists of legend out of which

[1] Chandragupta reigned B.C. 322–298.

the one great figure of Asoka dimly looms, the Scythians a the Turks rode through the northern mountain pass helped themselves to northern India and set up their kir doms there. And the native Hindu mass, as years rolled merged its conquerors, both Scythian and Turk, into own body.

The fourth and fifth centuries, A.D., comprised the gr period of Hindu art and history – the age of the Gu Kings. Then again the hand grew lax that held the northe passes; and again down out of Central Asia poured w after wave of wild humanity, this time the terrible nor White Huns, brothers to the forces of Attila. Ravenous the wealth of the land, they had watched the frontier their hour. When it struck, leaping through like a loose torrent, they swept the country bare of all that had been social fabric.

By the beginning of the sixth century the northern half the territory we call India had become one of the provin of the Huns. And the impact of successive Hun hord striking down through the mountain barrier, had again thoroughly wiped out the past that no authentic family clan tradition of to-day can go behind that point.

The Huns, like the Scythians and the Turks before the were gradually absorbed in the native stock. Hinduism, time disputed by Buddhism, regained possession of the la Its disintegrating tenets and its cumulative millions of ter fying gods did their work. Henceforth, save during a f years in the seventh century, no successful attempt was ma north or south, to establish political unity or a perman state, while forces of disunion multiplied and grew stron

The history of northern India from the middle of t seventh century through the next five hundred years i ngled web of the warfare of little clans and states, conantly changing in size and in number with the changing rtunes of battle and intrigue. Small chiefs march and untermarch, raid, seize, annex, destroy, slay and are slain, ch jealous of each, each for himself alone, embroiling the tire northern and central part of the country in their nstant feuds.

Meantime, peninsular India remained always a place part, untouched by the currents of the north and defended erefrom by the buttress of her hills and jungles. Here ved the dark-skinned aboriginals, Tamils, without insion of Aryan blood, fighting their own fights and worripping the demons of their faith. And when at last Hindu issionaries sallied south along the coast, these recomended their creed, it would seem, by the familiar process f adding the local demons to the number of their own gods.

The Tamils had developed a rich native art; and in one at ast of their many and ever-changing little kingdoms they ad brought forth an elaborate and interesting system of illage government. By the end of the twelfth century, howver, this feature had utterly perished, crushed out. And it well to observe that, north or south, a history made up of ndless wars and changes of dynasty developed no municipal stitutions, no free cities, no republics, no political conciousness in the people. Each region lay for ever prostrate, upine, under the heel of a despot who, in his brief hour, did s he pleased with his human herds until some other despot ulled him down to destruction.

For a rapid survey of the next era in India's history one annot do better than turn to Sir T. W. Holderness's *eoples and Problems of India*:[1]

[1] Williams & Norgate, London, 1920, pp. 48–50.

'The first comers were Arabs, who founded dynasties i Sind and Multan as early as [A.D.] 800. . . . About [th year] 1000 the terror came. By that time the Tartar race had been brought into the fold of Islam, and the Turks, th most capable of these races, had started on the career whic in the West ended in their establishment at Constantinopl . . . In 997, Mahmud [a Turkish chieftain] descended upo India. His title, "the Idol-breaker," describes the ma Year by year he swept over the plains of India, capturin cities and castles, throwing down idols and temples, slaugh tering the heathen and proclaiming the faith of Muhamma Each year he returned with vast spoils [to his home i Afghanistan].

'For five hundred years, reckoning from A.D. 1000, suc cessive hosts of fierce and greedy Turks, Afghans and Mo gols trod upon one another's heels and fought for mastery i India. At the end of that time, Babar the Turk founded i 1526 the Mughal Empire; thenceforward for two hundre years the passes into India were closed and in the keeping c his capable successors.'

Says Holderness on another page:[1]

'The Mughal Empire . . . was of the ordinary type c Asiatic despotisms. It was irresponsible personal govern ment. For India it meant the substitution of a new set o conquerors for those already in occupation. But the ne comers brought with them the vigour of the north – the came from the plains of the Oxus beyond the Kabul hills - and they drew an unlimited supply of recruits from the fines fighting races of Asia. In physical strength and hardihoo they were like the Norsemen and Normans of Europe.'

[1] *Peoples and Problems of India*, p. 53.

To check the Islamic tide in its flood toward the south, a
:indu power, known as the Empire of Vijayanagar, sprang
) among the Tamils. Its rulers built a gorgeous city and
/ed in unbounded luxury. But here, as elsewhere all over
ıdia, the common people's misery provided the kings' and
)bles' wealth, and only their abject submission made
)ssible the existence of the state. Yet the glories of the
'indu stronghold soon eclipsed. In the year 1565 one blow
' Muslim arms, delivered by the sultans of small surround-
g states, slaughtered its people and reduced the splendid
ty to a heap of carven stones.

Yet the earlier of the great Mughal Emperors tolerated
e old religion. Their chief exponent, Akbar, even married
native lady, and admitted Rajput chiefs and Brahman
holars to place and posts. But the Mughals administered
ways as conqueror strangers; and though they made use of
.e talents or learning of individuals among the Hindus, they
ok care constantly to strengthen the Muslim hand from
.eir own transmontane source.

Then, in 1659, the Emperor Aurangzeb again brought
the Mughal throne an Islamism that would not counten-
ıce the idolatry of the Hindu mass. His heavy hand, des-
oying temples and images, broke the Rajputs' fealty and
used the Hindu low-caste peasantry of the Deccan – the
Iahrattas – in common wrath. So that when Aurangzeb,
his ambition for more power, more wealth, attacked even
ıe little Muhammadan kings of the Deccan, the Mahrattas
)se up as guerilla bands, and, under cover of the general
nbroilment, robbed, slew and destroyed on their own
:count, wasting the land. A half-century of Aurangzeb's
isjointing rule so weakened the Mughal Empire that, at
.s death, it fell asunder, leaving the Mahratta hordes, now

trained in raids and killings under their bandit chiefs, to pla a brief rôle as the strong hand in India.

Then again happened the historic inevitable, as happen will whenever the guard of the north is down. The Mugh Empire fallen, the door open to Central Asia, Central As poured in. First came the Persian, then the fierce Afgha who, in a final battle delivered in 1761, drove the Mahratt with wholesale slaughter back to their Deccan hills.

Now, in the scanty official records of all these trouble centuries, little indeed is said of the common people. Th histories are histories of little kings and tribal chiefs, the personal lives, ambitions, riches, intrigues, fights and dowr falls. Such glimpses as appear, however, show the populac generally as the unconsidered victims of their master's gree be that master Hindu or Muhammadan. Hungry, nake poverty-stricken, constantly over-ridden by undiscipline mobs of soldiers, bled of their scanty produce, swept b exterminating famines and epidemics, our clearest know ledge of them comes from the chronicles of strangers wh from time to time visited the country.

Many western travellers – French, Dutch, Portugues Spanish – have left records of the country, north and south as it was during and after Akbar's day. All agree in th main points.

The poor, they say, were everywhere desperately poo the rich for ever insecure in their riches. Between commo robbers and the levies of the throne, no man dared count o the morrow. The Hindu peoples constituted the prostrat masses. The nobles and governing officials, few in number were almost all foreigners, whether Turks or Persian Their luxury and ostentation arose, on the one hand, from a insatiable hunger for sensual pleasure, and, on the other m the necessity not to be outshone at court. All places l favours were bought by costly bribes, and the extrava-ıce of life was increased by the fact that, in northern India east, whatever a rich man possessed at the time of his th reverted to the royal treasury.

To acquire means to keep up their gorgeous state the cials, from the pro-consuls down, had but one method – squeeze the peasantry. They squeezed.

n Madras, wrote van Linschoten, who saw the country he decade between 1580 to 1590, the peasants [1]

. are so miserable that for a penny they would endure to whipped, and they eat so little that it seemeth they live by air; they are likewise most of them small and weak of bs.'

When the rains failed, they fell into still deeper distress, dered like wild animals in vain search of food and sold ir children for 'less than a rupee apiece,' while the slave-ket was abundantly recruited from those who sold their ı bodies to escape starvation, of which cannibalism, an inary feature of famine, was the alternative.

The Bádsháh Námah of 'Abd Al Hamid Láhawrí bears ness that in the Deccan during the famine of 1631 unded bones of the dead were mixed with flour and sold. Destitution at length reached such a pitch that men an to devour each other and the flesh of a son was pre-ed to his love. The number of the dying caused obstruc-ı in the roads.' The Dutch East India Company's repre-tative in the same year, recorded that in Surat the dearth so great that 'menschen en vee van honger sturven . . .

The Voyage of John Huyghen van Linschoten to the East Indies. Edited he Hakluyt Society, 1884.

moeders tegen natuer haere kinderkens wt hongersnoot gegeten hebben.' Two years later Christopher Read ported to the British East India Company that Mesulapat and Armagon were 'sorely oppressed with famine, the li inge eating up the dead and men durst scarcely travel in country for feare they should be kild and eaten.' And Pe Mundy wrote from Gujerat during the same period that ' famine it selfe swept away more than a million of the Com or poorer Sort. After which, the mortallitie succeeding as much more among rich and poore. Weomen were se to rost their Children; . . . A man or woman noe soo dead but they were Cutt in pieces to be eaten.'

These testimonies will be found and at greater length the text and Appendix of the Hakluyt Society's edition the *Travels of Peter Mundy.* Other old chronicles corro rate them.

Slaves cost practically nothing to keep and were theref numerous in each noble's household, where their little va ensured their wretched state. The elephants of the nob wore trappings of silver and gold, while 'the people,' says contemporaneous observer, de Laet,[1] 'have not suffici covering to keep warm in winter.'

Merchants, if prosperous, dared not live comfortab dared not eat good food, and buried their silver deep un ground; for the smallest show of means brought the turers to wring from them the hiding-place of their wea

The village masses constituted practically the only p ductive element in the land. All their production, save th bare subsistence, was absorbed by the State. As to its distribution, that took a single route, into the pockets of extremely small body of foreigners constituting the rul

[1] *De Imperio Magni Mogolis.* J. de Laet. Leyden, 1631.

s. None of it returned to the people. No communal efits existed.

A very few bridges and such roads as are made by the lding of bullocks' feet through dust and mud comprised communication lines of the land. No system of popular cation or of medical relief was worked, and none of legal ence. Fine schemes were sometimes set on paper by rs and their ministers, but practically nothing was ually done toward the economic development of the ntry; for if any one ruler began a work, his successor troyed it or let it decay.[1]

Fifteen years after the death of Akbar, or in the year 1620, Hollander, Francisco Pelsaert, began that seven-years' dence in India of which he left so valuable and so curious cord. In the course of his narrative Pelsaert writes:[2]

The land would give a plentiful, or even an extraordinary d, if the peasants were not so cruelly and pitilessly ressed; for villages which, owing to some small shortage roduce, are unable to pay the full amount of the revenue-n, are made prize, so to speak, by their masters or gov-ors, and wives and children sold, on pretext of a charge of ellion. Some peasants abscond to escape their tyranny and consequently the fields lie empty and unsown and w into wildernesses.

. . . As regards the laws, they are scarcely observed at all, the administration is absolutely autocratic. . . . Their s contain such provisions as hand for hand, eye for eye,

[1] *India at the Death of Akbar*, by W. H. Moreland. Macmillan & Co., lon, 1920, gives an elaborate and heavily documented digest of contem-neous authority on this general subject.

[2] *The Remonstrantie of Francisco Pelsaert*, translated from the Dutch by I. Moreland and P. Geyl. Heffers, Cambridge, 1925, pp. 47–59.

tooth for tooth; but who will ex-communicate the Pc And who would dare to ask a Governor "Why do you rul this way or that? Our Law orders thus." . . . In every there is a . . . royal court of Justice . . . [but] one n indeed be sorry for the man who has to come to ju ment before these godless "un-judges"; their eyes are blea with greed, their mouths gape like wolves for covetousn and their bellies hunger for the bread of the poor; every stands with hands open to receive, for no mercy or compas can be had except on payment of cash. This fault should be attributed to judges or officers alone, for the evil is a versal plague; from the least to the greatest, right up to King himself, every one is infected with insatiable greec

'. . . It is important to recognize that [the King, Jal gir] is to be regarded as king of the plains or the open rc only; for in many places you can travel only with a str body of men, or on payment of heavy tolls to rebels [and] there are nearly as many rebels as subjects. Tal the chief cities, for example, at Surat the forces of Raja Pi come pillaging up to, or inside the city, murdering the pe and burning the villages, and in the same way, near Ahn abad, Burhanpur, Agra, Delhi, Lahore, and many o cities, thieves and robbers come in force by night or day open enemies. The Governors are usually bribed by thieves to remain inactive, for avarice dominates m honour, and, instead of maintaining troops, they fill adorn their *mahals* with beautiful women, and seem to l the pleasure-house of the whole world within their wal

The observant Dutchman[1] repeatedly dwells on disastrous contrast between

[1] *The Remonstrantie of Francisco Pelsaert*, p. 60.

e manner of life of the rich in their great superfluity and solute power, and the utter subjection and poverty of the nmon people – poverty so great and miserable that the of the people can be depicted . . . only as the home of rk want and the dwelling-place of bitter woe.'

Nevertheless, he says, having discovered the numbing luence of the doctrines of fate and caste: [1]

'The people endure patiently, professing that they do not serve anything better; and scarcely anyone will make an ort, for a ladder by which to climb higher is hard to find, cause a workman's children can follow no occupation other in that of their father, nor can they inter-marry with other tes. . . . For the workman there are two scourges, the st of which is low wages. . . . The second is [the oppresn by] the Governor, the nobles, the Diwan . . . and other al officers. If any of these wants a workman, the man is t asked if he is willing to come, but is seized in the house in the street, well beaten if he should dare to raise any jection, and in the evening paid half his wages or nothing all.'

Forty years after Pelsaert's departure from India came a ench traveller, François Bernier. His stay covered the riod from 1656 to 1668. His chronicle perfectly agrees th that of other foreign visitors, and gives a vivid picture men, women and things as he found them in the reigns of ahjahan and Aurangzeb – the climax of the Mughal npire. Speaking on the subject of land-tenure and taxon, this observer writes: [2]

[1] *The Remonstrantie of Francisco Pelsaert*, p. 60.

[2] *Travels in the Mogul Empire*, François Bernier, Oxford University Press 6, p. 224.

'The King, as proprietor of the land, makes over a cert quantity to military men, as an equivalent for their pay. . Similar grants are made to governors, in lieu of their sala and also for the support of their troops, on condition t they pay a certain sum annually to the King. . . . The lan not so granted are retained by the King as the peculiar mains of his house . . . and upon these domains he kee contractors, who are also bound to pay him an annual ren

Bengal, he thinks probably 'the finest and most fruit country in the world.' But of the other regions he writes

'As the ground is seldom tilled otherwise than by co pulsion, and as no person is found willing and able to rep the ditches and canals for the conveyance of water, it happe that the whole country is badly cultivated, and a gre part rendered unproductive from the want of irrigation. . The peasant cannot avoid asking himself this questio "Why should I toil for a tyrant who may come to-morr and lay his rapacious hands upon all I possess and value . . . The Governors and revenue contractors, on their pa reason in this manner: "Why should the neglected state this land create uneasiness in our minds? and why should expend our own money and time to render it fruitful? W may be deprived of it in a single moment and our exerti would benefit neither ourselves nor our children. Let draw from the soil all the money we can, though the peasa should starve or abscond, and we should leave it, when co manded to quit, a dreary wilderness." . . . It is owing this miserable system of government . . . that there is city or town which, if it be not already ruined and deserte does not bear evident marks of approaching decay.

[1] *Travels in the Mogul Empire*, pp. 226–7, 230.

'The country is ruined by the necessity of defraying the ·rmous charges required to maintain the splendour of a nerous court, and to pay a large army maintained for the ·pose of keeping the people in subjection.'

Now, to touch as briefly as possible on the history of ropean powers in India: At the time of Akbar's accession 556 – the Portuguese were already rooted and fortified the western coast of the Peninsula, at Goa, which, with environing territory, they had taken from the Muhamdan kinglets of the Deccan. Thence they controlled the rchant traffic of the Arabian Sea and the Persian Gulf. other European power had yet secured a base in the land, l no Englishman had yet set foot on the soil of India.[1]

The Portuguese hand in India soon weakened, on lines of auchery and cruelty. Thus came the decay that, in the ly sixteen hundreds, let fall all the Portuguese settlements e only Goa itself, into the hands of the Dutch.

Dutch and English merchants, at that period, were equally :n for the trade of the East. The Dutchmen's main inest, however, lying with Java and the Spice Islands, their glish rivals soon stood in India practically alone.

British merchant adventurers, by charter and concessions nted by Queen Elizabeth and by the Mughal Emperor, v from time to time established trading stations along the st coast. Their post in the Bay of Bengal antedated by : years the settlement of Boston by the Puritans. Nine rs later the first English proprietary holding in India was ured, by agreement between the local Hindu ruler and the overnor and Company of Merchants of London, Trading h the East Indies.' By this treaty the latter were allowed

[1] *Oxford History of India*, p. 348.

to rent and fortify as a trading post a bit of rough shorela now the site of the city of Madras. Here, presently, was come Elihu Yale, once of Boston in Massachusetts, Governor in the Company's behalf. Here was earned means to benefit the Connecticut University that bears name to-day. And here, in the old house where Briti Governors of Madras still dwell, hangs Elihu Yale's portr looking placidly out upon the scene of his labours.

French merchants, they also desirous of the trade of Ind during the latter half of the seventeenth century secur several small *points d'appui* along the southern coasts. Th commerce never equalled that of the English; but th aspirations and the national clashes in Europe alike led th into a series of anti-English intrigues with small Indi rulers, resulting in hostilities of varying result. So that wh the English colonists of New England and New York, w the aid of Indian allies, were fighting 'French and Indi Wars' for control of the future, English colonists on t other side of the world, with the aid of Indian allies, we fighting French and Indian wars for the same purpose. A with a comparable outcome.[1]

The struggle which began, openly, in 1746, when t French took Madras, came to its close in 1761, when t French unconditionally surrendered Pondicherry, their ov headquarters, thus ending their effective career in India.

Until well into the eighteenth century, English holdin in India were limited to a few square miles in Madras, in t Island of Bombay, and at three or four other points; duri

[1] As Americans, we may here draw our critics' shot by admitting that wh we have done much to exterminate our Indians, and only in 1924 gran them citizenship though retaining guardianship over them (United States Nice, 241 U.S. 598—1916), our British cousins have multiplied theirs, a have led them into a large and increasing measure of self-government.

s period the English representatives in India occupied mselves with trade alone, taking no hand in local wars or itics. But with the death of the Emperor Aurangzeb, the lapse of the Mughal Empire, and the chaos of free-oting wars that then broke over the land, the Company set for the protection of its settlements a force of European ops, supplemented by Indian auxiliaries.

Thenceforward it grew toward the status of a governing poration. In 1784 the British Government, by Act of rliament, assumed a degree of control over the Company's ocedure. With such authority behind it, the Company uld enlarge its activities and proceed toward establishing ace in a country teeming with anarchy.

This meant reducing to order a host of robber gangs, of rauding chieftains, of captains of the old Mughal *régime* w out of a job and swarming like migrating bees looking new kingdoms and new plunder. It also meant dissuad-g small reigning princes from their hereditary vocation of listing gangs of mercenaries and campaigning against eir neighbours. And if these movements, which the inces themselves often requested, usually resulted in nexing more territory to the sphere of British influence or ntrol, they also brought an increasing semblance of unity the country.

Once the work of pacification was well in hand, began the empt to build up civil institutions and public privileges d to introduce law, justice and order, a thousand years and ore unknown in the land. The Company was still a trad-g company, with a trader's chief preoccupation. But it cepted the responsibility for the people's welfare implied the authority it now held.

A human enterprise covering two centuries of human

progress, the name of the East India Company was som times dimmed by mistaken judgment or by unfit agen Some of these were overbearing, some tactless, some wav ing, one or two were base and a few succumbed to t temptation to graft. Of their defects, however, not a lit nonsense is spun.

The Company, on the whole, was honoured in the quali of its officers. As time passed, a more sensitive public co science at home made it increasingly alive to critical obse vation. Its affairs were reviewed by Parliament. And, wi the general rise in world-standards, rose its standards administration. Its inclusive achievement was courageou arduous and essential towards the redemption of the countr Whatever its faults, it cleared and broke the ground for pr gress. And it lighted the first ray of hope that had ev dawned for the wretched masses of the Indian peoples.

The abolition of ancient indigenous horrors, such as t flourishing trade of the professional strangler tribes, t Thugs; the burning alive of widows; the burying alive lepers, lie to the credit of the Company. And no briefe summary of the epoch-making elements of its concer could be forgiven a failure to cite the gist of Section 87 the Parliamentary Act of 1784, which reads:

'No native of the said territories, nor any natural-born su ject of His Majesty resident therein, shall, by reason only his religion, place of birth, descent, colour, or any of ther be disabled from holding any place, office or employme under the Company.'

A bomb, indeed, to drop into caste-fettered, feud-fille tyrant-crushed India! Nor was this shock of free weste ideas without its definitely unsettling influence. The Sik ellion in 1845, the Indian Mutiny in 1857, were in no ll degree direct fruits of that influence. And with the clusion of the latter England felt that the time had come lo away with the awkward Company-Parliament form of ernment, to end the control of a great territory by com- cial interest, however safeguarded, and to bring the ninistration of India directly under the Crown.

n the year 1858 this step was taken. Shabby, threadbare, and poor, old Mother India stood at last on the brink of ther world and turned blind eyes toward the strange new above her head. It carried then, as it carries to-day, a dge that is, to her, incredible. How can she, the victim slave of all recorded time, either hope or believe that her st master brings her the gift of constructive service, nocracy and the weal of the common people?

CHAPTER XXII

THE REFORMS

THE roots of the form of government now gradua working out in British India ramify into past centuries a are visible through continuous growth. For the purpose this book they may be passed over, to reach the briefest o line of the present evolutionary phase.

The supreme power over India, to-day, is the people Great Britain represented by the British Crown and Parl ment, acting through the Secretary of State in Council India, sitting in India Office, in London. The supre government in India is that of the Governor-General-i Council, commonly called the Government of India. T Governor-General, or Viceroy, is appointed by the Crow His Council, similarly appointed, consists of seven Depa mental heads – the Commander-in-Chief of the Forces, t Home Member, the Finance Member, the Member Railways and Commerce, and the Members for Educati Health and Lands, for Industries and Labour, and for La Of this cabinet of seven members the three last named a Indians.

Next in the structure of the Central Government com the 'Indian Legislature,' with its Upper Chamber 'Council of State,' and its Lower Chamber or 'Legislati Assembly.'

The Council of State comprises 60 members, of whom are elected, while 26, of whom not over 20 may be Gover ment officials, are nominated by the Viceroy.

The Legislative Assembly consists of 144 members,

ıom 103 are elected. Of the remaining 41, all nominated the Viceroy, 26 must be members of Government, while : rest are named to represent the minor interests in the ıntry, as, the Christian Indian population, etc. Both ambers are heavily Indian, and both are constituted with view to due representation of the several provinces into ıich, for purposes of administration, the country is divided.

British India is thus divided into 15 provinces, each with separate administration. Of the 9 major divisions – adras, Bengal, and Bombay Presidencies, the United ovinces, the Punjab, Behar and Orissa, the Central ovinces, Burma, and Assam – each is controlled by a overnor with his Executive Council. These act in conınction with a Provincial Legislative Council, a legislature which 70 per cent. (in Burma, 60 per cent.) at least must elected by the people.

The electorate is intended to give fairly balanced separate presentation to the various races, communities and special terests. The scale varies from province to province, with rying local conditions. In Madras, for example, it stands follows:

Class of Constituency	Number of Members Returned
Non-Muhammadans (meaning Hindus, Jains, Buddhists, etc.)	65
Muhammadans	13
Indian Christian	5
Europeans (including British)	1
Anglo-Indian	1
Landholders (zemindars)	6
University	1
Commerce Industry	6

The qualification for voters also varies in the seve provinces. In general, however, the franchise rests on minimum property qualification. The law, thus far, h given the vote to some seven and a half million persons [1] a has conferred upon all the major provinces the right enfranchise their women.[2]

The effort to decentralize – to magnify the responsibiliti of provincial governments for the purpose of training ar stimulating Indians to handle their own affairs, stands o pre-eminent in the present scheme. In part and as applie to the nine major divisions, this makes of the provinci government a two-branched machine operated from t office of the Governor. The Governor and his Executi Council, all Crown appointees, form one branch. Counc membership is commonly divided between British ar Indians. The Governor and his Ministers of Departmen form the second branch. These are appointed by the Go ernor from the elected members of the legislature and a themselves responsible to that body. All ministers a Indian. Between the two branches the various functions government formerly handled by a single arm are no divided, under the heads of 'reserved' and 'transferre subjects.

Reserved subjects, save for the ultimate power of t Central Government, lie in the hands of the Provinci Governor in Council. Transferred subjects are assigned the provincial legislatures, and are operated by the Minister

The list of transferred subjects represents authority r signed by the British people in favour of the peoples India. The intention of the plan is, if the experimen

[1] *The India Office*, Sir Malcolm C. C. Seton. Putnams, London, 192 p. 59.

[2] See Appendix II.

:ceeds, to enlarge the list of subjects transferred. On the ıer hand, where the Ministerial machine fails to work, ·vernors-in-Council may resume control of a subject eady transferred. Transferred subjects at present comse Education, Public Health, Management of Public orks other than irrigation and railways, Development of dustries, Excise, Agriculture, Local Self-government and ıers. Reserved subjects include Maintenance of Law and der, Defence of India, Finance, the Land Revenue stem, etc.

Of the provincial legislatures, known as Legislative uncils, a recent authority[1] says:

'The Councils have very wide powers of legislation and : annual provincial budgets are submitted to them. In ansferred subjects they possess the power of the purse, but : Governor may restore grants for purposes of the Reserved .e of the administration if he considers it essential to : discharge of his responsibility that money refused by the uncil should be provided. He can disallow an Act or reve it for the Governor-General's consideration, and has : exceptional right to enact on his own authority a measure ·ovided that it deals with a Reserved subject only] the ssage of which he certifies to be essential to the discharge his responsibility. This special power has hitherto been :rcised only once.'

Turning from provincial legislatures to that of the Central ·vernment, the same authority summarizes:[2]

'The Indian legislature, subject to the preservation of the wers of Parliament, has power to make laws "for all

[1] *The India Office*, Seton, pp. 59–60.
[2] *Ibid.*, pp. 60–2.

persons, for all courts, and for all places and things, witl British India," for British officials and subjects in Indi States, for "native Indian subjects of His Majesty" beyo British India, and for officers, soldiers and followers of t Indian Army wherever serving. But it requires the sancti of the Governor-General for the introduction of measu affecting the public debt or revenues, religion, military d cipline, foreign relations, or for measures treating on matt relegated to provincial governments. . . .

'The power of the purse has been very largely entrusted the Legislative Assembly. . . . The annual budget is la before both Chambers, and the consent of the Legislati Assembly is sought for the grants required on most matte though certain heads of expenditure are classed as "no votable."'

The Viceroy and the Crown hold the power of veto; a the former may enact a bill into law, subject to disallowan by the Crown, without the consent of either Chamber. A emergency measure, such a step would be taken only extreme cases.

It will scarcely be necessary, in this place, to go furth into the machinery of the present government of Briti India.

Commonly known as 'Dyarchy,' or 'The Reforms,' it is essence no new thing, but merely an accelerated unfoldi of the original British theme whose *motif* is the drawi of Indians into responsible participation in governme India's outburst of loyalty in the World War, her whol hearted contribution of men and means from every provin and state save Bengal, prompted a responsive flood of feeli in Britain and a desire to requite one demonstration of co ence and sympathy with another in kind. But Parliament s, in reality, only re-phrasing the original principle em-died in the Proclamation of Queen Victoria in 1858, was ly pursuing the line of the Indian Councils Act of 1909, en, in the Preamble of the Act of 1919, the Act now ictioning, it declared its policy.[1]

'. . . to provide for the increasing association of Indians in ery branch of Indian Administration, and for the gradual velopment of self-governing institutions, with a view to the ogressive realization of responsible government in British dia as an integral part of the empire.'

The scheme in its shape of to-day has not the stability the slow-growing oak, root for branch, balanced and chored. Rather, it is a hothouse exotic, weedy, a stranger its soil, forced forward beyond its inherent strength by the it of a generous and hasty emotion. An outsider sitting day through sessions of Indian legislatures, Central or ovincial, somehow comes to feel like one observing a omful of small and rather mischievous children who by cident have got hold of a magnificent watch. They fight d scramble to thrust their fingers into it, to pull off a wheel two, to play with the mainspring; to pick out the jewels. ey have no apparent understanding of the worth of the chanism, still less of the value of time. And when the cher tries to explain to them how to wind their toy up, y shriek and grimace in fretful impatience and stuff their tterscotch into the works.

As to the relation of these people to their supposed job, its st conspicuous quality, to-day, is its artificiality. Adepts the phraseology of democratic representation, they are, in

[1] *Cf.* pp. 179 and 258, *ante*.

fact, profoundly innocent of the thought behind the phra Despotisms induce no growth of civic spirit, and the peop of India, up to the coming of Britain, had known no rule b that of despots. Britain, by her educational effort, has grad ally raised up an element before unknown in India - middle class. But this middle class – these lawyers and p fessional men – are in the main as much dominated to-day were their ancestors five hundred years ago by the law of ca and of transmigration – completest denial of democra They talk of 'the people' simply because the word bul large in the vocabulary of that western-born representati government which they now essay.

A village head man knows and feels infinitely more th do these elected 'representatives' as to the duties and respo sibilities of government. An Indian prince has the inherit habit of ruling, and, whatever his failings, whatever his pu pose, keeps his people somewhere in mind. And an Am ican, unconscious of his own civic debt to his spiritual blood-lineal ancestors, from Plymouth Rock to Runnyme may be brought to a wholesome state of humility by a f days' watching of the anchorless legislators of India.

Off and on, during the winter session of 1926, in Delhi listened to Assembly debates. Hour after hour, day aft day, the Swarajist bench spent their energies in steri obstructionist tactics, while for the most part the rest of t House sat apathetic save for an occasional expression weary contempt from some plain fighting man out of t north. Little or nothing constructive emanated from par benches. The simplest piece of essential legislation propos by Government evoked from the Swarajist orators fantas interpretations as to sinister intent. The gravest concer elicited from them only a bedlam of frivolous and abusi tter. 'We do not trust you,' they would repeat in effect; know your motives are bad.' 'We believe nothing good your thrice-damned alien government.' And, coming wn to specific arraignments, they could solemnly produce h theories as that the Supreme Court of the United States ys, in its decisions, the will of the British Crown.[1]

Patient, unruffled, always courteous, the Government mbers answered back. Not once was there a sign of irri- ion or annoyance or fatigue, much less of despair of the iation thrust upon them.

One day I took up this subject with one of the most able members of the Assembly, an Indian, of superior lities, whose dislike of Britain is probably as sincere as t of any of those who attack her on this floor.

'Your fellow-legislators of the opposition make terrible usations against the good faith of Government,' I said. ley impugn its honesty; they accuse it of trying to set ndus and Muhammadans by the ears, on the principle of vide and rule"; they allege that it tramples Indian in- ests under foot, that it treats Indians themselves with dis- pect, and that it sucks or cripples the resources of the intry for its own selfish interests.'

'Yes,' he replied, 'they say all that, and more.'

Do they mean it?' I asked.

How could they?' he replied. 'Not a man in the House ieves anything of the sort.'

To an American having America's Philippine experience sh in mind, this repetition of history was infinitely sadden- . One remembered the words of the King-Emperor's ssage to the Indian Legislature and Councils at the open- of the first Sessions held under the Reforms Act:

[1] *Legislative Assembly Debates*, Vol. VII, p. 278.

'On you, the first representatives of the people on the n Councils, there rests a very special responsibility. For on y it lies, by the conduct of your business and the justice of yc judgment to convince the world of the wisdom of this gr constitutional change. But on you it also lies to rememb the many millions of your fellow-countrymen who are r yet qualified for a share in political life, to work for th upliftment and to cherish their interests as your own.'

What meaning had such language in the ears of th to whom it was addressed? What relation did they fe between themselves and poor old Mother India? What du toward their own cause, to exhibit capacity and thereby command further concessions?

The history of British administration of India shows th reactionary disorders follow attempts at speeded progre The East resents being hustled, even in reforms. It was pe haps specially unfortunate for 'Dyarchy' that its birthd should fall in the season of Mr. Gandhi's ill-starred adve ture into politics, when he could turn upon it the full flo of his non-co-operative gas attack. His influence in Beng and the Central Provinces was enough at the time to stop t experiment completely, and although that influence has n everywhere lapsed into negligibility as a political factor, crippling and embittering after-effects still drag upon t wheels of progress.

Without presuming to offer a criticism of the Refor Act, it would seem that its chief obstacle lies deeper in t roots of things than any enmity can reach. The wh structure of the Reforms is planned to rest on the foundati of a general electorate which, through its directly elect legislators, controls in each province the Ministers w ndle the people's affairs. And the difficulty is that while structure hangs waiting in mid-air, the foundation de-ned to sustain it yet lingers in the blue-print stage – does t in fact exist. India has no electorate, in any workable nse of the word, nor can have on the present basis for many nerations to come. And of this statement the natural com-ment is also true: India's elected representatives are as profoundly unaware of the nature of the duties incumbent on their office.

Reasons for the non-existence of an electorate will have en gathered in the foregoing pages of this book. One of chief among them is, that while less than 8 per cent. of peoples can read at all, that literate fraction is concen-ted almost entirely in the large towns and cities, leaving great masses spread over the great spaces of the land, reached and unreachable by the printed word.

This illiterate peasantry, these illiterate landholders, have access to and no interest in the political game, nor in any rizon beyond that which daily meets their physical eyes. e town politician, the legislator actual or aspirant, rarely mes near them unless it be at election time or, as in the riod of the 'non-violence' agitations, to stir them with some port of evil to rise in blind revolt. When, recently, Swara-members of the legislative councils decided to try to block wheels of government by walking out, not one of them, far as I was able to learn, took the previous step of con-ting his constituents. The constituency is as yet too gauzy igment, too abstract a theory, too non-oriental a concep-n, to figure as an influence in their minds.

No one who has studied the course of events in the Central d Provincial governments during the last six years can ape the conclusion that the British government officials charged with administering the new law have striven w honesty, sincerity and devotion, to make it a success. Tl work against great difficulties, straining their faith a power and patience to bridge wide voids of experience a development. Their success sometimes seems dim a slight. But one of the finest executives of them all used, my hearing, these words:

'I would ask only this: "Leave us alone. Don't always resurveying, reinvestigating, pulling up the plant to look its root. Each year that we get through is a gain, one y more of peace for the people, of public works protected a advanced, of justice given. The longer we can go on, nc without any great storm, the better the chance of Coun and Ministers discovering that when we oppose them is in obedience to our conception of a law higher than t of personal ambition or clan advantage." '

In the last clause of the paragraph just quoted lies h hidden one of the greatest stumbling-blocks in the way sympathy and just judgment between India and the W To us it seems radically obvious that personal advantage a nepotism, as motives of the acts of public officials, can mean, the world over, shame and disgrace. Therefore suggestion that Indians find difficulty in sharing that vi carries, to our ears, the taint of moral snobbery; and so search our own minds for other explanations of certain p nomena that follow India's autonomization of Governme

But we should be fairer to the Indian as well as wiser o selves if we looked in his mind, rather than in ours, for li on causes. Then we should see that no white man in of ever labours under such a handicap as does the aver Indian official, or ever is so largely foredoomed to defeat, effort toward disinterested public service.

With the Hindu comes, first, the ancient religious law of : family-clan; because of this system the public office-lder who fails to feather the nest of his kin will be branded all his world not only a fool but a renegade, and will find ither peace at home nor honour abroad. No public opinion stains him.

Second, beyond the family line comes the circle of caste. ne Hindu office-holder who should forget his caste's in-ests for interests lying outside that circle would bring wn upon his head the opprobrium, perhaps the discipline, his orthodox fellow caste men. And this, be it remem-red, means not only temporal discomfort, but also dire nalties inflicted upon his soul, determining the miseries future incarnations.

Third, the political struggle between Hindu and Muslim, will be seen in later chapters, brings tremendous pressure bear upon the official from either camp, practically com-lling him to dispense such patronage as he enjoys among s co-religionists only.

With these points in mind, one views with more charity d understanding the breakdown of allegiance to western eals that generally occurs in even the staunchest of Indian iblic officials when the British superior officer who has cked him through thick and thin in free work for general od, is replaced by an Indian, himself subject to the ancient de.

It is stiff work to maintain, alone and accursed, an alien ındard among one's own people.

Yet with all its increased expense and diminished effi-ency, the new constitution is, somehow, turning the wheels. aking the shorter view, it has improved the position of dians in the services. It has opened to them the height of office along many lines. It has made Government m directly responsive to the sentiment of vocal India, to such extent indeed that the onlooker is tempted to wonder whet Government's sense of proportion is not impaired, whethe has not been nervously stifling its conscience to save its ea whether it is not paying more attention to the spoiled bab shrieks for the matches than it is to the vital concerns of whole big, dumb, helpless and infinitely needy family.

A 'hard-headed American' long resident in India, hims a person of excellent standing, told me this incident:

One of the principal Swaraj politicians had just deliver himself of a ferocious public diatribe against the Viceroy

'Now tell me, Pundit,' said the American, privately, 'h can you shout like that in view of the fact that only a f weeks ago this very Viceroy went far out of his way to courteous and accommodating to you and to get you wh you wanted?'

'How can I shout like that?' laughed the Indian. 'W shouldn't I shout? Of course I shout, when every time shout he gives me something.'

Thus in taking information from the Indian, at home abroad, a vital preliminary step is to appreciate and ke always in mind the definition and value that he assigns 'truth.'

The Indian may be a devoted 'seeker after truth' in t sense of metaphysical speculation; he may be of a splend candour in dealing with most parts of most subjects which you speak together. And yet he may from tir to time embed in the midst of his frank speech statemer easily susceptible of proof and totally at variance with t facts.

Having repeatedly come across this trait, I took it up f

.mination with a distinguished Bengali, one of the most)ad-minded of Indian public men. Said he:

'Our *Mahabharata* preaches truth above all. If we have viated it is because of the adverse circumstances under ich we long lived. If we lie it is because we are afraid to e the consequences.'

Then I laid it before a great mystic, spiritual teacher of ltitudes, who had favoured me with a classic and noble taphysical discourse. His reply was:

'What is truth? Right and wrong are relative terms. You ve a certain standard; if things help you, you call them)d. It is not a lie to say that which is necessary to produce)d. I do not distinguish virtues. Everything is good. thing is in itself bad. Not acts, but motives, count.'

Finally, I carried the matter to a European long resident India, and of great sympathy with the Indian mind.

'Why,' I asked, 'do men of high position make false statents, and then name in support documents which, when I them out, either fail to touch the subject at all or else ve the statement to be false?'

Because,' he replied, 'to the Hindu nothing is false that wants to believe. Or, all matter being nothingness, statements concerning it are lies. Therefore he may melessly choose the lie that serves his purpose. Also, en he presents to you the picture that it suits him to offer, never occurs to him that you might go to the pains of cking his words at the source.'

In the same line, a well-informed New York journalist, in winter of 1926–27, asked certain Indians who had been)licly talking in the city: 'Why do you make such egreusly false allegations about conditions in India?'

Because, said one of them, speaking for the rest, 'you

Americans know nothing of India. And your missionari when they come back for more money, tell too much tru and hurt our pride. So we have to tell lies, to balance up."

As his metaphysics work out, it is no shame to a Hir to be 'caught in a lie.' You do not embarrass or annoy h by so catching him. His morality is no more involved in matter than in a move in a game of chess.

Now, in the name of fair play, it cannot be too stron emphasized that this characteristic, this point of view, t different evaluation, constitutes not necessarily an inferiori but certainly a difference, like the colour of the skin. Yet a difference involved in the heart of human intercourse must constantly be reckoned with and understood; else t intercourse will often and needlessly crash.

CHAPTER XXIII

PRINCES OF INDIA

HUS far we have been dealing mainly with British India, distinct from the Indian Empire composed of British dia and the Indian States. Of the total area of the Indian npire – 1,805,332 square miles – 39 per cent. belongs to Indian States. Of the total population of the Empire – 8,942,480 – the Indian States hold 23 per cent., or about ,000,000 persons.[1] Individually, the states vary in size m properties of twenty square miles or less to a domain as ge as Italy. Each is governed by its own prince, or, if the nce be a minor, by his regent or administrator. Some of ruling houses are Hindu, some Muhammadan, some kh, or, in accordance with their history.

The territorial integrity, as well as the sovereign rights of princes within their territories, was made the subject of ecial pledge in Queen Victoria's Proclamation of 1858 on umption of the Paramount Power. Laying down the nciple that Britain not only desired no extension of territory herself, but would permit no aggression from any quarter on the domains of the Indian States, the Queen added:

'We shall respect the rights, dignity and honour of the tive Princes as our own; and we desire that they, as well our own subjects, should enjoy that prosperity and that cial advancement which can only be secured by internal ace and good government.'

[1] See *Statistical Abstract for British India from* 1914–15 *to* 1923–24, 3–5.

The relation between the British Government and ruling chiefs is a treaty relation, not that of conqueror a conquered. It leaves the princes free to determine their o types of government, to levy their own taxes, and to wi the power of life and death within their territories. The ba of the relation, on the part of Britain, is (*a*) non-interfere in the states' internal affairs, excepting in cases of grave ne while exercising such progressive influence as may be ta fully possible; and (*b*) the safeguarding of the interests of country as a whole, in matters of an Imperial charac Foreign relations and negotiations between state and sta must, however, be conducted through the Paramount Pow A British political officer, called Resident, is stationed in e of the larger states, to advise the Ruling Chief. The sn states, by groups similarly, have their British advis members of the political branch of the Viceregal Gove ment.

Once a year the Chamber of Princes, under the chairm ship of the Viceroy, convenes at Delhi for discussion common policies. This assembly is a brilliant, stately a dignified function. And if, in ordinary times, no gr weight of business confronts it, owing to the self-contair nature of the elements represented, its convocation nev theless serves a wise purpose. For it tends, through perso acquaintance under favourable auspices, to harmonize r tions between the ruling houses, while affording a medi for rapid common action in case of need. Nevertheless this meeting two or three of the greatest of the princes h never yet been persuaded to come, on the ground, it is sa that occasions would arise on which for mechanical reas some one of their number must cede precedence.

In visiting Indian States it is extremely difficult to arr

an idea of the actual nature of the administration. One is : guest of the prince, enjoying a lavish hospitality. Like y private host, the prince is showing off the estate, ex-)iting those parts that are, to him, most noteworthy. From cient palaces to modern improvements, there is much of :at beauty and interest to occupy one's eyes. And one ırcely demands of one's host, East or West: 'Now, where : the defects of the picture?'

Nevertheless, it is definitely visible that several states are ll-governed, that most are fairly governed, including some ıt are backward, and that a few are governed badly. These t exhibit the famous 'Golden Age,' preserved like a fly in .ber. Their court life and the life of the people are sections m the unexpurgated *Arabian Nights*. On the one side ange outbreaks of rage, jealousy, violence, the sudden and al disappearance overnight of a favourite minister, lurid nishments and poisonings, and the endless mortal in- gues of the *zenana*. On the other side a populace too life- s even to complain of the burden that crushes it.

The old normal relation of the prince to the people was : relation of a huge-topped plant to a poor, exhausted, over- ed root. He squeezed his people dry, giving little or hing in return. And under such a prince, unless he be outrageous, the people may to-day be fairly content. For ir whole historic experience tells them little or nothing of ossible other mode of existence. And they dearly love the ade, the great ceremonies and brilliant spectacles of birth- rs, marriages and religious fêtes, that their princes so ularly provide but which, because of the tax burdens in- ved, are rarely afforded under British rule.

On the whole, however, it is obvious that the tendency of te government is to level up. This is largely due to the growing ambition of the chiefs for the condition of th properties. Or again, progress is effected when the remo of an unfit ruler leaves the administration of the State in t hands of the Resident, with, it may be, a regent, during t minority of the heir. A measure of comparison is there established, favouring the birth of active discontent if a ret grade government follows, and tending gradually to force its quality from below.

As a particular instance, one may cite the case of a certa prince whose minority lasted twenty years. During t period the British Resident administered the State, and, f the first time in its history, its revenues went to the service the people. Good roads and bridges were built, schools we opened, a modern hospital was established and endowed wi a competent staff; order was secured; trade and manufa tures were fostered; the exchequer made solvent, the reser funds built up, justice was put within the reach of all. An all the years of this pleasant novelty, the people sighed f the day when their prince, not only dearly beloved but al ritualistically half-divine in their eyes, should come hor and rule over them as his fathers had done over their fathe

The day dawned. The boy took over. The wives and t concubines, the Court officials, the dancing girls and t ambitious relatives at once laid hold on him, plying him wi every soft temptation that could dissolve his energy and wi power, sap his manhood and make him easy to control. three years' time he had ruined the work of the precedi twenty. The treasury reserves were gone. Taxes shot u Public services went flat. The excellent doctor, who co £100 a month, had been replaced by a sixty-shilling deal in charms and potions. The competent hospital staff w replaced by useless hangers-on. The hospital itself h ned into a kennel; and so on, through the departments, ıbbiness and decay overwhelming them all. No justice s to be had and no appeal could be taken against bought :isions, for there was none who cared to hear, except at a ce. Graft did everything, and the people were bled to pro-.e money for their young ruler's extravagances and vices. At last they came to their old friend, the Resident, ading:

'We did long to have him come to live among us and rule er us. But we knew not how it would be. We can bear no re. Let the Sahib return and give us peace and justice l the good life we had before.'

The people had begun to think.

Scandalous tales are told of the cruelties and monstrous :ds of certain princes, and a measure of ground work bably underlies many such tales. But none of them can accepted without specific proof, for the reason that the lian anti-Government Press seizes upon every suggestion such material, spreading it broadcast, elaborated and gnified without regard to facts. It provides a pretext to ack Government for laxness in permitting such things to ; although where Government have intervened the same ments are often quick to raise the cry of 'alien despot.'

The boy born to the throne comes into the world with a rful handicap. All want his favour, and the ancient high-d thereto is the ministration to unbridled sensuality, ogance and extravagance. But sometimes there is a strong l intelligent Queen-mother who defends her son. And netimes the heir is sent to a public school in England; or, may spend some years in one of the four Chiefs' Colleges India, where, also, wholesome influences are brought to ır.

One of these influences is the give-and-take of life amo his peers. In his home he has no equal within reach, and therefore, always with inferiors or elders. A second influer for good is the constant effort to rouse him from physical a mental sloth and to get him to work and to play acti games, especially games such as tennis, which he can ca back to his home. Not the least factor that the school wie in his favour is the understanding friendship of the Briti headmaster, his appreciation of the boy's difficulties, prese and to come, and his quiet instillation of that active ideal princely pride which is the pride to serve.

In some cases the work of education seems completely lo in the boy's later life. But the development of character others is definitely lifting the whole standard of governme in the Indian States.

An outstanding example is that of the State of Myso a principality of size nearly equal to that of Scotland, wi some six million inhabitants. The father of the prese prince was carefully trained for his duties under Briti guidance. Acceding to a government which, during minority, had been set in order by British supervision, proceeded, with the aid of a good Dewan,[1] to administer w and faithfully to the interest of his people. Dying in 18 he left a minor heir, so that again the State, in the hands the Queen-regent, came under British guidance, while ag a young prince went into training for coming responsibiliti In 1907 this prince was enthroned. Since that time he h given a high example of unselfish and intelligent devoti to his duties.

A devout orthodox Hindu, his recent choice of Muhammadan Persian, Mirza Ismail, C.I.E., O.B.E.,

[1] Premier.

wan, may be taken as a proof of his single-eyed desire for good of his State. The city of Mysore, with its wide, ded avenues, its fine modern public buildings, its parks l gardens, and its floods of electric light, is a model town, an and bright. A large technical college, a large Univer- building with its separate library, an extensive hospital, among the many conspicuous and handsome edifices. A irrigation scheme is nearing completion. The State's rich neral resources, its agriculture and its peasant industries l manufactures are being developed on progressive lines. ges of both skilled and unskilled labour have doubled in years. A system of bringing the people, through elected presentatives, into periodic communication with the head the State on the State's affairs, is in successful operation. d finally, to dismiss so pleasant a subject too briefly, two ts on the picture are being removed.

First: An Edict has gone forth that, as between two ndidates for administrative office, the office shall go to the ter qualified man rather than to the man of higher caste. d, second, the State's health record being too low, the nce, through his Dewan, has not stopped short of reaching the best the world affords. He has asked the International Health Board of the Rockefeller Foundation to help n make Mysore the cynosure of India.

The request, the second [1] of its sort to come from any part the Indian Empire, has been gladly honoured. The outme will be of extraordinary interest.

All the princes keep armies, according to the needs of ir domains. Thus the Nizam of Hyderabad, with his

[1] The first request to the Rockefeller Foundation to advise a government in ia came from that of the Madras Presidency. An officer of the Foundation ow stationed there.

State of nearly 83,000 square miles, maintains an army about 20,000 men, while the Maharaja of Datia, with 911 square miles, commands a full company of Infantry a battery of seven field guns. Infantry, cavalry, artillery, transport corps compose the larger commands.

Here is a story, from the lips of one whose veracity never, I believe, been questioned. The time was that stor period in 1920 when the new Reforms Act was casti doubt over the land and giving rise to the persistent rum that Britain was about to quit India. My informant, American of long Indian experience, was visiting one of more important of the princes – a man of great charm, c tivation and force, whose work for his State was of the fi order. The prince's Dewan was also present, and the th gentlemen had been talking at ease, as became the old frier that they were.

'His Highness does not believe,' said the Dewan, 't Britain is going to leave India. But still, under this n regime in England, they may be so ill-advised. So, H Highness is getting his troops in shape, accumulating mu tions and coining silver. And if the English do go, th months afterward not a rupee or a virgin will be left in Bengal.'

To this His Highness, sitting in his capital distant fr Bengal by half the breadth of India, cordially agreed. H ancestors through the ages had been predatory Mahra chiefs.

The Swarajists, it would appear, forget that, the mome government were placed in their hands, the princes wo flash into the picture as powers in the land, severally to reckoned with exactly as they were a century ago; and t the Indian Army, if it hung together at all, might be mc ly to follow one of the outstanding princes rather than commands of a Legislative Assembly composed of a type t India has never known or obeyed.

Che Indian mind is cast in the mould of autocratic aris-racy. A natural war means a princely leader and un-ited loot. If His Highness above had set out for Ben-, the man-power of the countrysides, barring Britain's sence, would surely have romped after him.

3ut the princes know well that if Britain were to withdraw m India, they themselves, each for himself, would at once in annexing territory; that all would be obliged to live ler arms, each defending his own borders; and that the sent-day politician would in the first onset finally dis-ear like a whiff of chaff before flame.

Che princes, however, want no such issue. They frankly that they enjoy the *pax Britannica*, which not only relieves m from the necessity of sustaining larger military estab-ments, but which gives them the enjoyment of public ities, as railroads, good high-roads, ports, markets, mail, l wires, while permitting them to develop their properties peace. Their attitude during the War was wholly loyal, l they contributed munificently of money, men and goods the Empire's cause. In a word, they are a company of h-spirited, militant aristocrats strongly interested that the tish Crown shall remain suzerain in India, but absolutely using to carry their complaisance so far as to admit the lian politician of the Reforms Government as an agent to ir courts.

Their supreme contempt of that class is not unmingled h distinct irritation that the Power to which they acknow-ge fealty stoops to parley with what seems to them an oudent and ridiculous *canaille*.

'Our treaties are with the Crown of England,' one them said to me, with incisive calm. 'The princes of In made no treaty with a Government that included Beng *babus*. We shall never deal with this new lot of Jacks-office. While Britain stays, Britain will send us Engl gentlemen to speak for the King-Emperors, and all will as it should be between friends. If Britain leaves, we, princes, will know how to straighten out India, even princes should.'

Then I recall a little party given in Delhi by an Ind friend in order that I might privately hear the opinions certain Home Rule politicians. Most of the guests we like my host, Bengali Hindus belonging to the Weste educated professional class. They had spoken at length the coming expulsion of Britain from India and on the fut in which they themselves would rule the land.

'And what,' I asked, 'is your plan for the princes?'

'We shall wipe them out!' exclaimed one with convicti And all the rest nodded assent.

Part Five: Into the North

OHAT, guarding the mouth of Kohat Pass – just one le post on the long line of the North-West Frontier de- ces. All compact and tight-set, fit for the grim work it es. Beds of blue violets along its streets. Beds of blue lets in gardens, for somehow your Briton will have flowers, erever you strand him. Barbed wire entanglements gird- g the town. Lights every hundred paces, and heavy- ned sentries. Big arc searchlights at each corner of each use, turned on full blaze at dusk. No shrubs, no trees or ıer cover for skulkers, allowed too near a dwelling. No ite woman permitted outside the wire after daylight begins fail; not because of fears, but because of things that have ppened. Army officers' wives they are, the few white men in Kohat; the quiet, comradely sort that play the ole game to the finish.

And not one moment of any day or night, in this or any ontier post, is free from mortal danger.

Under the wing of the Post, an Indian town, ringed about high mud walls. Bazaars, mosques, temples, blind-faced uses in pinched and tortuous streets, where hawk-nosed n in sheepskin coats, with rifles lying in the crook of their ns, shoulder bullocks and asses for passage. Hundreds of le stalls, like booths in a country fair, reflect the Afghan undary. Wonderful shining slippers, heelless and curly- d, for the little feet of Muslim ladies; Persian bed-posts, ly lacquered; beautiful gauzes; block-printed silks and tons; vessels inlaid in tin and brass or copper; peacock ttery; fine fox-skins from the mountains; red rugs from khara; meat, for this is a Muslim country; rice and curry l sugar, because certain Hindus have ventured in, lending money while they sell their wares and getting always ric with their money-lending. Getting too rich, maybe, a little too confident. For though the hawk-nosed man the big sheepskin coat may not be their match in play with money, that lurks in his half-humorous, wholly pierc hawk-eye which should warn the boldest.

Besides, this hawk-nosed, hawk-eyed citizen is here in own country. And no more than a gun-shot away, in grey, impending crags of the Frontier mountains lurk brother Muslims, the wild tribes who call no man king master, who know no business other than that of raiding, whose favourite year-round sport is the kidnapping of Hi money-lenders to hear the queer sounds they emit in course of the subsequent entertainment.

In all this world, say the men who, day and night, year year out, guard the frontier of India – in all this world are fighters better than the tribesmen. Also, behind them Afghanistan, like a couchant leopard, green eyes fixed on glittering bait of India. And behind Afghanistan – nay, Kabul itself, lurks 'the Man that walks like a Bear,' finger gold and whispering ceaselessly of the glories of a rush acr the border that shall sweep the Crescent through the str Muslim Punjab, gathering Islam in its train; that shall ra the Muslims of the South and so shall close from both sid like a tide, for ever, over the heads of the Hindus.

'Why not?' asks the Bear. 'Are you feebler men th your fathers? What stops you? The English? But look worry them on the other flank, stirring up the silly Hind north and south, against them. Already these English re their hand, as the councils of their home-country weak And I, the Bear, am behind you. Look at the loot and killings! Drive in your wedge! Strike!'

CHAPTER XXIV

FIREBRANDS TO STRAW

OUGHLY speaking, three-quarters of the population of itish India are Hindus, if the 60,000,000 Untouchables computed with the Hindus.[1] Roughly speaking, one arter of the population of British India is Muhammadan. d between the two lies a great gulf whence issues a con-uous threatening rumble, with periodic destructive out-rsts of sulphur and flame.

This gulf constitutes one of the greatest factors in the esent Indian situation.

Its elements formed integral parts of the problem that the itish Crown assumed in 1858. And if for the first half-ntury of Crown rule they remained largely dormant, the son is not obscure. During that half-century, govern-ent was operated by British officers of the Civil Service, th in the administrative and in the judicial branches. ese officers, in the performance of their duties, made no ference between Hindu and Muhammadan, holding the neral interest in an equal hand. Therefore, being in the joyment of justice and of care, man by man, day by day, d from an outside authority that neither Hindu nor uhammadan could challenge, neither party was roused to lousy, and religious communal questions scarcely arose.

[1] The Census of India of 1921 shows about three and a quarter million hs and about one and a sixth million Jains, of both of which sects many mbers call themselves Hindus. The Buddhists, numbering eleven and alf millions, are largely confined to the Province of Burma, outside the lian Peninsula.

In 1909, however, the wind switched to a stormy quart
The Minto-Morley scheme was enacted by Parliament
the 'Indian Councils Act.'

The effect of this measure was instantly to alarm
Muhammadan element, rousing it into self-consciousness
a distinct and separate body, unorganized, but suspicio
militant in spirit and disturbed about its rights. For it sa
clearly enough, that in any elected legislature, and in a
advantages thereby to be gained, the Hindu was practica
sure to shoulder the Muhammadan out of the path.

Now in order to understand how this situation came abo
it is necessary to recall that Muhammadanism first came
India as the religion of the conqueror; that for five hundr
years its arm controlled the greater part of India, duri
which period Persian was the language of the Court, t
language of literature and verse, the language of the la
But the Muhammadan, though he learned his Koran and
Persian verse, was as a rule an open-air sort of man w
would rarely bother his own head with pens or books if
could find another to do the job for him. Therefore, whe
ever some Brahman, with his quick brain and facile memo
acquired a knowledge of Persian and thereby released
further store of learning for the master's use, he was apt
find a desirable niche in Government service.

Consequently, for five centuries or so, the Brahman d
much of the paper work, while the Muhammadan co
manded the country.

The history of the interval between Islam's effecti
dominance and the assumption of direct administration
the British Crown has been elsewhere outlined.[1] It w
twenty-one years previous to the latter event – back in t

[1] See pp. 255 *et seq., ante.*

s of the East India Company – that a little seed was sown h whose fruit we now deal.

This was the changing of the language of the Courts of tice from Persian to English.

The change took place as a logical part of the Westernizing ndian education. It looked simple. Its results have been ple, like the results of a clean stroke of the axe. The cutta University Commission thus suggests the initial cess:[1]

'The influence of the Act of 1837 and the Resolution of 44 [giving preference in Government appointments to lians who had received a Western education] upon the ndu *bhadralok*[2] from among whom all the minor officials l long been drawn, was bound to be decisive. They had g been in the habit of learning a foreign language – sian – as a condition of public employment; they now nt English instead. It was, indeed, the Hindus who ne took advantage of the new opportunities in public ication in any large numbers. The Musalmans naturally tested strongly against the change; which was, indeed, istrous for them. Hitherto their knowledge of Persian l given them a considerable advantage. They refused to e up learning it. It was for them the language of culture. take up English in addition would be too heavy a burden; reover, they had learnt to think of English as associated h Christian teaching, owing to the activity of the mis-aries, and they were less willing than the Hindus to ose their sons to missionary influences. Their pride and ir religious loyalty revolted; and they stood aloof from movement.'

[1] *Report*, Vol. I, Part I, pp. 37–8.

[2] Professional classes.

Literate or illiterate, the Muhammadan is a passio monotheist. 'There is but One God.' His mosques are c of images. His frequent daily prayer is offered straigh the invisible One Omnipotent. And although he resp Christianity as a revealed religion and reverences Chris an inspired teacher, the doctrine of the Trinity constitute impossible heresy. His faith is his highest possession, he would not willingly open the door to what he consid impure doctrine by learning its vehicle, the English ton

Deeply hurt by the alternatives forced upon it, Is withdrew into itself, little foreseeing the consequences o withdrawal.

As long as British officials administered the affair India in town and village the potentiality of the situa thus created remained obscured. But the first gun of Minto-Morley 'Reforms' rent the curtain, and the star Islamic chiefs, their hands on the hilt of the sword a-ru the scabbard, peered forth half-awake upon a world with shapes of ill-omen.

And so, greatly at a disadvantage, the Muslims as a p tical entity re-appeared in the field. Yet over the v country, in the villages and the hamlets, the stir scar reached. For there, still, the British official alone represe Government, dealing justice and favour with an even ha and Muslim and Hindu, side by side, lived at peace.

Then came 1919, the extension of the 'Reforms' of 19 the transfer of much power, place and patronage fr British into Indian hands, and the promise, furthermore a reviewal of the field at the end of a third ten-year inter with an eye to still further transfers.

From that moment, except in country districts unreac by agitators, peace between the two elements became a n ie – an artificial appearance maintained wholly by the ish presence. And now, as 1929 draws nigh, the tension y increases, while the two rivals pace around each other ircles, hackles up, looking for first toothhold.

'or a time during the political disturbances that followed War a brief farce of unity was played by the leaders of day. Mr. Gandhi embraced the Khilafat [1] agitation as oodied in those picturesque freebooters, the Ali brothers, hereby the Muhammadan weight might be swung with own to embarrass the British administration. But the ilafat cause itself died an early death. And a single in- ent of the Gandhi-Ali alliance may be cited to illustrate actual depth of the brotherhood it proclaimed.

Up on the mountains overlooking the Malabar coast, ong a population of about two million Hindus, live a ple known as the Moplahs, descendants of old Arab lers and the women of the country. The Moplahs, who mselves number about a million, live in surprisingly clean well-kept houses, have often intelligent, rugged faces l, according to my own experience, are an interesting and ndly primitive folk.

But, zealot Muhammadans, they have ever been prone to breaks of religious passion in which their one desire is to sent to Paradise by a bullet or a knife, first having piled the longest possible list of non-believers dead by their ds.

Among these simple creatures, in the year of disorders 21, the political combination above indicated sent emis- ies preaching a special edition of its doctrines. Govern-

[1] An Islamic movement, aiming at the restoration of Turkey to pre-war s, including her reconquest of the emancipated Armenians and Arabs, her recovery of Palestine, Syria, Thrace and the Dardanelles.

ment's hand, these proclaimed, was raised against the places of Islam. Government was 'Satanic,' an enemy of Faith. Government must and would be driven out of I and that right soon. Swaraj must be set up.

From mosque to mosque, from hamlet to hamlet, f coco-nut grove to coco-nut grove, the fiery words pas And, whatever meaning they might bear for an abst philosopher, to the simple Moplah, as, in those miser years, to so many millions of simple Hindus all over the l they meant just what they said – War.

But the point that Mr. Gandhi missed, whatever humorous Ali brothers may privately have thought abou was this: Swaraj, to a Moplah, could only mean the con of the earthly Kingdom of Islam, in which, whatever happened or failed to happen, no idol-worshipping Hi could be tolerated alive.

So the Moplahs, secretly and as best they could, n store of weapons – knives, spears, cutlasses. And on Au 20, 1921, the thing broke loose. As if by a prelimi gesture of courtesy to the sponsors of the occasion, European planter was murdered at the start. But wit further dissipation of energy the frenzied people then c centrated on the far more congenial task of communal First blocking the roads, cutting the telegraph wires tearing up the railway lines at strategic points, ther isolating the little police stations scattered through mountains, they set to work, in earnest and in detail establish a Muslim Kingdom and to declare a Swaraj a their own hearts.

Their Hindu neighbours, though outnumbering th two to one, seem to have stood no chance against them. Hindu women, as a rule, were first circumcised – 'forci verted,' as the process is called – and were then added to plah families. The Hindu men were sometimes given choice of death or 'conversion,' sometimes flayed alive, etimes cutlassed at once and thrown down their own ls. In one district, the Ernad Taluk, over 900 males were cibly converted' and the work spread on through the intain-slopes.

As rapidly as possible police and troops were thrown into country, by whose work, after six months of trying ser-, the disorders were quelled. But not until some 3,000 plahs had cast away their lives, without reckoning the idus they accounted for, not until much property had n destroyed and many families ruined, and not until a long of prisoners awaited trial for guilt that certainly belonged heads higher than theirs.

Meanwhile, the circumcised male Hindus wandered up down the land calling upon their brethren to take ning.

A trained American observer, agent of the United States ernment, chanced to be in the region at the time. His ement follows:

I saw them in village after village, through the south and of Madras Presidency. They had been circumcised by eculiarly painful method, and now, in many cases, were ering tortures from blood poisoning. They were pro-ming their misery, and calling on all their gods to curse araj and to keep the British in the land. "Behold our erable bodies! We are defiled, outcasted, unclean, and because of the serpents who crept among us with their son of Swaraj. Once let the British leave the land and the me that has befallen us will assuredly befall you also, idus, men and women, every one."

'The terrors of hell were literally upon them.

'And the Brahman priests were asking one hundred to hundred and fifty rupees a head to perform the purifica ceremony which alone could save the poor creatures' so

'This ceremony consisted in filling the eyes, ears, mo and nose with soft cow-dung, which must then be was out with cow's urine, after which should be administe *ghee* (clarified butter), milk and curds. It sounds simple, can only be performed by a Brahman, and with proper r and sacred verses. And the price which the Brahmans r set upon their services was, to most of the needy, prohibit Their distress was so desperate that British officials, for o interfering in a religious matter, interceded with the Br mans and persuaded them, in view of the large number c cerned, to accept a wholesale purification fee of not c twelve rupees a head.'

I have not verified the final item in this statement. informant, however, besides having been on the spot at time, is professionally critical as to evidence.

If there was anything particularly Muhammadan in outbreak, it was in the feature of 'forcible conversion' rat than in the general barbarity educed. Less than six mon before the Moplah affair began, occurred the Chauri Cha incident in the United Provinces, far away from Malal

An organization called the 'National Volunteers' lately been formed, more or less under pay, to act as a mil for the enforcement of the decrees of the Working Co mittee of the Indian National Congress. This 'Congress a purely political organization, and was, at the time, un the control of Mr. Gandhi.

On February 4, 1921, a body of National Volunte followed by a mob whom their anti-Government propaga inflamed, attacked the little police station at Chauri ura, within which were assembled some twenty-one ce constables and village watchmen, the common guars of the rural peace. The peasantry and the 'Volunteers,' bering altogether some three thousand men, surrounded police station, shot a few of its inmates dead, wounded rest, collected the wounded into a heap, poured oil over n, and fried them alive.

'his was as Hindu to Hindu.

gain, in the Punjab during the disorders of 1919, antiernment workers launched a special propaganda for the ation of foreign women.

ts public declarations took the form of posters such as e: 'Blessed be Mahatma Gandhi. We are sons of India Gandhi! We the Indians will fight to death after you;' 'What time are you waiting for now? There are many es here to dishonour. Go all around India, clear the ntry of the ladies,' etc., etc.[1]

'his was as Indian to white man.

uch language, to such a public, could carry neither a rative not a second import. Had time been given it to do vork, had a weak hand then held the helm of the Punjab, mbearable page had been written in the history of India. And if these three instances are here brought forward n among the scores of grim contemporaneous parallels a which they can be diversified and reinforced, it is not the purpose of shaming the Indian peoples, but rather to nt out the wild, primitive and terribly explosive nature of elements that politicians and theorists take into their ds when they ignite those people's passions.

See *Disorders Inquiry Committee*, 1919–20, *Report*. Chapter VII, for rds posted in and around Lyallpur, in April, 1919.

In most rural regions even now no developed Hin Muhammadan animosity exists, and the two elements together amicably enough as neighbours, unless out political agents have disturbed them.

Instances occur, to be sure, such as that in the Distric Bulandshahr, near Delhi, in the year 1924, when the Gar flooded. It was a disastrous flood, sweeping away wh villages and their inhabitants, man and beast. Upon cer Hindu ferrymen and fishermen, the local owners of bo depended the first work of rescue. And these made us the opportunity to refuse to take a single drowning Muh madan out of the water.

But, on the other hand, I recall visiting a village nig school, set up by Muhammadans for their own boys wh was in part supported by contributions from the Hi neighbours. This was in Nadia District, in Bengal, wh the villagers of the two religions seemed to bear no sor ill-will toward each other, and where an ever-active Bri Deputy Commissioner was their confidant and chosen co sellor in all their affairs.

Something, again, is to be learned from the simple hist of a park designed for the city of Lucknow. When ground came to be surveyed, it was found that a little Hin temple lay in one corner of the allotted area. Following th established policy in such matters, the British authorities the temple undisturbed.

Then came the Muhammadans of the city, saying: 'W too, desire a place in this fine new park wherein to say prayers.'

So the Municipal authorities arranged that a suitable o space be set aside at the opposite corner of the park the Muhammadans. And the Hindus worshipped in th ıple, and the Muhammadans worshipped in their open ce, both quite happily and innocently, for a matter of ht years.

n the interval came the 'Reforms,' came the fruit of the forms,' came a tension, stiffening steadily.

For Lucknow is a Muhammadan city, in the sense that all important people, all the old families, all the great buildings and monuments, are of the ancient Muhammadan gdom of Oudh. Wherefore the Muhammadans felt that he control of India was about to revert to Indians' hands ir city of Lucknow ought to revert to them.

But, though the history and the aristocracy of Lucknow indubitably Muhammadan, in the population of Luck- the Hindu outnumbers the Muhammadan three to one. erefore the Hindus, filled with sudden fear of the future, v asked each other:

If this Swaraj is indeed coming, where will it plant Hindus of Lucknow? Under Muhammadan masters? ter were we all dead men!'

Upon which they began to organize, to assert themselves, haps rather aggressively and offensively, and particularly lo so each evening, toward sunset, in that little old temple the park.

Now, sunset is an hour appointed for Muslim devotion. eight years the Muslim prayer-rugs had been spread, minutes before sunset, in that same little park, and the hful, kneeling in rows, had said their vespers there. Nor ıld they submit to interruption by obstreperous Hindus v. So, they issued an edict: The Hindus, hereafter, must ose for their temple meeting a time that did not clash h the Muhammadans' evening prayer.

The Hindus resented the edict of the Muhammadans.

The Muhammadans resented the resentment of the Hind
Tinder smouldered up to flame. And presently big gangs
each religion gathered in the park at one and the same h
to fight the thing to a finish.

In the matter ensuing, the Muhammadans seem to h
been the more skilful, since they swept the field quickly
human impedimenta and were about to smash the offens
temple itself, when a detachment of police, reinforced
British troops, intervened.

Thus this particular incident came to a standstill, such
the combatants as were able dispersing to their homes. I
an intense and really dangerous feeling, bred of the bat
and of the fear and jealousy in the air, survived in full vigo
If a small lurking party of the other side saw a Hindu o
Muhammadan pass in the street, that party would dash o
seize and beat him. To restore confidence it was necess
for two or three days to patrol the city streets with Brit
cavalry.

Enter, then, the British District Commissioner –
cities, as well as rural parts, have their commissioners. A
the Commissioner, obviously, must 'arrange.' For t
quarrel was literally ruining the town. Trade was sufferi
small shops were failing, the people were boycotting ea
other, and fresh broils and violence, promising any erupti
disfigured every day.

So the Commissioner invited the leaders of the factions
come to his house and talk it over – because his house w
the only place where they would meet in peace. They can
and sat, and came again. They sat and talked and talk
again. And neither party would yield an inch.

The Hindus insisted that they must begin to beat th
prayer drums five minutes before sunset. The Muhamm

ıs as firmly maintained: 'At exactly five minutes before set we must begin our evening worship, which you ndus shall not disturb.'

Yet at last the Commissioner prevailed. For he elicited m the Hindus a concession of five minutes, and from the ıhammadans a concession of five minutes. Then, with his ıbined winnings safe under his feet, he proceeded to ract from the Hindus a promise that, during the last ten ıutes before sunset, they would not play music in their ıple; and from the Muhammadans a promise that on the of the first of the silent ten minutes they would begin ir ten-minute vesper prayer.

For, during the conferences in the Commissioner's wing-room, the fact had developed that the Muhamdans' objection lay, not to the Hindus' praying, but to the they made at their prayers, hammering temple gongs and ıms.

Those joint conferences in the Commissioner's drawingm lasted, altogether, fifteen hours. As the fifteenth hour sed, the Commissioner's dinner-gong rang in the hall. ıereupon one of the Hindus pondered aloud:

'That gong's voice, over in our temple, wouldn't reach so '

'Will you try it and see?' asked the Commissioner quickly. d to this day the Hindus of that Lucknow temple worship the low and mellow voice of the British Commissioner's ner-gong.

But that experienced official is by no means deluding him- with the notion that he can now go to sleep on his post.

CHAPTER XXV

SONS OF THE PROPHET

In December, 1916, a political body called the All-In
Muslim League united with the Indian National Congr
already mentioned, in proclaiming the identity of Muha
madan and Hindu interests, and in asserting their comm
desire for Swaraj.

The white light of the Moplah uprising remained
veiled on the knees of the future, but at the joint act of t
two organizations, the Muhammadans' instinct of se
preservation, far and wide over India, took alarm. So t
when, in the autumn of 1917, Mr. Montagu, Secretary
State for India, sat in Delhi to receive from Indian intere
their views on the subject of his proposed Reforms, assoc
tion after association came forward to deplore or to repudi
the act of the All-India Muslim League; and the langua
they used was simple enough. Said the United Provin
Muslim Defence Association:[1]

'. . . any large measure of self-government which might c
tail the moderating and adjusting influence of the Briti
Government could be nothing short of a cataclysm.'

Said the Indian Muslim Association of Bengal:[2]

'In the existing backward condition of the majority
Hindus and Muslims, with their divergent creeds, castes,

[1] *Addresses Presented in India to His Excellency the Viceroy and the Ri Honourable the Secretary of State for India.* London, 1918, p. 10.

[2] *Ibid.*, p. 30.

utions and clashing interests, the differences which separ- the Hindu from the Muslim cannot but be reflected in ir dealings and relations with each other. . . . No careful erver will be deluded by the deceptive unanimity of the tional Congress and the Muslim League . . .

'The Indian Muslim Association . . . does not agree to wisdom of any catastrophic changes likely to weaken the manence and stability of British rule in India, upon the ad foundations of which rest all our hopes and aspirations constitutional and administrative progress.'

Said the Association to Safeguard the Muslim Interests in Province of Bihar and Orissa:[1]

We cannot deprecate too strongly the want of foresight played by some of our co-religionists in endorsing in their irety, the views and claims of the Congress. Already re is strong tendency visible in certain quarters to oppress terrorize the Musalmans and ignore . . . their interests. e guiding principle of the English rule up to now has ays been to administer the affairs of Indian Empire with partiality in the presence of diverse religions and nationali- of which it is composed. . . .'

The South India Islamia League[2] presented a plea in ich they reminded Mr. Montagu that, being a minority nmunity, they

. realize the value of the British Government in holding scales even between different classes in this country . . . d] are opposed to any scheme of political reconstruction ich tends to undermine the authority of British Govern-

[1] *Addresses, etc.*, p. 40. [2] *Ibid.*, pp. 62–3.

ment in India, but are strongly in favour of gradual progı sive political development.'

The Muttialpet Muslim Anjuman, a Muhamma educational society of Madras, implored Mr. Montagı stay his reforming hand:[1]

'The Britisher alone can hold the scales even between various communities. Whenever our interests collide w those of other communities, it is to him we look up as embodiment of justice and fair play. Whatever reforms r be introduced, we trust that nothing will be done to unc mine the authority of the British Government in India.

The Muhammadans of the Bombay Presidency presen an anxious appeal which read in part:[2]

'It is freely asserted that in no distant future the Eng bureaucracy will disappear and an Indian majority in Councils will take its place. Whatever may have been defects of that much abused bureaucracy in the past, it m be admitted that it has had one redeeming merit, viz., t of holding the balance even as between the two princ communities in India, and thus protecting the weak aga the strong.'

But in view of the nature of Muhammadan though more ominous weight lay in a simpler pronouncement. Ulema is the body of official interpreters of the Koran wh on occasion of doubt, delivers decisions that guide Muslim world. The solemn verdict of the Ulema of Mad

[1] *Addresses Presented in India to His Excellency the Viceroy and the Honourable the Secretary of State for India.* London, 1918, p. 63.

[2] *Ibid.*, pp. 78–9.

w laid before the British Secretary of State for India, was pressed in three closely similar dicta, one of which follows:[1]

'Verily, Polytheists are unclean.' In case the British Government were to hand over the administration, as desired the Hindus, it would be contrary to the Sacred Law of usulmans to live under them, Polytheists.

SAIYID MUHI-UD-DIN
Trustee of the endowments of the Amir-un-Nisa Begum Sahiba Mosque.
One who is forgiven!

The comparative numbers of the Hindu and the Muhammadan element in the major provinces of British India may seen from the following table:[2]

Province.	Hindus.	Muhammadans.
Madras	88·64	6·71
Bombay	76·58	19·74
Bengal	43·27	53·99
United Provinces	85·09	14·28
Bihar and Orissa	82·84	10·85
Central Provinces and Berar	83·54	4·05
Assam	54·34	28·96
Punjab	31·80	55·33
North-West Frontier Province	6·66	91·62

Now, in view of the militant character developed in any ople by the Islamic faith, it appears that British India's uhammadan factor, even where it is weakest, is strong ough to make trouble. Always an international rather than

[1] *Addresses, etc.*, 63–4.
[2] *Statistical Abstract for British India, from* 1914–15 *to* 1923–24, pp. –15.

a nationalist, all over India the Muhammadan is saying day: 'We are foreigners, conquerors, fighting men. Wha our numbers are small! Is it numbers, or men, that cou When the British go, *we* shall rule India. Therefore it hoves us quickly to gain such ground as we can.'

The Hindu, on his side, wittingly misses no step to c solidate his own position. And so wherever choice rests Indian hands, every office must be filled, every decisi taken, every appropriation spent, on religious commu lines, while the other side fights it, tooth and nail, and t actual merits of the matter concerned disappear from t picture.

Heavily as this condition in all directions handicaps t public service, nowhere is its influence more stultifying th in the judiciary. Always an eager litigant, the Indian fin in his religious quarrels endless occasions for appeal to la But, if the case must be tried before an Indian judge, one si or the other is in despair. For, though he were, in fact miracle of rectitude, he is expected to lean, in his verdict, the side of his own creed, and nothing can persuade the li gant of the other faith that he will not do so.

The Bench of India has been and is graced by some nati judges of irreproachable probity. Yet the Indian is tra tionally used to the judge who accepts a fee from either si in advance of the trial, feeling that probity is sufficien served if, after the verdict, the fee of the loser is return Bought witnesses are also a matter of course; you may them to-day squatting before the court-house waiting to hired. Theoretically I know it is irregular,' said c western-educated barrister of Madras, 'but practically cannot leave that advantage entirely in my opponent's han It is our custom.'

3ut when the matter of the Hindu-Muslim conflict enters all else as a rule gives way. 'How shall any judge decide inst his gods?' moans the unfortunate. 'And does he not d court in the midst of my enemies? Take me, therefore, ore an English judge, who cares naught for these matters will give me upright judgment, though I be right or ong.'

A freakish case was that of an old, experienced Muhammadan District Magistrate of the United Provinces before om, last year, were brought certain police officers of his rict. These men had grossly failed in their duty during tain religious riots, entailing thereby the death of several sons. They richly deserved a severe sentence. But they e Hindus. Therefore the judge, fearing the accusation eligious animosity, let them off with a sentence so light as amount to an unjust award and an offence against the blic service.

More usual is the spirit illustrated in another incident, ich occurred in February, 1926. An old Muhammadan stant engineer who had long served in the Irrigation partment under a British superior, suddenly found him- taking orders from a Hindu. This young man, just out college and full of new ideas, set himself to worry his ior, baiting and pin-pricking till his victim could bear no re.

So, accompanied by his son, the old Muslim sought out major British official, asking for counsel.

Sahib, can't you help my father? Surely it is a shame, r all his years of service, to treat him so!' exclaimed the , at the end of the story.

But the Briton could not resist his opportunity. 'Mahud,' said he. 'You have always wanted *swaraj*. You see, in this, what *swaraj* does to you. How do you feel ab it?'

'Aha!' replied the youngster. 'But I've got a Dep Collectorship now. I take office shortly, and when I do, (help the Hindus I get my hands on!'

The Muslim comprises but a bare quarter of the pop tion of British India. But that percentage is growing. gains indicate both superior fecundity and superior vita His brain is not quick, but he has often a gift of horse-se He is beginning to see that he must go to school. Gran time, opportunity and a sense of security, he may wipe his handicaps and fit himself for full participation in administration of the country. Thrown into the arena to- he would see but one recourse – the sword.

And it should never for a moment be forgotten that w the Muslims of India draw the sword, it will not be as isolated body but as the advance line of an energy banked up, like the waters of a brimming reservoir, by Frontier Defence of the Army.

A glance at the map shows a strip of territory some miles long by from 20 to 50 miles wide, lying along northern boundary of the Punjab. This strip is the No West Frontier Province. Beyond it lies a parallel strip similar dimensions, tribal territory occupied by independ Muhammadan clans, superb fighters whose sole busin since time began, has been the business of raiding. Beh this, again, lies Muhammadan Afghanistan and Muh madan Asia, a huge primeval engine always to be swung one great hammer by the call to loot and a Holy War.

To release that force needs at any moment but a wo Its ceaseless pressure along the thin steel line of the front its tenseness, its snapping, stinging electric current, ırcely realizable until one sees and feels it for one's lf.

Few Hindu politicians do realize it. 'The Afghan has pt off us these many long years. Why should he come rough now? Bah! It is a child's bogy!' they say with dull es, as unaware of their own life-long protected state and w it is brought about as the oyster on its sea-bed is unrare of the hurricanes that blow.

The North-West Frontier Province, 95 per cent. Mummadan, lies to-day quiet and contented with its government, a buffer State between, on the one hand, the rich, partindu Punjab and the vast soft Hindu south, and on the her hand, the hungry Muslim fighting hordes whose gers twitch and whose mouths water to be at them. The ntentment of the North-West Frontier Province with ings as they are is invaluable to the peace of India.

I talked with many leading men of that province. All emed of one mind in the matter. Here, therefore, are the act words of a single representative – a mountain-bred an of Persian ancestry some genera ons back – big, lean, wk-nosed, hawk-eyed, leader of many, sententious until s subject snatched the bridle from his tongue:

'The whole province is satisfied now and desires no ange. As for those little folk of the south, we have never lled them men. There is far more difference between us d them than between us and the British. If the British thdraw, immediate hell will follow, in the first days of hich the Bengali and all his tribe will be removed from the rth. I can account for a few, myself, with much pleasure. -operation between the British and us is our one course. hey have given us roads, telephones, good water where no ater was before, peace, justice, a revenue from trade made possible only by their protection, safety for our families, ca for our sick and schools for our children. None of the things did we have till they came. I ask you, is it likely v shall throw them all away because a coward and a sneak ar our own inherited enemy calls for "boycott," and "non-c operation"? Nothing was ever gained and much lost by th stupid "non-co-operation." India is a big country and nee all our united strength can do for it. Muslims and Briti and even Hindus. But without the British no Hindus w remain in India except such as we keep for slaves.'

On December 26, 1925, over eight years after the Indi National Congress and the All-India Muslim League pr claimed their united demand for the self-government India, the former, or Hindu body, assembled for its annu session. Its president, this time a woman, a product European life and education, opened the proceedings wi an address that deplored the

'. . . sharp and importunate sense of aloofness on the pa of my Muslim brothers, which, to the profound alarm a resentment of the Hindu community, manifests itself in growing and insistent demand for separate and preferent rights and privileges in academic, official, civic and politic circles of life.'

A few days later the All-India Muslim League convene And the address of its president, Sir Abdur Rahim, comi as a tacit reply to the earlier pronouncement, was so clea hewn as to constitute a landmark in Indian history. It repa study at length.[1]

[1] Sir Abdur Rahim's address was published in pamphlet form by Kar Bux Brothers, Calcutta.

'Hindus and Musalmans are not two religious sects like : Protestants and Catholics in England, but form two dis-ct communities or peoples. . . . Their respective attitudes vards life, their distinctive culture, civilization and social bits, their traditions and history no less than their religion, vide them so completely that the fact that they have lived the same country for nearly a thousand years has con-buted hardly anything to their fusion into a nation.'

Referring to recent Hindu movements set on foot to oselyte Musalmans, and to train Hindus in the arts of f-defence, the speaker said:

'The Muslims regard these movements . . . as the most ious challenge to their religion which they ever had to eet not even excepting the Christian crusades whose main jective was to wrest back from the Muslims some places cred to both. . . . In fact, some of the Hindu leaders have ked publicly of driving out the Muslims from India as e Spaniards expelled the Moors from Spain. . . . We all, undoubtedly, be a big mouthful for our friends to allow. . . .

'Any of us Indian Musalmans travelling, for instance in ghanistan, Persia, Central Asia, among Chinese Muslims, abs, Turks . . . would at once be made at home and ould not find anything . . . to which we are not accus-med. On the contrary, in India, . . . we find ourselves in social matters total aliens when we cross the street and ter that part of town where our fellow Hindu townsmen e. . . .

'It is not true that we Muslims would not like to see a self-verning India provided the Government . . . is made as ich responsible to the Muslims as to the Hindu. . . .

Otherwise, all vague generalities such as swaraj, or commo wealth of India, or home-rule for India have no attracti for us. . . . But as a first step we must . . . definitely che the baneful activities of those Hindu politicians who und the protection of Englishmen's bayonets and taking adva tage of their tolerance and patience are sowing trouble in t land to attain swaraj, the full implications of which they not understand and would never face. . . .

'The real solution of the problem . . . is to bring abou state of things in which the conditions of life of the enti population – Hindus, Muslims, Sikhs, Parsis and Christia the peasants, labourers and Hindu untouchables – will be improved economically and intellectually and the politic power so distributed in the general population, that domi ation by a class of monopolists and intelligentsia, will ha disappeared and with that all strife between the differe communities.

'It has been my lot to be in daily contact with educat Englishmen, for nigh upon 35 years as practising barrist as Judge, . . . and last of all as Member of the Executi Council of Bengal. . . .

'I wish to acknowledge without reserve that I found tha had much to learn from my English colleagues at every sta of my career. . . . I have also been associated with ma eminent countrymen of mine in the discharge of public duti and I believe they will admit that most of the progressi measures were originated by the initiative of Englishme . . . In the Government, I cannot recall even a single occ sion when there was agreement on any question among Indians that our opinion was disregarded. . . . I have n known anyone who has seriously suggested that the people this country left solely to themselves would be able at prese set up a government of their own and maintain it against tside attacks. . . . It is best for us all to recognize frankly ıt the presence of the English people . . . is justified by cessity. . . . England owes a great moral debt to India and : only way she can discharge that debt is by taking all pos- le measures to help her to become self-reliant and strong. ıe best men of England recognize this obligation. . . . I not know whether the revolutionaries have any political ogramme; if they have, they have not divulged it. Their mediate objective, apparently, is to overthrow the British *ime*, and with it the entire present system of government. e can, however, dismiss the revolutionaries because there not the least possible chance of their success.

'We Muslims whose history for 1,300 years and more has en one of constant struggles and wars, spreading over Asia, rica and Europe, cannot but regard as extremely foolish d insane the men who think that by throwing a few bombs w and then, or shooting one or two Englishmen from be- ıd, or by razing and looting the houses of unsuspecting d defenceless Indian villagers and by killing and torturing :m, they are going to shake the foundations of British wer in India. . . . We Muslims cannot regard boys or :n suffering from hysteria as serious politicians and the :t is significant that not a single Muslim has joined :m. . . .

'Political measures are not the sole means of building up a tion. At present we have not even a vernacular name for : people of India including Hindus, Muslims and others, r a common language. . . . It is neither by the English ne nor by the Hindus or the Musalmans acting singly, t by the earnest and united efforts of all that the 300 llions of India's population can be led to a higher destiny.'

Sir Abdur Rahim's plain words brought down a storm accusation from the Hindu leaders and their Press, while t rancour between the two camps grew stronger.

Meantime, grim potentialities were beginning to dimly perceived. The Calcutta Riots broke out. By mi summer, 1926, thirty-one murderous explosions h occurred since the beginning of the year, some with hea casualties.[1] It was already evident that both sides, Musli and Hindu, were becoming sobered by the situation in which their mutual fears had brought them. The c Gandhi-ist accusation that the secret hand of Britain br their dissensions still found its mouth-pieces; but thes commonly, were of the irresponsible firebrand type who h no stake in the country save such as might best be serv under cover of smoke. Thinking men of either party saw t untenability of the idea and began, however reluctantly, declare the need of a strong and impartial suzerain to gi them security in the advantages already in their possessio advantages which, they now saw clearly enough, had the roots in the British presence and would be drowned in blo on the day that presence was withdrawn.

The Summer Session of the Indian Legislative Assemb met in a mood to talk reason. Said Maulvi Muhamm Yakub, a Muhammadan member, speaking on the twent fourth day of August:[2]

'I do not agree with those who think that the Governme have a hand in fomenting communal riots and commun feelings. I also do not think that the Government of Ind

[1] For the list, see *Legislative Assembly Debates,* Vol. VIII, August 1926, p. 12.

[2] *Ibid.,* August 24, 1926, pp. 280–3.

ve ever shown partiality towards any community in dealing h communal matters, and, Sir, I take this opportunity blicly to enter my strong protest against the pronouncement recently made by Lord Olivier in this connection the House of Lords. It is very surprising that an *ex*-cretary of State for India should be so ignorant of the thods of administration in this country. I am sure his rdship did not appreciate the result of his announcent. On the one hand he has been very unfair to the vernment of India, and on the other he has done great ustice to the Musalmans in this country, who are already ouring under very disadvantageous conditions. . . .

'There can be no two opinions that communal bitterness . has now assumed an all-India importance. . . .

'Sir, we are fed up with these communal frictions, and the uation has become so very difficult that we cannot enjoy r home life happily, nor do our festivals bring any joy to . . . Is not the time ripe, . . . when we should ask the vernment to come forward and help us, since we could not ve the question ourselves?'

A few months earlier such words could scarcely have been oken on that floor without rousing a flurry of rebuttal. To-y not a voice opposed them. Instead rose that king-pillar orthodox Hinduism, our old friend the Diwan Bahadur Rangachariar of Madras, not to rail at an 'alien governnt,' not to accuse it of clumsy or arrogant interference in dian affairs, but to acknowledge that [1]

. facts are facts, and they have to be faced by us like men. . I admire the sincere spirit in which my Honourable

[1] *Legislative Assembly Debates*, August 24, 1925, pp. 283–4.

friend Maulvi Muhammad Yakub has come forward. I feels the soreness of this disgraceful position . . . and I f it likewise. I am glad, and the whole country is glad, th His Excellency Lord Irwin has taken it up in right earne . . . We cannot achieve the results which we have at he without the co-operation of all people, official and non-offic alike. I want a majority of the people whose hearts are rea bent upon changing the situation.'

The doctrine of non-co-operation with the establish Power led nowhere, as all now see. The mystic doctrine spiritual war, a war of 'soul-force,' that uses the language hate while protesting theories of love, had logically and i sistently projected itself upon the material plane in the for of the slaughter of men. The inability of individuals to su ordinate personal, family or clan interests and to hold t gether for team-work, had been demonstrated. And the fa had been driven home to the hilt that neither Hindu n Muhammadan could think in terms of the whole people.

For the moment, some of them see it. Can they hold t vision? To have seen it at all marks gain.

CHAPTER XXVI

THE HOLY CITY

›WIN ARNOLD has written beautifully about Benares. ındreds of people have also written about Benares. urists, enraptured with its river-front panorama, have ıausted their vocabulary in admiration.

And small wonder, for the scene is beautiful, instinct with our and grace and with that sense of souls' uplifting that rounds the high altar of any part of the human race.

Benares is the Sacred City of the Hindu world. Countless ıples adorn it, set like tiers of crowns above and among broad flights of stairs that ascend from the Ganges, Holy ver. Chains of yellow marigolds are stretched across that er to welcome Mother Ganges as she comes. And as the rshippers, clad in long robes of tender or brilliant colours, ıring their water-jars upon their heads or shoulders, trail and down the high grey steps, they seem so like figures in vision of a prophet of Israel that one almost hears the ıg they sang as 'they went up by the stairs of the city of vid, at the going up of the wall.'

But my visit to Benares was made in the company of the unicipal Health Officer, a man of whom no artist-soul is to think.

This gentleman is an Indian. Before taking up his present ties, he made preparatory studies in America, in the enjoy-nt of a Rockefeller Foundation Scholarship in Public alth. Without attempting to convey an idea of his whole blem, one may indicate here a few of its points.

The normal stationary population of Benares is about

200,000, of whom some 30,000 are Brahmans connec with the temples. In addition, 200,000 to 300,000 pilgri come yearly for transient stays. And upon special occasio such as an eclipse, 400,000 persons may pour into the c for that day, to depart a few days later as swiftly as th came.

To take care of all this humanity the Municipality allo its chief Health Officer an annual sum equal to ab £2,000, which must cover his work in vaccination, regist tion of births and deaths, and the handling of epidemics a infectious diseases.

Much of his best work lies in watching the pilgrims they debark from the railroad trains, to catch cholera patie before they disappear into the rabbit-warrens of the tov Let that disappearance once be effected and the case will concealed until a burst of epidemic announces the preser of the disease. For, although the municipality pays higher officials and the foremen of the Public Health Depa ment fairly well, it allows a mere pittance to its menial st with the result that, if contagion is reported and disinfecti is ordered, the subordinates harass the people for what th can wring from distress.

Benares is an old city. Some of its drains were built the sixteenth and seventeenth century. No one now kno their course except that, wherever they start, their outl give into the river. Constructed of stone, their location sometimes disconcertingly revealed by the caving-in of th masonry beneath a building or a street. Sometimes, si choked at the outlet, their mouths have been unwittingly unthinkingly sealed in the course of river-wall repairs. N a few still freely discharge their thick[1] stream of house-sewa

[1] 'Thick' in particular because of the little water used in Indian hou

Photo: M. M. Newell.

HINDU HOLY MEN—THE FIRST IS A BRAHMAN

) the river anywhere along its humanity-teeming front. most, having become semi-tight cesspools, await the ᴧnpours of the rainy season, when their suddenly swollen tents will push into the city's sub-soil with daily increas- force.

Che city stands on a bluff, her streets about seventy-five above river level. The face of the bluff, for a distance of e miles or more along the river front, is buttressed by rs and by high walls of stone. These, because of their tinuity, bank up the sub-soil water, which, from time to e, bursts the masonry and seeps through into the river, along its famous templed front. There, among the wor- ping drinkers and bathers, among the high-born pilgrim es the painted holy-men, the ash-pasted *saddhus* and s, you may see it oozing and trickling down from those g zigzag cracks that so mellow the beauty of the venerable nes.

Against bitter religious opposition, the British, in 1905, ceeded in getting a partial sewage system and water pipe- into the city. Its main pumping station is at the south of the town, not much habitation lying above it. The er is settled in a tank, filtered, and then put into general ribution, the Municipal Health Officer himself doing eekly chemical and bacteriological analysis from each r.

But the devout will not drink this filtered water. Instead, y go daily to the river, descend the stairs of some bathing- t, scoop up a vesselful in the midst of the bathers under seepage-cracked wall, and carry it home to quench the st of the household. All warnings and protests of the alth Officer they meet with supreme contempt.

It lies not in the power of man to pollute the Ganges.'

And 'filtering Ganges water takes the holiness out,' t reply firmly.

Now, whoever bathes in the Ganges at Benares and dri Ganges water there, having at the same time due regar the needs of the priests, may be cured of the worst dis that flesh is heir to. Consequently upon Benares are delil ately focussed all the maladies of the Hindu millions. Ag whoever dies in Benares, goes straight to heaven. Theref endless sick, hopeless of cure, come here to breathe their l if possible, on the brink of the river with their feet in flood.

Many of the incidents connected with this tenet exquisitely beautiful and exalted in spirit. But the th to public health needs little emphasis.

One such has to do with the over-burdened burni ghats.

The main burning-ghat lies directly in the middle of populous waterfront. 'Nothing on earth can move it fr there,' says my conductor, 'because the place is of partic sanctity. So all I can do is to try to see that all bodies completely burned.'

But complete burning takes a lot of wood. Not every will or can face so heavy a cost. And the Indian-run mun pality, thus far, has been unable to interest itself in the ma to the extent of giving an additional quantity of wood w necessary to complete incineration.

'See those dogs nosing among the ashes. There – has found a piece!' said I to the doctor, as we stood lo ing on.

'Yes,' he answered. 'That happens often enough. they burn bodies here, sometimes rather incompletely, a hours of day and night. Still, if the dog hadn't got that would simply have got into the river, to float down ong the bathers. As the dead babies do, in any case. No ndu burns an infant. They merely toss them into the eam.'

There are no latrines along the water-front. The people efer to use the sandy places at the water's brink among the hing stairs. Thus and otherwise one typhoid or cholera rier may, during his stay, infect 10,000 persons. The er banks are dried sewage. The river water along the nks is liquid sewage. The faithful millions drink and bathe the one, and spread out their clothes to dry upon the other. en in due time, having picked up what germs they can, ey go home over the length and breadth of India to give em further currency, carrying jars of the precious water to ve through the year.

Also, the beautiful and picturesque temples do their part. is may be sufficiently indicated in the words of a dis-guished Brahman pathologist, educated in European iversities and an annual visitor to London and Paris. Said , with deep feeling:

'The temples of Benares are as evil as the ooze of the river-nks. I myself went within them to the point where one is liged to take off one's shoes, because of sanctity. Beyond the shrines, rising out of mud, decaying food and man filth. I would not walk in it. I said *No*! But hun-eds of thousands do take off their shoes, walk in, worship, lk out, and put back their shoes upon their unwashed et. And I, a Hindu and a doctor, must bear witness to at!'

The position of Public Health Officer of Benares, one key the health of India, means so large and difficult a task that would seem to confer honour and distinction upon any man to whom it is entrusted. The present incumbent appeared be confronting his job in a good spirit, determined to pi out his little means with his wits. But I found in the attitu of an Indian brother doctor a differing view. This man, a a Rockefeller Foundation scholar, said: 'That fellow ha rotten job.'

'Why rotten?' I asked, sincerely surprised.

'Because it is so hard. But chiefly because of the indign that he, a Rockefeller scholar, should have to serve unde white man. The Minister is an Indian, of course. But immediate superior, the Director of Public Health, is Briton. It is a miserable shame!'

Curiously enough, this remark was made while, with speaker, I was visiting an Indian attempt at sanitary self-he The attempt was not brilliant, but at least it was a beginnin and the workers were simple, eager, unpretentious little fe hungry and thirsty for encouragement. Seeing whi hunger, our Rockefeller scholar, now an official and to th a great luminary, slowly, thoroughly, and without a glimm of sympathy, impaled them on the toasting-fork of laughing scorn.

Other holy cities exist in India, other centres of pilgri ages. Each, automatically, is a reservoir and a potential d tributing point of disease, demanding the utmost vigilan and the utmost tact in handling.

But the public health problem presented by an ordina Indian city is stiff enough. Take, for example, Lahore. T European section of the town has something about it western America – all of one age, new, roomy, airy, w certain of its good modern buildings erected by the pub spirit of that fine old Punjabi, Sir Ganga Ram. But Kin Lahore, the old Indian quarter, where the crowds live a ve, and in particular its bazaar, where the crowds adore :ongregate, is the danger-point that keeps the Director of alth awake at night.

Streets about eight feet wide, twisting like earth-worms r a rain, straight up from whose edges rise solid lines of elling-houses sometimes several stories high. At their e, on either side, a row of little open-fronted shops, their :ons, brasses, holy pictures, embroideries, silks, grain-s, jewellery, exposed on their floors or walls. Many :ety wooden platforms, built of intermittent slats, project n the front edge of the shop floors, at street level, to the e of the street. Close under these platforms, on both es of the road, runs an open gutter about a foot wide. The ter is in steady and open use as a public latrine. Heaped he slats of the wooden platforms, just escaping the gutter, messes of fried fish, rice cakes, cooked curry, sticky etmeats, and other foods for sale. All the food-heaps lie ctically underfoot, exposed to every sort of accident, while , dirty hands, the nosing of dogs, cows, bulls and sheep, scurrying rats constantly add their contributions; as do babies and children with sore eyes and skin diseases, ing and rolling in the midst of it all, enveloped in clouds lust and of acrid smoke.

And you must be careful, in walking, not to brush against wall of a house. For the latrines of the upper stories and he roofs drain down the outside of the houses either in :ing pipes or else from small vent-holes in the walls, pping and stringing into the gutter slow streams that just r the fried fish and the lollypops.

Mr. Gandhi, whose early sojourn in England has in-nced his general point of view in more ways, perhaps, than he knows, has repeatedly written on this subject. says, for example:[1]

'Some of the [Indian] national habits are bad beyond scription, and yet so ingrained as to defy all human eff Wherever I go this insanitation obtrudes itself upon gaze in some shape or another. In the Punjab and Sind total disregard of the elementary laws of health we dirty terraces and roofs, breeding billions of disease-produc microbes and founding colonies of flies. Down south we not hesitate to dirty our streets, and early in the mornin is impossible for anyone in whom the sense of decenc developed to walk through the streets which are lined w people performing functions of nature which are meant be performed in seclusion and in spots which human bei need not ordinarily tread. In Bengal the same tale in vary form has to be told; the same pool in which people h washed their dirt, their pots, and in which cattle have dru supplies drinking water. . . . These are not ignorant peo they are not illiterate; many have travelled even beyond borders of India. . . . No institution can handle this pr lem better and more speedily than our Municipalities. T have . . . all the powers they need in this direction, and t can get more if necessary. Only the will is often wantin

And again:[2]

'Whilst the Government has to answer for a lot, I kr

[1] *Young India*, October 29, 1925, p. 371.

[2] *Ibid.*, November 19, 1925. Mr. Gandhi on 'Our Insanitation,' p. In its issue of January 21, 1926, *Young India* all too clearly shows the sanitary habits of the body of Hindu political delegates just assem at Cawnpore in the Indian National Congress are identical with the w that Mr. Gandhi elsewhere describes.

t the British officers are not responsible for our insanita-n. Indeed if we gave them free scope in this matter, they uld improve our habits at the point of the sword.'

Mr. Gandhi's judgment of the attitude of Indianized unicipal governments was corroborated by my own obser-:ions in big and little towns in many parts of India.

The city of Madras, for example, the third largest city in : land, completed its present water system in 1914. The chment area, in the hills, includes several villages. The ter, as it reaches the city plant, is about as foul as water n be. By the design of the system it is here passed through w sand-filters into a pure-water tank at the rate of ,000,000 gallons a day.

But the population of Madras has increased and the pacity of the plant is now 4,000,000 gallons short of the ily needs of the town. Detailed plans for the construction adequate new filters, backed by British experts, have been d before the Municipal Council. But these sixty leaders d guardians of the public weal, Indians all, have adopted simpler scheme. As I saw and heard for myself from the dian Superintendent on the spot, they now filter ,000,000 gallons of water a day, run it into the pure-ter tank, then add 4,000,000 gallons of unfiltered sewage, d dish the mixture out, by pipes, to the citizens of the wn.

In judging this performance, one must remember that it kes longer to outgrow race thought and habits of life than does to learn English. The well-dressed man who speaks ith an easy Oxford accent may come from a village where, they desire a new well, they do to-day what their fathers d a thousand years ago; they choose the site not by the slope of the land but by throwing a bucket of water ove goat. The goat runs away. The people run after. A where the goat first stops and shakes himself, though it in the middle of the main street, just there the new wel dug.

CHAPTER XXVII

THE WORLD-MENACE

.ITISH INDIA has half a million villages made of mud. ›st of them took all their mud from one spot, making reby a commensurate hole, and built themselves on the e of the hole.

The hole, at the first rains, filled with water and became village tank. Thenceforward for ever, the village has hed in its tank, washed its clothes in its tank, washed its s and its pans in its tank, watered its cattle in its tank, wn its cooking water from its tank, served the calls of ure by its tank and with the content of its tank has nched its thirst. Being wholly stagnant, the water breeds squitoes and grows steadily thicker in substance as it porates between rain and rain. It is sometimes quite utiful, overgrown with lily-things and shaded by feath-l palms. It and its uses pretty generally ensure the nocratization of any new germs introduced to the village, . its mosquitoes spread malaria with an impartial beak – ugh not without some aid.

Witness, small Bengali babies put out to lie in the buzzing ss near the tank's edge.

Why do you mothers plant your babies there to be eaten e?'

Because if we protect our babies the gods will be jealous l bring us all bad luck.'

One of the most popular and most glorious gifts that beral rich man can make to his own village is the dig-g of an extra tank. One of the fondest dreams of the British Public Health official is to get all tanks fil up.

Nobody knows the exact incidence of malaria in India, village vital statistics are, perforce, kept by primitive vill watchmen who put down to 'fever' all deaths not due snake-bite, cholera, plague, a broken head or the few ot things they recognize. But a million deaths a year fr malaria may be regarded as a conservative estimate of Indi loss by that malady.

Malaria originates in many places apart from tan There is, for example, the water-front of the city of Bomb needless and deadly poison-trap for the sailors of the wor There are railway embankments built without suffici drainage outlets, asking for remedy. There is the wat logged country in the Punjab; there is the new farm-land the United Provinces, cut out of the tiger haunts of the Hin layan foot-hills – both by nature heavily malarial, but bo being ditched and drained as a part of the huge agricultu irrigation schemes now under development by Gover ment.

Malaria, altogether, is one of the great and costly cur of the land, not alone because of its huge death-rate but ev more because of the lowered physical and social conditio that it produces, with their invitation to other forms disease.

Under present conditions of Indianized control, gover mental anti-malarial work, like all other preventive sa tation, is badly crippled. Yet it generally contrives to ho its own, though denied the sinews of progress.

And one recognizes with satisfaction, here and there. few small volunteer seedlings springing up, strangers a aliens to the soil. Pre-eminent among these is the An laria Co-operative Society of Bengal, an Indian organ-ion now trying to bring control of malaria into the lives he people, through educating the villagers in means of tecting their own health. Much praise is due to the ıusiasm of its chief exponent, Rai Bahadur Dr. G. C. ıtterjee, with his ardent co-adjutors, Dr. A. N. Mitra and u K. N. Banerjee. Not only are these gentlemen, whom sited at their centre in Nimta, trying to do anti-malaria k, but also they are raising funds to make available to the gali villagers the services of Indian doctors properly ned in western medicine.

ıpart from its precious tank a village may have a well. depth of the wells averages from twenty to forty feet. ir content is mainly surface seepage. A little round plat-n of sun-dried brick usually encircles the well, a log lying ss the orifice. Squatting on that platform and on that at all hours of the day you may see villagers washing their hes, taking their baths, cleaning their teeth and rinsing r mouths, while the water they use splashes back over r feet into the pit whence they drew it.

lso, each person brings his own vessel in which to draw water he wants – an exceedingly dirty and dangerous el from a doctor's point of view – which he lowers into well with his own old factotum rope. When he returns is house, he carries his vessel with him, filled with well-er for the family to drink.

)ne of the great objectives of the British Sanitary Admin-ıtion is to put good wells into the villages and to educate people in their proper use. Now, not infrequently, one s such *pucca* wells. But, exactly as in the Philippines, the ple have a strong hankering for the ancestral type, and, re they can, will usually leave the new and protected water-source for their old accustomed squatting- and goss ing-ground where they all innocently poison each other

As for pumps, the obvious means to seal the wells a facilitate haulage, some have been installed. But, as a ru pumps are impractical – for the reason that any bit of mac nery is, to the Indian, a thing to consume, not to use and care for. When the machine drops a nut or a washer, no c puts it back, and thenceforth that machine is junk.

Now, this matter of Indian wells is of more than Ind importance. For cholera is mainly a water-borne disea and 'statistics show that certain provinces in British In are by far the largest and most persistent centres of chol infection in the world.' [1]

The malady is contracted by drinking water infected w the fæces of cholera patients or cholera carriers, or fr eating uncooked or insufficiently cooked infected food. finds its best incubating grounds in a population of l vitality and generally weak and unresisting conditic There is a vaccine for preventive inoculation but, the dise once developed, no cure is known. Outbreaks bring a m tality of from 15 to 90 per cent., usually of about 40 per ce The area of Lower Bengal and the valley of the Ganges is, India, the chief cholera centre, but 'the disease is very g erally endemic in some degree throughout the greater p of the whole [Indian] peninsula.' [3]

Since the year 1817, ten pandemics of cholera h

[1] *The Prevalence of Epidemic Disease . . . in the Far East.* Dr. F. Nor White, League of Nations, 1923, p. 24.

[2] Cf. *Philippine Journal of Science*, 1914. Dr. Victor G. Heiser.

[3] *A Memorandum on the Epidemiology of Cholera.* Major A. J. Rus Director of Public Health in Madras Presidency, League of Nations, 1 which see for the whole topic.

:urred. In 1893 the United States was attacked, and in s explosion the speed of travel from East to West was more id than ever before.[1]

In ordinary circumstances, in places where the public ter supply is good and under scientific control, cholera is : to be feared. But the great and radical changes of dern times bring about rapid reverses of conditions; such, example, as the sudden pouring in the year 1920 of ndreds of thousands of disease-sodden refugees out of ssia into Western Europe.

Without fear of the charge of alarmism, international blic Health officers to-day question whether they can be e that local controls will always withstand unheralded icks in force. With that question in mind, they regard lia's cholera as a national problem of intense international port.

In estimating the safety of the United States from in- tion, the element of 'carriers' must be considered. Each demic produces a crop of 'carriers' whose power to spread disease lasts from one hundred and one days to per- nency.[2] Moreover, the existence of healthy carriers is iclusively proved. And India is scarcely a month removed m New York or San Francisco.

'Whenever India's real condition becomes known,' said American Public Health expert now in international vice, 'all the civilized countries of the world will turn to League of Nations and demand protection against her.'

Bengal, one of the worst cholera areas, is about the size of

Recent Research on the Etiology of Cholera. E. D. W. Grieg, in *The Edin- h Medical Journal*, July, 1919.

E. D. W. Grieg, in *Indian Journal of Medical Research*, 1913. Vol. I, 59–64.

Nebraska. It has a village population of over 43,500,c persons, living in 84,981 villages. In the year 1921, a m cholera year, the disease was reported from 11,592 of th villages, spread over 26 districts, the reported deaths totalli 80,547.[1] Imagine the task of trying to inoculate 43,500,c persons, scattered over such an area, in advance of hour of need; bearing always in mind the fact that the vir of a cholera preventive inoculation lasts only ninety da Imagine also the task of disinfecting all these village we when first you must persuade, not compel, the incredulo always fatalistic and often resisting people to permit process.

In the winter of 1924–5 sporadic cases of cholera appea in the Indian state of Kashmir. The British authorities what they could to induce those of Kashmir to act, but latter, Indian fashion, could see no point in disturbing the selves about ills yet only in bud. Consequently, in Ap came an explosion, killing in a single month 2 per cent the entire population of the State. Across the border British India, in the Punjab, the hasty Indianization of Public Health Service had already so far proceeded that o one British officer remained in the department. Result: the first time in thirty years the deadly scourge overflo the Kashmir border and reaped a giant harvest among Punjabi peasantry.

In the normal course of events, however, the main dan source for widespread cholera epidemics is the periodic c centration of great masses of people in fairs and festivals in pilgrimages to holy cities. During the past twelve year

[1] *Statistical Abstract for British India*, 1914–15 *to* 1923–24, pp. 2 382; and 54*th Annual Report of the Director of Public Health of Be* Appendix I, p. xxviii.

re, the British sanitary control of the crowds, in transit . also in concentration, where temporary latrines are lt, pipe-lines for water laid, wells chlorinated and doctors . guards stationed, has been so efficient as greatly to lessen risks. Of the possibilities of the future the Kashmiri dent speaks.

Hookworm, an intestinal parasite, saps its victim's vitality, ntually reducing him, body and mind, to a useless rag not th his keep to himself or anyone else. Hookworm is con- ted by walking with bare feet on ground contaminated h the fæces of persons infected. The procedure against kworm is (*a*) to get the people to use proper latrines, and to get them to wear shoes.

As Mr. Gandhi has shown, Hindus, anywhere, dispense h latrines, but are not, beyond that, always greatly con- ned as to what they use. In one town I found from the nicipal chairman that latrines had been built obediently the Health Officer's specifications and desire; but the ple, he said, were leaving them strictly alone, preferring lo as they had always done, using roads, alleys, gutters . their own floors.

This was in part because the town was short of outcastes therefore had no one to remove night-soil – a thing ch no caste man would do though he smothered in his dirt; and in part because it was easier so to observe the du religious ritual prescribed for the occasion concerned.[1] agers, in any case, always use the open fields immediately ounding their village, fields over which they continually k.

To sum up in the words of Doctor Adiseshan, Indian istant Director of Public Health of Madras: 'How are

[1] See *Hindu Manners, Customs and Ceremonies*, pp. 237–40.

you to prevent hookworm when people will not use latrin
and when no orthodox Hindu, and certainly no woman, v
consent to wear shoes?'

Under such circumstances it appears that, although
cure for hookworm is well established, absolute, simple a
cheap, it would be an indefensible waste of public mon
to administer that cure to patients sure to be immediat
reinfected.

It is estimated that over 80 per cent. of the people
Madras and 60 per cent. of those of Bengal, harbour ho
worms. And in this connection Dr. Andrew Balfour ma
an interesting calculation. As to India, he says:[1]

'A conservative estimate shows that 45,000,000 wa
earners in that country are infected with hookworm. In 1
the Statistical Department calculated the average wage o
able-bodied agricultural labourer in Bengal at 10 rup
monthly (14*s.*). . . . Assuming that the average yearly w
of the 45,000,000 infected labourers is 100 rupees e
these men are at present earning Rs. 4,500,000,000 annua
Now the managers of tea estates in the Darjeeling dist
estimate that the Rockefeller anti-hookworm campaign th
. . . has increased the labour efficiency of the coolies fr
25 to 50 per cent. Suppose that in India gener
only 10 per cent. increased efficiency is achieved. E
so the Rs. 4,500,000,000 [£309,500,000] bec
Rs. 4,950,000,000 [£334,600,000].'

Bubonic plague was first introduced into India in 18
coming from China. To-day India is the world's c
reservoir of infection,[2] and has lost, since 1896, s

[1] *Health Problems of the Empire*, pp. 193–4.
[2] *Prevalence of Epidemic Disease in the Far East.* Dr. F. Norman White, p

,000,000 lives by that cause alone. The case mortality is ɔut 70 per cent. Of pneumonic plague, which sometimes ·elops in conjunction with the other form, only an occanal case survives.

Plague uncontrolled at its source may at any time become international scourge, a danger to which international ılth officers are the more alive since latter-day observations ıtinue to show the disease breaking out in regions where occurrence has been unknown before.

Plague, unlike cholera, is not communicated by man to n, but to man by fleas from the bodies of sick rats. The bites the man and leaves a poisonous substance around bite. Man, scratching the bite, scratches the poison into skin and the deed is done. When plague breaks out in a lage, the effective procedure is to evacuate the village at :e and to inoculate the villagers with plague vaccine.

In most countries you simultaneously proceed to real ıtrol by killing the rats. But this, in a Hindu land, you ınot effectively do, because of the religion.

The constant obstacle in the Public Health Officer's path characteristically, a negative one – the utter apathy of the lian peoples, based on their fatalistic creed. The interttent obstacle, acute of latter years, is the political agent o runs here and there among the villages, whispering that evil Government is bent on working harm. To such a ch have these persons from time to time wrought their tims, that the latter have murdered the native health :nt entrusted with the task of getting them out of an ected site.

With repeated examples, however, of the results of follow- Government's behests, a degree of improvement has :en place. In some parts where plague has struck often.

the people have begun to evacuate of themselves, when r begin to die, and to flock into the nearest dispensary begg for inoculation. But in general the darkness of their mi is still so deep that the agitator can easily excite them resistance, even to violence, by some tale of wickedn afoot.

When the first Indian lady of the district can say to English lady doctor brought to her bedside: 'Why shoul show you my tongue when the pain is so much lower do And besides, if I open my mouth like that a lot more de will jump in'; or when the chief landlord of the district tie a great ape just beyond claw-reach of his ten-day-old and then torment the ape to fury to make it snatch and sn at the child, to frighten away the demon that is giving h convulsions, what is to be expected of the little folk squatt by the tank?

In the winter of 1926 I went through a plague-infes district in company with a British Public Health officer tour. The first village that we visited was a prosper settlement of grain-dealers, shop-keepers and mon lenders – the market town for the surrounding farm Each house was stored with grain in jars and bins, and r swarmed. The rats had begun to die. Then two men died. And on that the British District Commissioner ordered the people out.

Now they were all gathered in a little temporary 'str village' a few hundred yards beyond their town gate, ther await spring and the end of the scourge. As the docto Scotchman thirty years in the Indian Medical Serv approached the encampment, the whole lot, men, women children, rushed forward to greet him and then to ask advi

'Sahib, if we build fires here to cook our food, and

nd comes, it will blow sparks and burn these straw houses have made. What, then, shall we do to cook our food? :ase arrange.'

'Build your fires over yonder, behind that mound.'

'Ah, yes, Sahib, to be sure.'

'Sahib, if while we sit here, outside our gates, bad folk :ep into our houses and steal our grain, what then?'

'Even so, is it not better that bad men die of the plague ın that the plague kills you? Also, you may set watchmen a distance.'

'The Sahib is wise. Further: there is, in a tent near by, a anger of no merit who wishes to push medicine into our ns. Is it good medicine? Shall we listen to him? And ıat is the right price?'

'The man in the tent is sent by Government. The medi-ıe is necessary to all who wish to live. It is free medicine. ıere is no price.'

A pause, while the people exchange glances. Then the adman speaks:

'It is well, indeed, that the Sahib came.'

'It looks,' says the doctor, as we move on, 'as if my little spenser fellow had been squeezing those people for money fore inoculating them. They *will* do that! And then, if : people won't satisfy them, they report that inoculation is used. Except in the case of soldiers and police, we have authority to compel inoculation. It is a risky business, s fighting wholesale death with broken reeds!'

Later we find the 'stranger of no merit' squatting in his ıt, a travelling dispenser of the Public Health Department .ined and charged to do minor surgery, well disinfection d plague inoculation, to give simple medicines for simple ments, to lecture, and to show lantern slides on health propaganda. By his own showing he had sat in this tent a month.

'I call the people every day to be inoculated, but t refuse to come forward,' he complained. ' "Plague-docto they say, "now that *you* are here the plague *must* come!" they laugh at me. They are a backward and an ignor people.'

The doctor inspects his equipment. On the inner lid his plague box the dosage is written. Within are the ser tubes, the needles, the disinfectant equipment, undisturb Also his medicine chest – 'Dyspepsia Powders,' 'Cour Medicines,' simple drugs in tablets.

'Let me see your instruments,' says the doctor. All rusty, several are broken and useless.

'You should have sent those in, each one as soon as broke it. You know it would have been replaced at on says the doctor patiently. 'Now you have nothing to w with.'

'Ah, yes, I meant to send them. I forgot.'

CHAPTER XXVIII

'QUACKS WHOM WE KNOW'

r is better to sit than to walk, to lie down than to sit, to ep than to wake, and death is the best of all,' says the ahman proverb.

Taking into consideration the points with which the pre- ling chapter is concerned, the question naturally arises as how the Indian is affected by his own peculiar sanitary bits. That question may be answered in the words of an nerican scientist now studying in the country:

'From long consumption of diluted sewage they have ually acquired a degree of immunity. Yet all of them are lking menageries of intestinal parasites, which make a ivy drain upon their systems and which inevitably tell en some infection, such as pneumonia or influenza, nes along. Then the people die like flies. They have no istance.'

These conditions, added to infant marriage, sexual reck- sness and venereal infections, further let down the bars to ysical and mental miseries; and here again one is driven to culate as to how peoples so living and so bred can have ntinued to exist.

A reply is thus couched by one of the most eminent of ropean International Public Health authorities:

'It is a question of adaptation, and of the evolution of a -grade of existence on which they now survive. The tish are to blame for the world-threat that they constitute. the British had not protected them, the virile races of the th would have wiped them out.'

The superior virility of the northern races – including t Sikhs, and more especially the Pathans and other Muha madan stocks – is favoured by their superior diet. Th hardy out-door folk are all large meat-eaters, and consu much milk and grain. The diet of the southern Hindu l little in it to build or repair tissue. He subsists mainly sweets and carbohydrates, and, to the degree that he is ab he leads a sedentary life. Diabetes is often the incident tl brings to its early close the career of the southern Ind public man.[1]

Lieutenant-Colonel Christopher, I.M.S., Director of t Central Research Institute of the Government of India, i paper called 'What Disease Costs India,' has said:[2]

'The deaths in India annually number about 7,000,0 i.e., very nearly the population of greater London. . . . N all men must die, but it is to be hoped that each will hav run for his money. . . . During the first year of life, [Indian's] expectation of life is . . . about twenty-th years. At the age of five it is thirty-five years, the high expectation at any age.'

And Colonel Christopher further points out that so he a mortality inevitably indicates a background of widespr and continuous sickness, of reduced productivity, of hanced costs of administration, and of penalized trade, wh combined tax upon the resources of the country, thou difficult to calculate, cannot but be an enormous moral a economic burden to support, a heavy drag upon prosper

For this great field of need the lack of means is alw

[1] For an extended exposition of this subject see *The Protein Elemen Nutrition*, Major D. McCay, I.M.S. London, Edward Arnold, 1912

[2] *Indian Medical Gazette*, April, 1924, pp. 196–200.

nspicuous. For 1925–26, some of the provincial budgets owed the following items:[1]

	Education	Public Health
ombay Presidency	£1,450,000	£200,940
adras Presidency	1,294,000	219,700
nited Provinces	1,190,200	102,850
ngal	900,400	183,350

The open road to better conditions is clear, and, alas, ntrodden. One finger-post reads thus:[2]

'The necessary preliminary to any satisfactory advance . is the growth among the educated classes of a missionary d humanitarian spirit which will lead them to consecrate ne, money and energy to the task of ameliorating the contions in which their less fortunate brethren live. . . . India n never be safeguarded from a disastrous death rate, puncated by heavy epidemics, until her people can be weaned om their tenacious adherence to social observances which e as diametrically opposed to public health as they are to onomic prosperity.'

But that humanitarian spirit does not to-day exist.

Curiously lucid contributions on this line come from Mr. andhi; speaking as of Hindu medical men, he says:[3]

'It is worth considering why we take up the profession of edicine. It is certainly not taken up for the purpose of

[1] *Indian Year-Book*, 1926, pp. 89, 97, 107, 118.

[2] *Statement Exhibiting the Moral and Material Progress . . . of India ing the Years 1923–24*. London, 1924, pp. 211–12.

[3] Mr. Gandhi's statements quoted in this chapter will be found in his *dian Home Rule*. Ganesh & Co., Madras, 1924, pp. 61–2.

serving humanity. We become doctors so that we m obtain honours and riches.'

After which he affirms:

'European doctors are the worst of all.'

Amplifying his accusation, Mr. Gandhi continues:

'These [European] doctors violate our religious instin Most of their medical preparations contain either animal or spirituous liquors; both of these are tabooed by Hin and Mahomedans.'

And again, more specifically:

'I overeat, I have indigestion, I go to a doctor, he gives medicine. I am cured, I overeat again, and I take his pi again. Had I not taken the pills in the first instance, I wo have suffered the punishment deserved by me, and I wou not have overeaten again. . . . A continuance of a cou of medicine must, therefore, result in loss of control over t mind.'

'In these circumstances,' he concludes, 'we are unfit serve the country.' And therefore 'to study Europe medicine is to deepen our slavery.'

Whatever may be thought of Mr. Gandhi's judgment, sincerity is not questioned. Holding such an opinion of motives and value of Western medical men in India, it scarcely surprising that, in the period of his 'non-co-ope tion' campaign against Government and all its works, excepting its educational efforts, he should have exhort medical and public health students to desert their classes a to boycott their schools.

Boy-fashion, they did it – for a time – and at what a c to India!

The other side of this phase of Indian nationalism is its ıthusiasm for the Ayurvedic or ancient Hindu system of edicine under which a large part of the native population to-day being treated, more particularly in Bengal and in ntral and southern India.

This system is held to have been handed down from the ›ds in earliest times, and to be of spiritual and inspired ıture. Some hint of its quality may be gathered from an ccerpt from the Sushruta Samhita, one of the two venerable orks on which the system is based.[1]

'The favourable or unfavourable termination of a disease ıay be predicted from the appearance, speech, dress and de-ıeanour of the messenger sent to call a physician, or from ıe nature of the asterism and the lunar phase marking the me of the arrival, or from the direction of the wind blow-ıg at the time, or from the nature of omens seen by him on ıe road, or from the posture or speech of the physician him-ılf. A messenger belonging to the same caste as the patient imself should be regarded as an auspicious omen, whereas ne from a different caste would indicate a fatal or an un-ıvourable termination of the disease.'

Several works on modern Ayurvedic practice have been ublished. These make the claim that the Sushruta anatomy nd surgery of two thousand years ago were far superior to ıose of modern Western science, and deduce that as Ayur-edic methods have undergone no serious change since that me, they must be practically perfect. Says Sir Patrick Iehir:[2]

[1] Translation of Kaviraj Kunja Lal Bishagratna, p. 270.

[2] *The Medical Profession in India*, Major-General Sir Patrick Hehir .M.S. Henry Frowde and Hodder & Stoughton, London, 1923, p. 104.

'One of the principles of the system is that diseases are t result of the operations of evil spirits who have to be pacifie by various offerings and propitiated by incantations. R garding the diseases of children it is stated [1] that these "a due to the action of certain spirits who were belated in o taining lucrative posts in the retinue of the Destroyer ar were compelled, to secure power, to tax sorrowing parent who might have committed any of the hundred-odd ritu faults by afflicting their offspring." One searches in vain f anything approaching definite and rational therapeutics i this system. We have [here] in a *modern* Ayurvedic work complex combination of drugs extolled as being able to cu such diverse conditions as obesity and gonorrhea, an another extensive combination alleged to effect a cure in a diseases of women however caused.'

My personal inquiry into Ayurvedic surgical cases w limited to two instances. The first was that of a little bo who walked into a Madras Presidency hospital one day i 1925, carrying his own forearm as a parcel, with a reque to the British surgeon in charge, from a well-known Ayu vedic doctor, to sew the forearm in place.

The history of this case was that the arm had sustained compound fracture, the bone sticking through the flesh i an open wound. The Ayurvedic doctor had first applied cov dung to the open wound and then had clapped on splint which he bound tight with strips of freshly-peeled tree-bar The weather being hot and dry, the bark had contracte rapidly and produced extreme pressure. The circulatio stopped, dry gangrene set in and the arm sloughed off at th elbow. Seeing which, the Ayurvedic man thought it time t

[1] Quoted from Kaviraj Nagendra Nath Sen Gupta, *The Ayurvedic Syste of Medicine*, 3 vols., Calcutta, 1909.

voke the courtesies of the profession and to suggest the /estern needle.

The second case occurred in 1926, in the same province. n Ayurvedic doctor attempted to operate according to his de upon a man having an enlarged gland in the groin. olding his patient down, and without an anæsthetic, he ɔened the gland. As the knife went in, the patient jumped, artery was cut and the peritoneal cavity slit open. The ɔctor, knowing no anatomy, then took his patient to the earest Government dispensary. But there the little dispenry man in charge, an Indian, out of sheer terror pushed ıe risk away.

'I am not meant for this sort of thing,' he protested. 'I n only meant for minor surgery. Take the man on to a ɔspital.'

But before reaching the hospital the man died.

Action for manslaughter was brought by the police gainst the Ayurvedic physician. But an association of Indian ɔctors holding Western degrees, many of whom were in overnment employ, defended his case and paid the exenses. 'Our fine old Indian system must not be attacked,' ıey said. Their lawyers first got the defendant off on a chnicality; and then secured the prosecution of the little spensary man for criminal delay.

The common arguments in favour of the old system are ıat it is cheaper for the people, that it particularly suits ıdian constitutions and that it is of divine sanction and rth. Leaving the last tenet aside, as not in the field of disıssion, we find that the cost of running an Ayurvedic disensary is much the same as that of running a dispensary on /estern lines;[1] and that no material difference has ever been

[1] *The Medical Profession in India*, p. 116.

discovered between white man and brown, in the matter of reaction of medicines upon the system.

The Montagu-Chelmsford Reforms, however, have occasioned a great recrudescence of native medicine. Provincial ministers dependent on popular vote are prone to favour spending public money to erect Ayurvedic and Unani[1] colleges, hospitals and dispensaries. With the Indian National Congress claiming that Ayurvedic medicine is 'just as scientific as modern Western medicine,' with such men as Sir Rabindranath Tagore, the poet, fervently declaring that Ayurvedic science surpasses anything the West can offer; and with Swarajists in general pushing it forward on patriotic grounds, you get the melancholy spectacle of the meagre appropriations allotted to medicine and public health, in this most disease-stricken of lands, being heavily cut into to perpetuate a 'science' on the same level as the 'voodoo doctoring' of the West Indian negro.

That the old native systems still exert a strong hold on the imaginations of the masses cannot be questioned. Also, like the voodoo doctors, they teach the use of a few good herbs. These two points enable their practitioners to induce enough 'cures' to keep their prestige alive.

But once upon a time it chanced that Mr. Gandhi, having widely and publicly announced that 'hospitals are institutions for propagating sin';[2] that 'European doctors are the worst of all,' and that 'quacks whom we know are better than the doctors who put on an air of humaneness,'[3] himself fell suddenly ill of a pain in the side.

As he happened to be in prison at the time, a British

[1] The ancient Arabic school of medicine.

[2] *Indian Home Rule*, p. 61.

[3] *Ibid.*, p. 62.

geon of the Indian Medical Service came straightway to him.

Mr. Gandhi,' said the surgeon, as the incident was re-ted, 'I am sorry to have to tell you that you have appen-itis. If you were my patient, I should operate at once. t you will probably prefer to call in your Ayurvedic ysician.'

Mr. Gandhi proved otherwise minded.

'I should prefer not to operate,' pursued the surgeon, cause in case the outcome should be unfortunate, all your nds will lay it as a charge of malicious intent against us ose duty it is to care for you.'

'If you will only consent to operate,' pleaded Mr. Gandhi, will call in my friends, now, and explain to them that you so at my request.'

So, Mr. Gandhi wilfully went to an 'institution for pro-gating sin'; was operated upon by one of the 'worst of all,' officer of the Indian Medical Service, and was attentively rsed through convalescence by an English Sister whom he understood to have thought after all rather a useful sort of rson.

CHAPTER XXIX

PSYCHOLOGICAL GLIMPSES THROUGH THE ECONOMIC LEI

THE welfare of any people, we are wont to agree, m finally rest upon economic foundations. In the foregoi pages certain aspects of economic conditions in India ha been indicated. To these indications I should like now add a few more, disclaiming any pretence that they cc stitute a survey, and offering them merely for what they worth as scattering observations made in the living fie entirely non-political both in character and in purpose.

The Indian, aside from his grievances earlier describ has other explanations of what he calls his depressed stat in large part covering them with the elastic title of 'eco mic drains' upon the country. Compared with the matt already handled, these considerations seem superficial, se ing mainly to befog the issue. The principal drains, as th appear to me, have been shown in the body of this bo But the Indian native politician's category comprises none them. He speaks, instead, under such headings as cott tea, interest on Government bonds, export of grain, ar maintenance, and the pay of British Civil Servants in Ind

The attempt carefully to examine these or any compara point with the Indian intelligentsia is likely to end in d appointment and a web of dialectics – for the reason that, the question grows close, the Indian, as a rule, simply dro it and shifts to another ground where, for the moment, has more elbow-room. To touch briefly on the items ju enumerated will, however, illustrate his mode of thoug

Of cotton, his persistent statement is that the country's v crop, selfishly cornered, is sent to England to give ployment to Lancashire spinners, and then, brought back cloth, is forced upon Indian purchasers.

The facts are: (*a*) The English market stands sixth on : list of purchasers of the Indian cotton crop.[1] (*b*) Indian ton, being of poor quality, irregular, short of staple and 'sistently tampered with, to make weight, does not meet : requirements of English cotton cloth manufacturers. The cotton for the looms of Lancashire is supplied from nerica and the Sudan. (*d*) The little Indian cotton used the United Kingdom goes chiefly to making lamp-wicks, aning-cloths and other low-grade fabrics.

As affecting the present status of India's cotton import de, two mutually countervailing influences must be menned: On the one hand stands the recent handling by vernment of the old excise duty on Indian-milled cotton ods – an imposition which no Briton to-day defends; that :ise duty is now wiped out, and its disappearance would :urally serve to diminish importations and to stimulate es of home manufacture. On the other hand stand the ts that the people of India acquire, year by year, a little ore money to spend and a little more habit of spending it; .t they like fine cloths; and that the cloth from Indian lls is mostly coarse. Therefore, in spite of free markets, in te of Japan's growing competition in fine goods, in spite Mr. Gandhi's cottage spinning campaign and its rough oduct, India still chooses to indulge in a considerable iount of Lancashire's sheer fabrics.

Government, meantime, has been sparing no pains to prove the quality of the cotton crop. In the endeavour to

[1] See Appendix III A.

induce the growers to put more intelligence into the wo experimental farms and model stations have been establish in the cotton areas, inspectional teaching has been set up, a improved implements [1] and good seed [2] provided, with active propaganda as to the feasibility of higher prices.

'India is actually a better cotton country than is the Unit States,' an American authority has said, 'but the people w not put their backs into the work, and the Swaraj politici does what he can to discourage improved production, on t ground that "India must not help England by growi cotton that Lancashire will use." '

Whether unaware or regardless of the facts just recount the foremost of Indian politicians repeatedly assured that 'England takes our raw cotton away to give work to l own unemployed, brings the cloth back here and foists upon us. So all the profit is hers and India is robbed. country can stand such a drain.'

'But America raises cotton, some of which England bu makes into cloth and sells to America again. We gladly s to our best bidders, and we buy where we find what we wa Also, we make some cloth ourselves. Where is the diff ence,' I asked, 'between your case and America's?'

'But consider the question of tea,' replies the Ind economist quickly. 'We raise great crops of tea, and alm the whole is swept out of India – another exhausting dr upon the country.'

'Do you sell your tea, or give it away?'

'Ah, yes – but the *tea*, you perceive, is *gone*.'

The third 'drain' upon the country, as named above, is

[1] Originally imported from America, but now made by Indian labou the Government agricultural stations.

[2] From American stock.

erest upon Government's Public Utility bonds, paid to ndon. The calibre of the complaint may briefly be shown ough the single instance of railways.

The first line of railway in India was finished in 1853. At end of March, 1924, India had a total length of 38,039 es of open system,[1] which in 1925 carried over four and alf times as many passengers per mile of steel as did the lways of the United States.

Taking the respective viewpoints of Americans and of lians in the matter now in hand, we get further light on Indian economist. When America built her railways, had not sufficient means to do so without borrowing. nsequently she borrowed from Europe, largely from eat Britain, about half the money that built her railway tem, well content to pay what it cost in view of benefits pected from the opening of the country. These costs, in normal course, continued until about 1914. When India ilt her railways, she also failed to find the money at home; in her case not because money was lacking, but because dian capitalists would lend only at huge rates of interest. nsequently India borrowed from her cheapest market, ndon, practically all the money that built her railways, ying from 2·5 to 5 per cent., with an average of 3·5 per nt. on the loans – the lowest rates that the world knows.

It is the payment of the annual interest on these loans that Indian critic is constantly describing as an insupportable ievance, 'a drain' of the country's resources.

But the net profits to the Government of India brought in the railways after payment of interest, sinking funds, nuity charges, etc., were, in 1924–25, £12,237,200.[2]

[1] *Statistical Abstract*, p. 413. See also Appendix III B.

[2] *Statesman's Year Book*, 1926, p. 139.

Mr. Gandhi's views on railways, being a conspicuc feature of his anti-British propaganda, may be notic here:[1]

'Good travels at a snail's pace – it can, therefore, ha little to do with the railways. Those who want to do gc ... are not in a hurry. ... But evil has wings. ... the railways can become a distributing agency for the evil c only. It may be a debatable matter whether railways spre famines, but it is beyond dispute that they propagate e ... God set a limit to man's locomotive ambition in the cc struction of his body. Man immediately proceeded to d cover means of over-riding the limit. ... Railways are most dangerous institution.'

Yet Mr. Gandhi himself sets the example of braving th danger, in his many political tours, by rail, about the count And, despite his doubts on the point, one effect of the exi ence of the railroads has certainly been to wipe out the mor terror of famine in India. Whereas in the old days that thr hung always over the land, waiting only the failure of monsoon to reap its human harvest, deaths from this cau are now almost unknown; because Government's syste atized famine scheme is sustained by means to transp (*a*) men from famine areas to areas where labour is wante and (*b*) food and fodder whence both exist in plenty to plac where, to save life, both are needed.

Beyond the railheads runs the British-built network good highroads, speeding motor traffic where bullock ca alone used to creep and wallow.

'And every time I think of famine and the desperate wc and the wholesale death it used to mean,' said one c

[1] *Indian Home Rule*, pp. 45–8.

puty-District Commissioner, 'I say, "God bless Henry rd!" '

It is scarcely necessary to point out the further practical ·s of the railways, whether in equalization of prices, in ·ning of markets, or in development of trade with its con-quent increase of individual prosperity and of Government enues.

Turning now to the fourth item listed for consideration, e finds Mr. Gandhi and other Indian critics pointing to exportation of grain from a country where many regions from time to time short of food, as an intolerable 'drain' e to administrative ill-will, greed, or mismanagement. owever elaborately this idea is clothed, its bare bones tell lain story.

No man sells grain to-day that he needs to-day to put into mouth. If he sells grain, it is to get something that he lds more necessary or more desirable. Government, in last thirty years, has created great areas of rich grain land nere only desert existed before. Millions of Indians are sing on these lands quantities of grain far beyond their n consuming power or that of the regions in which they e. Roads, railways, and ships have brought the markets the world to their doors. They sell to the highest lder. If Government should clap an export duty on their oduce to keep it at home, what shame would then be cried on the despot whose jealous grip denied to labour the uit of its toil! Grain travels to and from India as it does erywhere else – in obedience to the currents of world ude.

For our fifth point: The cost of the army is always alleged be monstrous in proportion to the country's revenue. 'he army is too big,' says the politician.

'Is it too big for the work it has to do in keeping yc safety and peace?'

'I don't know. I have not looked into that,' is the us reply. 'But anyway, it costs an outrageous percentage India's revenue.'

In presenting this view of the subject it is the custom speak as of the Indian central budget only, which give figure of expenditure on defence amounting to about 59 p cent. of the total. To arrive at a just statement, the provinc budgets, which are entirely free from defence items, must reckoned in; it is then found that the proportion of gove mental revenues assigned to defence is about 30 per cen

The Indian peoples are taxed about 2*s.* 5*d.* *per capita* the defence of their country.[2]

The people of Great Britain pay about £2 14*s.* *per cap* on that count, the people of America about £1 1*s.*; those Japan pay for defence six times as much as the people India, implying a *per capita* tax on that score of over 14*s.* 7

India possesses 1,400 miles of constantly danger frontier, always actively threatened, and three times in t last century ablaze with open war. She also has an enormo and extremely vulnerable coast line, which without extra c to her is defended by the British fleet. And finally, she ha population which, time and again, in its sudden outbursts internecine fury, needs protection against itself. Taxes a light because the people are poor. Revenues are small b cause taxes are light. Costs of national defence look lar because revenues are small. The maintenance of order a

[1] *Defence of India.* Arthur Vincent. Humphrey Milford, Oxford Univ sity Press, 1922, p. 94.

[2] *India in 1924–25* p. 31.

[3] *The Statesman's Year Book*, 1926, p. xix.

ace is the prime duty of Government. On that duty any overnment must spend what it must. If the total revenue small, the less is left for other activities. The obvious ution is to increase the revenue.[1]

But the great weakness in the Indian's reasoning that the sts of the army constitute a 'drain' out of India of India's alth lies in the fact that practically all the pay of the Army ys in India. The pay of the great body of troops, which is dian, naturally does so. That part of British soldiers' pay at goes home to Britain is scarcely large enough to waste ords upon. British Army officers in India in practically all ses are spending their private means there, over and above eir pay. Equipment and stores, by order, are bought in dia whenever Indian firms can provide them in suitable ality and at a reasonable competitive price. Otherwise ey are bought abroad, by the High Commissioner for dia stationed in London, who is himself an Indian. In s matter of governmental purchase of stores, in whatever partment, a frequent disparity exists between the actual cords and the statements of the Indian politicians who, as own research proved, are wont to suit their allegations to eir convenience rather than to the facts.

The sixth conspicuous channel of 'drain' upon the untry's resources is the pay of the British members of the dian Civil Service. Here the relevant facts are that in the ginning it was necessary to offer good pay to get good men take on the job; and that, with all the upward rush of ices in the last quarter century, no comparable increase has ken place in that pay. India, to-day, is a costly place to live as any sojourner will find. She is not a white man's untry, in the sense that she frequently robs him of his

[1] See Appendix III C.

health if not of his life. In committing himself to her ser he must resign all home associations and privileges for l periods of time. If he marries he must part early with children, and maintain them separated from their parent a journey three weeks long. When he retires, after twe five to thirty-five years of active service, his pension £1,000 per annum loses 25 per cent. by taxes; and, last not least, the salaries paid to all but the few highest offic are large only from the point of view of the Indian, with greatly differing standard of living which few white would accept. The married British Civil Servant in Indi he has children to educate and no private resources on wh to draw, must live with watchful economy to make both e meet. And he can save little or nothing for a rainy day

Nevertheless, the unhappy peoples of India, says Sir Visvesvaraya,[1] speaking as does many another promin Indian, 'have not only to feed and clothe themselves, but to support one of the costliest administrations in the wor

To dissect this statement were, after one glance at the Table, a waste of time. 'One of the costliest administrati in the world' cannot be supported from such resources. cluding land revenue, which is properly to be listed as re rather than taxation, the total *per capita* tax paid by the in bitants of British India in 1923–24 was five and a half rupe (6*s*. 5*d*.) or nearly $1·82 in United States currency at then rate of exchange. The *per capita* taxation in the Phi pines for the year 1923, as shown in the Annual Repor the Insular Auditor, was $3·50, or 14*s*. 7*d*. sterling.

Even such a sum may seem large, in comparison with general poverty of the Indian people. Costs of Governm

[1] *Reconstructing India*, p. 7.

[2] *Statistical Abstract*, 1914–15 *to* 1923–24, p. 190.

luced to the irreducible are still high to a pauper. But servers are not wanting who believe that among the ises of India's poverty is this very lightness of taxation, ich deprives the Administration of means with which to rk.

Now, leaving matters of argument, let us face about and k at indisputable wastages of India's vital resources. The jor channels have been shown in earlier pages, but these ve untouched a list of points only second in importance, :h as caste marriage costs, the usurer, the hoarding of asure, and mendicancy.

Caste laws strictly limit the range of possible marriages, netimes even to the confines of half a dozen families, so ıt, despite his dread of sonlessness, a man may be forced to it till he is old for the birth of a girl within the circle ierein he may marry,[1] and then may be forced to pay nously to secure her. Or again, there is such a scramble husbands of right caste that, rather than sacrifice their n souls by leaving a girl unmarried, fathers strain their :dit to the snapping point to secure eligible matches for :ir daughters.

In Bengal, of late years, several cases have become public girls committing suicide at the approach of puberty, to 'e their fathers the crushing burden of their marriage wry.[2] And the chorus of praise evoked from Bengal uth by this act has stimulated further self-immolations. or do the father's finances greatly affect the case. Though nan prosper and take in much money, marriages in his nily still pull him down to ruin, for the reason that pride d custom for ever urge him ahead of his means.

[1] *Reconstructing India*, Visvesvaraya, p. 241.

[2] *Legislative Assembly Debates*, 1922. Vol. II, Part II, p. 1811.

Marriage expenses and funeral expenses, love of litig tion, thriftlessness and crop failures are among the ch roads that lead the Indian into debt. The Indian mon lender, or *bania*, is the same man as the usurer of the Phil pines. And, exactly as in the Philippines, the average Indi having a little money laid by, even though he be not a *ba* by caste and calling, will, if he be minded to lend, lend to neighbours at 33 per cent. and up, rather than to Gove ment at a miserable 3·5 per cent. so that Government m build him a railway. Let the silly folk in London do th

The *bania* is the man who, foreseeing a short crop, corn all the grain in his region, and at sowing-time sells se grain to his neighbours at 200 per cent. profit, taking t coming crop as security.

Once in debt to a *bania*, few escape. Clothing, oxen, a all purchased necessities are bought of the same wise spider. Compound interest rolls up in the good old way the years pass, and posterity limps under the load unto t third and fourth generation.

'The assumption that debt is due to poverty cannot entertained. Debt is due to credit and credit depends up prosperity and not poverty,' writes Calvert. Credit, in Ind is the creation of the British Government by the establis ment of peace and security of property, coupled with pub works that increase production and the value of land. T *abnia* in his fullest glory is therefore a by-product of Briti rule. In the Punjab, rich among provinces, we find him his paradise, 40,000 strong, collecting from the peo annual interest equalling nearly three times the total su that they annually pay to Government.[1]

Everywhere, whether openly or covertly, the usu

[1] See Appendix III D.

ɔoses the education of the people, because a man who can d will not sign the sort of paper by which the *bania* holds slave, and a man who can figure will know when his debt leared. As two Indian members of the profession warmly d me, the *bania* hates 'this meddlesome and unsympathetic eign Government that has introduced a system of co-:rative credit, which, wherever a Briton directs it, is ning our good old indigenous banking business. More-:r, not content even with that mischief, it is pushing in ht schools and adult-education schemes to upset the ɔple's mind.'

Intimately powerful as he is throughout the country, the *ia* exercises a strong undercurrent of influence in the arajist party, making it generally hostile to labour in-ests and currency reforms.

A third actual drain upon prosperity, seldom advertised, affecting not only India but the rest of the world, is lia's disposition of bullion. Since the early days of the man Empire, western economists have been troubled over lia's intake of precious metals, rather than of foreign ɔds, in payment for her produce. These metals she has ays swallowed up.[1]

In 1889 it was estimated that India held imprisoned 'a ck of gold bullion wholly useless for commercial purpose l increasing at the rate of nearly £3,000,000 sterling 14,000,000] annually, of the value of not less than 70,000,000 sterling [$1,312,000,000].'[2] This ever-:umulating treasure lies in the hands of all conditions and

See Appendix III E.

The Industrial Competition of Asia. An Inquiry into the Influence of rency on the Commerce of the Empire in the East. Clarmont John Daniell. ;an Paul, Trench, Trubner and Co., Ltd., London, 1890, p. 249.

orders of men, from the poorest labourer to the m eminent prince.

In 1927, Mr. D. C. Bliss, American Trade Commissio in Bombay, wrote of treasure in India:[1]

'Vast reserves have been accumulated . . . estimated amounting to more than five billion dollars – but they ha been jealously hoarded in the form of unproductive precic metals. Put to productive uses, or loaned out in the worl money-markets, they would suffice to make India one of t powerful nations of the world. The traditional "wealth the Indies" is there, but in such a form that it yields nothi to its possessors.'

From time immemorial it has been considered improp for any great heir to draw upon his father's hoard of precio treasure and equally improper for him not to build up hoard of his own. The late Nyzam of Hyderabad collect in his vaults jewels to immense values. The present prince understood to prefer bullion, of which his own accumu tions are said to reach to between 150 and 200 milli dollars. Equally, every peasant in the land secretly bur silver in the earth, and loads it upon his women's necks a wrists and ankles, for safe keeping. Forty per cent. of t world's total gold production, and 30 per cent. of the worl silver, is thus annually absorbed by India. None of this go is coined or goes into currency, and, says Mr. Bliss, of silve 'All of the absorption is in response to the demand for bulli for . . . ornamental uses.' 'Undoubtedly,' he adds, ' enormous quantity of bullion has been buried and forgotte The man heavily in debt to the *bania* commonly possesse

[1] *The Bombay Bullion Market.* Don C. Bliss, Jr. U.S. Bureau of Fore and Domestic Commerce, Trade Information Bulletin No. 457, pp. 5-

·e of hidden coin, yet continues borrowing. This custom s on the idea of being prepared for the rainy day and on rofound distrust of the human element in any scheme of ıking.

Ƭhe tendency of the world's gold and silver to concen- e in India and there to disappear from action tells its own ·y. On the one hand, an essentially poor country could bring such a thing about. On the other hand, no country t buries its wealth and then lies down and sleeps on the ve can be really prosperous.

Ƭurning now to the drain incurred through robbing the : India, as we know, is pre-eminently an agricultural ntry. But she has never fertilized her soil. Continually ing from it, she puts nothing back – and yet laments the ıness of her crops. Having but little firewood, she burns cow-dung for fuel. And, being under religious taboo inst the handling of dead animal substances, the Hindu jority will not use for bone-manure the cattle bones of ich they have such store, but, instead, sell them to be ·orted to foreign parts. And they cultivate with a little ɔden plough that barely scratches the surface of the ·und.

Suppose that, still respecting the taboo, they used some :heir idle buried cash, or the interest it would bring, put work, to buy fertilizer and machinery; what far-reaching ·fit might not that one step effect, did but their general of life permit enduring prosperity!

Ƭhe fragmentation of property through the ancient laws inheritance, until a man's holding is so split up into urdly shaped and widely scattered splinters that its useful tivation is impossible, is another formidable obstacle to people's welfare. Those interested in the subject will find it well developed in Calvert's *Wealth and Welfare of Punjab*, where also is treated the great restriction of pot tial revenue through lack of women's work.[1]

And here, too, though at cost of repetition, must be called the enormous dead loss incurred by the cour through the maintenance of its seventy-odd millions of profitable cattle, which, because of religious inhibitions, r but rarely contribute even hides and bones to the count profit.

Last on our list of drafts upon the wealth of India, we f the item of mendicancy.

The Brahmanic code commends renunciation of ac life and the taking up of a life of contemplation and begg as the proper terminal half of man's earthly career. At same time it teaches that he who gives to the beggar is reality a debtor to that beggar, in that he who receives affo the giver a priceless opportunity to establish credit in the to come. Therefore neither shame nor gratitude attache the beggar's part.[2]

In the Indian Legislative Assembly, on February 2, 19 Sir Hari Singh Gour said:[3]

'In the last Census Report . . . we find recorded as b gars, vagrants, witches and wizards . . . altogether 58 la [5,800,000]. . . . But in point of fact their number is s greater as to that class must be added saints and fakirs w live by beggary.'

Government's estimate of 1921 put the saints and fak then living by beggary at 1,452,174.

Now and again these privileged ones gather in groups

[1] See Appendix III F. [2] See Appendix III G.

[3] *Legislative Assembly Debates*, Vol. VII, No. 8, pp. 635–6.

ıdreds and stream across country feeding off the populace they go. The disciple that follows each holy man holds his master's begging bowl. And rarely is he denied. One s their encampments in moving about the country. One ets them on the road, almost or quite naked except for ir coat of ashes, their enormous mops of long snarled hair ached to the colour of ginger, their eyes reddened with ıgs. At great fairs they turn out in multitudes. A com- ent witness informed me that at the latest twelfth-year · of Madras, the two and a half miles of road from the city the bathing place was lined on both sides with religious ;gars sitting shoulder to shoulder, each with an attendant ıatting in front, calling out his master's claims to alms.

And now we come to a more obscure question, that of the sent economic status of the peoples in comparison with ir condition in past eras. Mr. Gandhi and his school rm that the peoples of India have been growing steadily ›rer and more miserable, as a result of British rule. To m a close surmise of the facts is difficult indeed. The sses have, as a whole, little ambition to raise or to change ual living conditions. Their minds as a rule do not turn the accumulation of things. They are content with their d huts. Given windows and chimneys, they stop them up. ther than keep the house in repair, they let the rains wash ıway, building a new one when the old is gone. Given ple space, they crowd in a closet. Rather than work der for more food, they prefer their ancient measure of ure and just enough food for the day.[1]

But their margin of safety is indubitably greater, their wer of resistance to calamity increased, and, allegations the contrary notwithstanding, means of enlarging their

[1] *Census of 1921*, Vol. I, Part I, p. 54.

income lie at all times, now, within their hands. In just su measure as desire for material advance awakens, one s this demonstrated in individual lives.[1] The question whet or not such desire is good underlies one of the prime diff ences between eastern and western thought and practice.

Now in assigning value to these factors, one must reme ber that the soil of India is to-day supporting the pressure over 54,000,000 more human beings than it sustained fi years ago, plus an estimated increase of 7 or 8 per cent. eve ten years.[2]

This, again, is a result of freedom from wars and disord and from killing famines; of the checking of epidemics; a of the multiplied production of food – all elements bound produce ever greater effect as essential features of an est lished government. And the prospects it unfolds, of sh volume of humanity piling up as the decades pass, is stagg ing. For, deprived of infanticide, of *suttee*, and of her ot native escape-valves, yet still clinging to early marriage a unlimited propagation, India stands to-day at that point social development where population is controlled by disea and disease only.[3]

[1] See Appendix III H.

[2] *Census of India*, 1921, pp. 7, 48. These figures of increase are reac after allowing for the factor of population added by annexation of territ

[3] *Ibid.*, 1921. Vol. I, Part I, p. 49.

CHAPTER XXX

CONCLUSION

ɪᴇ preceding chapters of this book state living facts of lia to-day. They can easily be denied, but they cannot be proved or shaken. That there are other facts, other umns of statistics, other angles left untouched by this earch I do not contest.

Neither do I wish to imply that some of the most untering things here affirmed of India are without countert in character and tendency, if not in degree, in certain tions of our western life. But India has carried the prinles of egocentricity and of a materialism called spiritity to a farther and wider conclusion than has the West. e results, in the individual, the family and the race, are y the more noteworthy. For they cast a spotlight toward end of that road.

Some few Indians will take plain speech as it is meant – as faithful wounds of a friend; far more will be hurt at art. Would that this task of truth-telling might prove so lically performed that all shock of resentment were finally sorbed in it, and that there need be no further waste of life d time for lack of a challenge and a declaration!

APPENDIX I

MEDICAL EVIDENCE

In the Indian Legislative Assembly of 1922, the following idence, introduced from the floor of the House as descrip- e of the conditions of the day, aroused neither question r opposition from any one of the assembled Indian gislators. The fact that, although thirty-one years old, it ll remained beyond challenge, carries a contributing gnificance. The evidence submitted consists of a list, mpiled in 1891 by the Western women doctors then actising in India, and by them laid before the Viceroy, th a petition for intervention on behalf of the children of dia. It is made up, they affirm, entirely of instances that ve come under the hands of one or another of their own mber, and whose like are continually revealed in their dinary professional experience.

A. – Aged 9. Day after marriage. Left femur dislocated, lvis crushed out of shape, flesh hanging in shreds.

B. – Aged 10. Unable to stand, bleeding profusely, flesh ıch lacerated.

C. – Aged 9. So completely ravished as to be almost yond surgical repair. Her husband had two other living ves and spoke very fine English.

D. – Aged 10. A very small child, and entirely un- veloped physically. This child was bleeding to death from e rectum. Her husband was a man of about forty years of e, weighing not less than eleven stone [154 lb.]. He had complished his desire in an unnatural way.

E. – Aged about 9. Lower limbs completely para- ed.

F. – Aged about 12. Laceration of the perineum tending through the sphincter ani.

G. – Aged about 10. Very weak from loss of blo Stated that great violence had been done her, in an unnatu way.

H. – Aged about 12. Pregnant, delivered by cranioto with great difficulty, on account of the immature state of pelvis and maternal passage.

I. – Aged about 7. Living with husband. Died in gr agony after three days.

K. – Aged about 10. Condition most pitiable. After c day in hospital, was demanded by her husband, for 'lawful' use, he said.

L. – Aged 11. From great violence done her person, v be a cripple for life. No use of her lower extremities.

M. – Aged about 10. Crawled to hospital on her ha and knees. Has never been able to stand erect since marriage.

N. – Aged 9. Dislocation of pubic arch, and unable stand or to put one foot before the other.

The list will be found in the *Legislative Assembly Deba* of 1922, Vol. III, Part I, page 919, Appendix. See a page 882 of the *Debates*.

APPENDIX II

ENFRANCHISEMENT OF WOMEN

In framing the Reform Bill of 1919, the British Parlia-
ent decided that the question of enfranchisement for the
omen of India could properly be determined only by the
dian peoples themselves. Parliament accordingly allowed
e old sex disqualification to remain in the Bill; but at the
me time so shaped the electoral rules as to leave it in the
wer of each province's Legislative Council to place women
the provincial electoral register by passing a resolution to
is effect.

Pursuant of this power, the Provinces of Madras, Bom-
y, Bengal, United Provinces, Punjab and Assam have
moved their sex disqualifications, granting the vote to
omen on the same terms as to the male electorate. Further,
e Central Legislative Assembly having passed a similar
solution, women may now vote not only for their Provincial
uncils but also for the Legislative Assembly. Under the
esent general qualifications, however, the total number of
omen entitled to vote throughout India does not exceed
00,000, or about 17 per cent. of the total electorate.

Sir Alexander Muddiman's Reform Enquiry Committee
1924, in opening the consideration of a further step –
at of women's candidature for elective office – reaffirmed
at [1]

e question went deep into the social system and suscepti-
ities of India, and . . . could only with any prudence be

[1] *Report of the Reforms Enquiry Committee*, 1924, p. 57.

settled in accordance with the wishes of the Indians the selves as constitutionally expressed.'

It was, however, upon the Muddiman Committe recommendation that the rules of candidature for Provinc Councils were lately amended, enabling the removal of t sex disqualification by vote of Provincial Council. To t invitation Madras and Bombay have already responded.

The Muddiman Committee next recommended that t electoral rules of both chambers of the Indian Legislatur the Council of State and the Assembly – be amended by t removal of the sex disqualification, so that constituencies provinces that have enfranchised their women might at w elect women to both Chambers. On September 1, 1926, t Indian Legislature so voted.

Thus far, however, it seems to be the British Provinc Governor rather than the Indian electorate that uses the n privilege. From 1922 to 1926, twenty-two women had b come Municipal Councillors or Members of Local Gover ment Boards, of whom only four were elected, the rest bei nominated by Government.[1]

The following statement is that of an Englishman deep conversant with Indian affairs, one who wields much mo influence in India, and who vigorously used that influence advocate the changes above indicated. It was elicited by r request for the grounds of his position and his view of t present status, and was elsewhere confirmed by ranki Indians.

'As for the reason for enfranchising Indian women, I c give you my own reasons, which I put before the Parl mentary Committee which framed the Act. In some plac

[1] *Indian Year Book,* 1926, p. 511.

men had long enjoyed the municipal franchise, especially Bombay. There were a considerable number of women, Bombay, who took a very useful part in our social work. erefore I pressed for the enfranchisement of women, both encourage and hearten these where actually so engaged, l to give others inducements to come forward. The *purdah* ıst be broken as fast as it can . . . its influence on the ılth of Indian women is disastrous. I looked on the franse as another nail in the *purdah* coffin.

'As for the effect of enfranchisement in the Bombay Presincy, so far as I can see, it has been slight; the women in blic life are the women who were there in one way or other before enfranchisement took place. In other parts of lia I should say the effect was smaller still. Until the social nditions have improved, the franchise can mean nothing to : Indian woman, for she dares not use it.'

In observing the position of the women of Bombay, outnding in India, one heavily contributing factor appears: ıis city is the great Parsi centre. Out of the total number Parsis in all India – 101,778 – nearly 93,000 are domi:d in Bombay Presidency.[1] Descendants of old Persian ck, the Parsis are practically all either merchants or nkers. Eight hundred per thousand of their men are :rate, as against the 115 literates per thousand of male ndus. The Parsis neither sequester nor suppress their men, but favour their adequate education. Thus 672 per ousand [2] of the women of the Parsis are literate, as against : 14 per thousand female literates of the Hindus.

The presence of such a body, occupying conspicuous sitions, cannot but influence the whole upper-class population.

[1] *Census of India*, 1921. Vol. I, p. 118. [2] *Ibid.*, p. 180.

APPENDIX III

A–INDIAN COTTON

The record of raw cotton exported from India in years 1924–25 is as follows, the unit being bales of 4 pounds:[1]

Japan	1,671,000
Italy	485,000
China (excluding Hong-Kong)	284,000
Belgium	201,000
Germany	174,000
The United Kingdom	162,000

Of the raw cotton exported to England the Lancash looms use little because of its inferior quality, buying, rath in Egypt and in America.

India's total raw cotton export, in 1924–25, 3,326,400 bales.[2] Her consumption in Indian mills dur that period was 2,050,891 bales.

Japan's purchase is mostly of the poorer grades of cot and is mainly used in competing in China with the prod of India's mills. In 1924 there were 337 cotton mills British India. These are nearly all Indian-owned and a rule have British superintendents and foremen, with Ind labour. The following figures[3] will further clarify situation:

[1] *Review of the Trade of India in 1924–25.* Calcutta, Governmen India Central Publication Branch, 1926, p. 73.

[2] *Ibid.*, pp. 21–2.

[3] *Review of the Trade of India in 1924–25*, p. 23.

	1913–14 Million Yards	1922–23 Million Yards	1923–24 Million Yards	1924–25 Million Yards
oduction in Indian mills of cotton piece-goods	1,164·3	1,725·2	1,701·6	1,970·5
port of Indian-milled piece-goods	89·2	157·0	165·3	181·5
ports of foreign-made cotton piece-goods, from all countries, including the United Kingdom, Japan, Italy, Netherlands and the United States	3,197·1	1,593·3	1,485·8	1,823·2

It will thus be seen that while the production and the port trade of India have been rising, the import trade is out half what it was before 1914.

B–RAILWAY STATISTICS

The following figures as of the year 1925 are based on tistics contained in *The Statesman's Year Book* of 1926:

	India	Argentine	United States	Canada
ileage open per 1,000 square miles of territory in	21	19	88	15
umber of passengers carried per mile of open railway	15,834	5,966	3,550	814

	India	Argentine	United States	Car
Tons of goods carried per mile of open railway	2,785	2,042	8,277	2,c
Total value of imports and exports carried per mile of open railway	£11,860	£15,227	£6,899	£7,4

C–MILITARY EXPENDITURES

An acknowledged authority thus puts the frame of matter:[1]

'The safe figure of a nation's military expenditure . . . fixed by considerations almost entirely beyond the countr control; by her geographical and ethnological boundaries, the power and attitude of her neighbours, by her natio resources in men and material, by her racial unity or d unity, and so on. . . . What requires investigation whether [India's] total budget . . . is worthy of her i mense territories and their prosperity. Were that total to increased largely, the defence item would remain virtua stationary, and the disproportion would disappear to point of making India one of the best-placed nations in t world for protective expenditure.'

[1] *The Defence of India*, Arthur Vincent, pp. 93–4.

APPENDIX

D-THE USURER

Of the Punjab *bania* Mr. Calvert writes:[1]

'He represents the richest single class. His profits prob-ly exceed those of all the cultivators put together. Beside m, the professional class is inconsiderable; the industrial ass is insignificant; even trade and commerce take second ace.'

But the usurer is by no means peculiar to the Punjab. he total rural debt of British India is estimated at approxi-ately £400,000,000, in the main unproductive. This ırden is largely due to the vicious usury and compound terest system, a trifling percentage is incurred for land provement, and the rest may be mainly attributed to travagant expenditures on marriages.

E-BULLION

The export of merchandise from India, in the year 1924–5 exceeded the import to the value of over £100,000,000.[2] uring that year the import of private treasure totalled 66,000,000.[3]

America, during 1924–25, imported Indian goods[4] to e value of £24,000,000. Yet she sold to India only 9,400,000 worth of goods and exported to India bars of lver on private account of approximately the same value nd gold to the value of £13,400,000. This process is

[1] *The Wealth and Welfare of the Punjab.* H. Calvert. Lahore, 1922, 130.

[2] *Review of the Trade of India,* p. 47.

[3] *Ibid.,* p. 48.

[4] *Ibid.,* pp. 48, 60–1, 76.

steadily increasing as the years pass, raising the worl
price of bullion.

F–LOSS OF WOMEN'S LABOUR

Calvert says, in his *Wealth and Welfare of the Punj*
p. 207:

'If there were in Western countries a movement aimi
at the exclusion of female labour from all except pur
domestic tasks, that movement would endanger the wh
economic fabric, and, if successful, would involve th
countries in ruin. . . . The fact that there are [India
tribes . . . which do not allow their womenfolk even
work in the fields is alone sufficient to explain their povert

The same point is recognized by the Hindu writ
Visvesvaraya, in his *Reconstructing India*, p. 246:

'The time has come when Indians must seriously consid
whether the passive life, to which they condemn women wi
a view of preserving the so-called proprieties and decenci
of life, is worth the appalling price the country is forced
pay in the shape of loss of work and intelligent effort fro
half the population of the country.'

G–MENDICANCY

On February 2, 1926, Mr. Abdul Haye, Muhammad
member from the East Punjab, introduced into the Indi
Legislative Assembly a resolution looking to the prohibiti
of beggary and vagrancy in India. Supporting it, he said
part: [1]

[1] *Legislative Assembly Debates*, Vol. VII, No. 8, p. 627.

'One wonders whether the stars in heaven are more in umber or the beggars in this country. . . . Barring agri-ulture there is no other profession in India which can claim ore followers. . . . I make bold to say, and without any ar of contradiction, that every twenty-fifth man in this untry is a beggar.'

Of these mendicants Lala Lajpat Rai says in his *National ducation in India*, p. 37:

'We find that to-day a good part of the nation (sometimes timated at one-fourth), having abandoned all productive onomic work, engages itself in . . . making the people elieve that next to becoming a Sadhú [a begging ascetic] mself, the best thing for man to do to avoid damnation is feed and maintain Sadhús.'

–ECONOMIC CONDITION OF THE MASSES

As general circumstantial evidence of increased means, ne sees the consumption by the peasants of non-essentials, nce beyond their dreams. Thus, at the fair at Aligarh, in ebruary, 1926, the turnover of cheap boots in one week mounted to £1,000, netting a profit of 20 per cent. Boots, the sort of people who snapped these up and put them on eir own feet, were, twenty years ago, an unheard-of luxury. ig stocks of umbrellas, lamps, and gaily painted steel trunks ere sold out and renewed over and over again, on the same ccasion, the buyers being the ordinary cultivators. Tea, igarettes, matches, lanterns, buttons, pocket-knives, mirrors, ramophones are articles of commerce with people who, fteen years ago, bought nothing of the sort. The heavy ird-class passenger traffic by rail is another evidence of money in hand. For railway travel, to the Indian peasar takes the place that the movie fills in America. In 1924–2 581,804,000 third-class railway travellers, as again 1,246,000 of the first-class, proved the presence of money spare in the peasants' possession. 'Where are they going?' I repeatedly asked, watching the crowds packing in the third-class carriages.

'Anywhere. Visiting, pilgrimage, marriage parties, litt business trips – just "there and back," mostly for the excit ment of going,' was the answer.

INDEX

A

B

INDEX

C

E

F

G

J

K

L

M

N

T

INDEX

U

V

W

Y

Z